I0554915

The BIG Book
of
Open-Ended Questions

Intentionally Supporting Young Children in Learning

Topics for Preschool thru 2nd Grade

By Angela Russ-Ayon

Online at AbridgeClub.com
E: AbridgeClub@aol.com

ISBN-13: 978-1-958627-07-5
IngramSpark Paperback

TABLE OF CONTENTS

TABLE OF CONTENTS

A Note from the Author

I wrote this book because most examples I found when searching for open-ended questions were not subject-specific. Many articles provided the beginning of a question, such as *"What would happen if...,"* leaving off the ideas for endings that would be most helpful, like *"What would happen if you let go of the ball?"* or *"What would happen if the ocean was full of trash?"*

I've touched on topics typically found in early childhood settings, providing questions in their simplest form to those more complex. Did I cover everything? No. There is no way for me to anticipate your experience. I expect your questions to grow along with your observations and conversations with the children. There are hundreds of open-ended questions in this book, along with very few helpful facts. It's up to you to dig deeper into subjects and get informed. Please note that during interactions, you may not need to ask a single question or more than one. Be sure to use appropriate pronouns, even when you don't see them.

Included are journal pages for writing new questions and ideas. Please share your contributions with me. I promise to keep the interior pages updated so everyone can benefit.

OPEN-ENDED QUESTIONS

A question is a sentence intended to get someone to provide information or think about something (MacNaughton & Williams, 2004). If you want to learn what children are thinking, you have to ask the right question. Not just any question will do. Questions can be open or closed.

Asking open-ended questions is one of the best ways to enhance children's curiosity and guide them through the learning process without telling them what to do. These questions encourage high-level thinking and meaningful exchanges because there are many possible responses (Lee, 2010). The way children respond will reveal what they feel, think, and comprehend as they share their ideas and opinions.

Adults who ask intentional thought-provoking questions that begin with who, what, when, where, why, and how can help expand children's discovery orbit. Open-ended inquiry encourages children to investigate further and participate in more diverse, deep, complex activities that build their knowledge. Children are inspired to see possibilities with no limitations.

For instance, what activity will expand on their experience after a child plays with water? How about asking questions about bubbles, transferring, measuring, squeezing with sponges, or floating and sinking objects? These are ideas children may not come up with on their own. The questions act as suggestions and permission all in one.

Research shows that most teachers tend to ask closed-ended and direct knowledge questions (Gall, 1984). Closed-ended questions are the kinds of questions one would answer on a test to prove they remember facts or have met standards. Teachers are pressured because "new state-standardized tests emphasize competence in various areas such as English language arts and deemphasize learning through curiosity, exploration, play, physical exercise, and creativity" (Gullo & Hughes 2010).

A conversation is usually a mix of **OPEN** and **CLOSED-ENDED QUESTIONS**. Closed-ended questions help determine specific facts and information. They serve their purpose by helping adults understand what children know or don't know about various concepts. They can be used to assess and evaluate what a child has learned. But, when children are asked closed-ended questions, they typically respond with one or two-word answers such as *"yes," "no," "fine," "two," "blue," "car,"* or other stunted replies. Whether speaking to a child or an adult, one-word responses tend to stop a conversation in its tracks and close the door to interaction.

Close-ended questions work well to transition into open-ended questions that keep a discussion flowing back and forth.

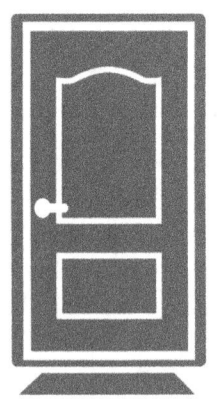

Have you ever made a wish? (closed)
What if your wish came true? (open)

Which book did you pick? (closed)
Why did you choose that one? (open)

What is your favorite shape? (closed)
What do you like about it? (open)

How many slices do you have? (closed)
How can you make sure everybody gets one? (open)

What colors did you use? (closed)
What happened when you mixed them? (open)

How many cups of sand will fit in the pail? (closed)
That's a good guess. How can you find out for sure? (open)

Which material will you use to build your structure? (closed)
How will you use it? (open)

Benefits of Open-Ended Questions

Open-ended questions help keep conversations flowing back and forth from adult to child. They encourage children to think about what they are doing, process the information, adapt, and share. Hidden in the children's responses will be little nuggets of knowledge that help adults understand where to lead them, so it's essential to know where children are in their stages of development.

Open-ended questions give children a chance to...

- communicate more effectively, expanding language skills (Walsh & Blewitt, 2006).
- describe and explain their actions.
- express their thoughts, feelings, opinions, and ideas.
- speak for longer periods of time (De Rivera et al., 2005).
- share their experiences and views with adults and peers.
- make thought-provoking decisions and take the initiative.
- imagine and think creatively.
- discover relationships between events.
- apply what they've learned and teach adults what they know.
- play and explore without limits.
- dig deeper into specific topics.
- work their way through the scientific process by predicting, experimenting, observing, examining, making adjustments, and concluding.
- recognize the need to make adjustments and changes.
- figure out how to solve their own problems.
- debate and defend their reasoning.
- gain confidence in their ability to interact with others.
- practice social skills - negotiate, consider others' perspectives, compromise, lead effectively, read social cues, regulate emotions, delay gratification, express empathy, assign roles and tasks, take turns, etc.
- recall what they did.

When is a good time to ask open-ended questions?

Open-ended questions support instruction across all domains anytime, but they can be particularly beneficial...

- when a child stops talking
- when a child is engaged in a project
- when play stalls
- when children become bored
- when introducing new ideas and materials, or complex levels
- when an argument ensues and escalates
- when encouraging involvement with peers for the practice of social skills
- after a project is complete

Let's say you see a child building with blocks. If you ask the child, *"What shape is this block?"* you will receive an answer like *"Triangle"* or *"Square."* And if you ask, *"What are you building?"* the child may answer, *"A bridge."* But if you ask a child, *"What can you tell me about your structure?"* the door is open for a wide range of responses.

Concealed in children's responses are invaluable clues as to what they are thinking and what they know. The conversation will move in surprising directions as children take the lead, and adults can learn what concepts need attention. For example, a child may describe their structure as "really wide" when it is actually tall and thin. Or, a child may estimate that there are more items in a set of pinecones than in a set of acorns, not because there are more pinecones but because pinecones are bigger.

This is how the cars get over the river.

Patience Pays Off!

Children require plenty of time to think about the questions and relate them to what they are doing.

They need time to:

- feel comfortable
- comprehend the language spoken
- process the question asked
- evaluate their actions and ponder ideas
- practice skills
- experiment and test their theories
- observe what is happening
- think critically
- make connections to what they already know
- problem-solve or make changes
- come to a conclusion
- formulate a response
- communicate their response

NOTES

> *"When you teach a child something. You take away forever the chance for him to discover it himself."*   - John Piaget

Responses to Open-Ended Questions

Not all children will respond to questions vocally. They may be shy, too young to understand the question, too young to speak, may speak a different language, or may have developmental delays. Look for nonverbal cues from these children, then physically demonstrate or use gestures and actions to help them understand the question.

You like the ball?
How can we make the ball roll?

Then, demonstrate rolling the ball.

Think about where children are developmentally. Does the child understand what the word "roll" means? Is the child old enough to be able to describe the ball? Expect children to explain what they observe in ways that make sense to them, using actions, terms, and language they know, which will vary from child to child. These differences can lead to productive discussions and richer learning.

Children experience little successes when prompted by open-ended questions because this type of inquiry is an invitation to make discoveries; they are a green light for children to do more with what they have.

Correctly planned and asked questions can improve the effective thinking of children (Duster, 1997). For this reason, the answers children provide can be both revealing and surprising to adults who observe and pay attention.

Consider how much goes into a child's response when asked a question:

- listening skills
- observation skills
- maturity
- temperament
- language
- learning style
- stage of development
- verbal and physical abilities
- disabilities
- cultural background
- experiences
- interests
- knowledge

Just as there are perfect times to ask the right questions, so too are there times when adults should just sit quietly and observe (Jones & Reynolds, 2011, Pg. 35).

Important Tips

This book is full of questions,
but you may not need to ask a single one.

1. Observe and actively listen. Take notice of what children are doing and saying before, during, and after an activity. You won't know what to ask them if you're not paying attention. Confirming their actions and restating their words with an inquiry that begins with, *"It looks like you are...,"* or *"I heard you say...,"* or *"Did you mean...?"* will help clarify what is happening and where to go next. You may miss a great follow-up question if you try to formulate the next question before hearing the answer to the first one.

- children may become intimidated and not answer the questions, especially if the questions are too complex.
- asking multiple questions can interfere with the natural back-and-forth flow of the conversation you wish to promote.
- asking questions too early or asking too many questions can interrupt children's thought processes. They might have been heading in another direction, but you'll never know.

Are you saying...?

2. Show you care. Demonstrate that you are interested in the children's responses by setting aside the cell phone, turning from distractions, dropping to their level, and making eye contact.

3. Ask questions responsively. Avoid bombarding children with question after question because...

- children won't have time to answer or think about one question before you fire off another.

4. Understand the make-up of children and their families, including developmental needs, disabilities, culture, religious beliefs, household status, income, parenting styles, native language, types of households, or community. Imagine asking a child a question about their house when they are homeless, asking about their mother when they are being raised by two fathers, or asking about an experience that costs money when their family lives in poverty. Does a child from the inner city know what a sheep is? Is a child who lives on a farm familiar with the subway?

5. Questions should span across a range of roles and transcend stereotypes. Conscious or unconscious biases may be extended toward any social group. Personal prejudices and stereotypes exist with regard to gender and gender identity, age, physical abilities, religion, sexual orientation, weight, and other characteristics. Respond in a similar fashion to boys and girls, children who are thin or portly, those who are mature and immature, etc.

6. Research topics that are of interest to the children. A Google search is at your fingertips. When developing open-ended questions, first become familiar with a subject. Knowing relevant information makes it easier to formulate questions, introduce related vocabulary terms, and guide children with wisdom.

Did you know that all bugs are insects, but technically, not all insects are bugs? A few characteristics distinguish bugs from other insects, but how would a person know which ones if they didn't research the information?

7. Do not force children into an activity. Children learn more by doing than by instruction. They should be free to approach tasks that interest them, exercising their autonomy. Let them know that they have control over themselves and their choices. As long as they are not putting themselves or others at risk or damaging the props, materials, or their surroundings, what they do with what they have is their choice. It's okay if the activity does not turn out exactly as planned.

8. Ask questions that fit the moment or activity without distracting children from what they're doing or intruding on their thoughts. Stay on the subject as they act and react. Questions should relate directly to what the child is doing. Why would you ask a child what they like about horses when they have just discovered a ladybug?

- *How do ladybugs move around?*
- *Really? A ladybug? Describe it to me.*
- *How do you think the ladybug got here?*
- *Why do you think ladybugs have spots on their bodies?*
- *Do you think the ladybug is afraid of you? Why? Why not?*

Connect what the child is seeing, hearing, touching, feeling, or doing, and expand on that. Here are a few examples:

⇒ It's music time.
  How can we move to these sounds?

⇒ The child picked up a book.
  What do you like about this story?

⇒ A block tower keeps falling.
  I wonder how you can make your tower more stable.

⇒ The child has found some sticks.
  How can you use your sticks to make shapes/numbers/letters?

⇒ The child has picked up various leaves.
  How are the leaves the same/different?

⇒ It rains.
  How do you feel about the rain?

⇒ The child draws a picture of his room.
  Tell me about where you live.

9. Open-ended questions don't have to make sense, but they should be interesting enough to provoke thought, expand vocabulary, create imagery, initiate an activity, or promote social awareness. A child's world is constantly evolving, just like your questions, so out-of-the-box thinking is required!

10. There is no perfect question, and there is no single right or wrong answer to correct, grade, applaud, or criticize. Focus on effort, not outcome. The fun is in the learning, and the learning comes naturally. Allow children to express their views openly, whether they make sense or not. Doing so makes them equal partners in the conversation without feeling they're being judged. They will learn that you trust them to have good ideas and to contribute in valuable ways.

11. Be sure to ask "Why" questions with a smile because questions such as, *"Why did you make it?"* or *"Why did you put it there?"* can sound accusatory or critical. Be sure to ask these types of questions less harshly.

12. Build on what children already know or can already do. Ask questions that extend children's investigations, add new ideas to their work, or take them to their next level of learning. Here is a simple scenario:

Scenario: A child draws a rough design for a tower. The child builds the tower. An adult takes a photo of the child's drawing and completed tower; a visual account of their work.

Select <u>one</u> prompt and see where it leads:

◊   *Tell me about your tower.*

◊   *How does your tower compare to the one John built?*

◊   *How can you measure your tower to see how tall/wide it is?*

◊   *How can you add rooms for the people who live in your tower?*

◊   *What if your tower was surrounded by water?*

◊   *How will people/animals get inside?*

◊   *How can you get this last piece on top?*

13. Plan for the mess, and don't be dissuaded. There will probably be a mess. Water spills, clay gets stuck in things, mud splatters, paint drips, and chalk is dusty. Messy play is also sensory play. Whether children are exploring indoors or outside, they will likely get dirty and make a mess. Dress them in old clothing, then give them a location and a green light to explore.

14. Allow children to respond to the question without interruption. They should not feel rushed or made to feel like they didn't respond fast enough. And they should be given ample time to carry out their intentions.

15. Reword and rephrase for better understanding. Children may not be familiar with the topic or vocabulary in the question. It may help if you simplify or restructure the sentence, use gestures or sounds, turn to visual aids such as books or pictures, or ask the question differently.

16. Introduce developmentally appropriate materials that are worth exploring. Support children's creativity by adding equipment that may take them to a new dimension of play. In order to take children to the next level of learning, there must be a next level. Introduce materials that give children a plethora of choices on how to use them. Providing children with open-ended materials increases the complexity of play and offers a variety of possibilities with no one correct way of using them (Grestwicki, 2016).

Materials like clay, blocks, sand, water, rocks, paint, loose parts, or dramatic play props don't come with directions. They can be played with, manipulated, designed, redesigned, taken apart, put back together, and transported in multiple ways. The children will determine how they'll use the materials, but the key term to remember is "age-appropriate" because small toys can also be eaten.

17. Vary and rotate materials and props. Put the old ones away for a while and replace them regularly. The greater the variety of materials, the more likely they will attract interest. Find the right balance between what's familiar and what's novel. Materials don't have to be expensive; they can just be different and interesting to the children. How long has the clay been sitting there with the same old molds and presses that are no longer exciting?

18. Provide enough materials. According to the NAEYC, the general rule is that there should be enough materials so that three or four children can engage in play. Offer alternative activities for those children who have to wait. If all else fails, separate the children into different rooms or spaces like indoors and outdoors.

19. Combine materials that typically would not be used together. Try adding one or a few at a time; enough to make things interesting and only what the children can handle.

◊ What would happen if clay molds and tools were rotated throughout the year to connect to books you read?
◊ What would happen if children were invited to play with clay sitting next to a bowl of shells, toothpicks, buttons, nuts & bolts, rocks, foil, or pipe cleaners?
◊ What would happen if children were encouraged to work with clay on a tarp spread on the floor instead of on a table?

20. Store and display materials in an appealing, organized manner. Present them in a well-defined area that is accessible to the children in a way that appeals to their senses. A disorganized or chaotic setting can be overwhelming for anyone. Be sure to add photos and name tags for second language learners and pre-readers.

21. Select one question, then wait to see what happens. You already know how a butterfly net works. Allow children to figure out how and teach you. To do this, they must have an opportunity to investigate, experiment, and test their ideas for as long as they are interested. Children discover new ways to use things without an adult's help. Let them take the lead in exploratory play. They will surprise you with their opinions, creativity, and view of the world.

◊ *Why do you think the butterfly is flying away from you?*
◊ *How can you catch the butterfly without hurting it?*
◊ *What will you do once you catch the butterfly?*

22. Leave room for the questions. Try not to give all of the specifics of an activity or details of an experience at once. Providing too much information leaves no room for discovery.

23. Avoid leading children to an answer. The questions in this book grow from the simplest forms to those more complex. The lists begin with questions that have a narrow focus and transition to those that are broader and more detailed. They are meant to be asked in response to what the children might typically say or do in the moment, which is something no one can predict.

A question should not be asked just because it's on the list. Doing so may lead children directly to the answer, or influence their response, robbing them of the opportunity to observe, discover, and explain for themselves. Here are several examples.

Let's say you have a bucket of water. If you ask the children, *"I wonder what would happen if you poured sand in the water?"* they are invited to pour sand into the bucket and see what happens, an action they may not have thought of themselves. The next question, *"What happened?"* should encourage observation and an eventual response, so wait.

Jumping in with a follow-up question such as *"Why did the sand sink to the bottom?"* cuts off the children's thought process and describes the adult's observation, not the children's. However, after the children say, *"It went to the bottom,"* is a good time to ask, *"Why do you think the sand sank to the bottom?"* A new vocabulary word is introduced, *sank*, and defined through hands-on experience.

When the children become fascinated by their shadows, you might ask, *"What do you notice when you move?"* rather than, *"Why does your shadow get bigger?"* The fact that the shadow got bigger is the adult's observation, not the children's.

When the children examine bubble wrap, you might ask, *"Why do you think people use bubble wrap?"* rather than, *"Why do people use bubble wrap to protect things?"* The latter question leads children straight to the answer unless they have already informed you that they know bubble wrap is used to protect things.

In addition, questions that begin with *"don't you?"*, *"can't they?"*, or *"isn't it?"* are not open-ended. They are questions soliciting agreement. Instead of asking, *"Isn't it a wonderful day?"* and waiting for a child to agree with you, you might ask, *"How is your day?"* and get more details.

24. Acknowledge children's attempts at reasoning by:

- actively listening
- expressing excitement
- offering positive feedback
- encouraging further exploration
- motivating continued efforts
- assisting and prompting only when necessary
- providing age-appropriate materials for new discoveries

25. There is a distinct difference between praise and encouragement.

Children who are praised tend to look for more opportunities to please someone other than themselves. They aren't making decisions because they want to, but because **you** want them to. They aren't thinking about how they feel about their work; they're thinking about how **you** feel about their work. In contrast, children who are encouraged respond to positive feedback by continuing on their path, persisting, trying new things, and looking for solutions.

Encourage children as they take the initiative, develop positive feelings about their capabilities, and understand how their actions affect others. When support is immediate, specific, and enthusiastic, children learn to believe that their contributions are valued and worthwhile.

Don't we want children to continue working because they feel good about their work, not because they want to hear praise? An open-ended question doesn't have to be asked in every situation, and a child doesn't always need to be encouraged. Simply stating what the child has done, and pointing out details, works just as well.

It is often difficult for adults to break old habits, especially when they have been taught to TEACH and PREACH. Here are a few tips that might help you in the area of encouragement:

- Memorize four reassuring phrases that fit a variety of situations.
  * one to encourage persistence
  * one for problem-solving
  * one for completion
  * one for positive social interaction

- A good rule of thumb is whenever you find yourself about to say the words *"I like,"* substitute them for the words *"I notice."*

- Children are reading your cues, so whatever you say, try to end comments on a positive note to invite future dialog, provide unconditional support, and prompt further action.

"Are our reactions helping the child to feel a sense of control over her life — or to constantly look to us for approval" (Kohn, 2001)?

NOTES

> *"In play, a child is always above his average age, above his daily behavior; in play, it is as though he were a head taller than himself."* - Lev S. Vygotsky

Samples of
Positive Support and Encouragement

1. Action: both arms straight up in the air like a cheer
2. Action: two thumbs up
3. Action: high five with child
4. You're off to a great start.
5. You remembered!
6. That's the way to use your mind.
7. It's fun to keep trying.
8. That's it!
9. You have found a creative way to do it.

· · · · · · · · · · ·

10. You are really trying hard.
11. You have gotten a lot done.
12. You're almost there.
13. You've almost got it.
14. You're so close.
15. You're almost finished.
16. I can see you're thinking hard about it.

· · · · · · · · · · ·

17. I can't wait to take a picture.
18. I'm sure you are going to write your name on that.
19. I can't wait to put that in your folder.
20. I bet you can't wait to show your family.

· · · · · · · · · · ·

21. Look what you can do all by yourself.
22. I'll bet you're super excited.
23. You must have been practicing.

· · · · · · · · · · ·

24. You solved the problem.
25. What a great way to solve the problem.
26. You fixed it.
27. I see how you improved your design.
28. You searched your mind and came up with something.
29. You did it!
30. Congratulations!

31. I'll bet you're proud of yourself.
32. I knew you could do it.
33. You did that all by yourself/on your own.
34. I knew you would figure it out.
35. You learned how to do it.
36. You worked extremely hard on that.
37. I'm so glad you kept working.
38. You made it very interesting.
39. I'll bet that feels good.
40. Nothing can stop you.
37. You handled that very well.

38. Wonderful teamwork.
39. You work very well together.
40. I noticed the way you helped each other.
41. Look how happy you made your friend.

· · · · · · · · · · ·

37. You explain things very clearly.
38. Your thoughts are very interesting. Tell me more.
39. Everyone enjoyed hearing your ideas.
40. I appreciate you explaining your work.
41. Thank you for your idea/suggestion.

Ask open-ended questions in different and thought-provoking ways:

- **Ask for a prediction:**
  - *What do you think will happen if you pour the sand through the strainer?*
  - *How will the water feel after you add ice?*

- **Ask for a solution:**
  - *How will you clean up the water?*
  - *What can you invent to take care of this?*

- **Ask about consequences:**
  - *How will you color if you break the felt tips off the markers?*
  - *What will happen to your teeth if you always eat candy?*

- **Ask for a real-life connection:**
  - *Have you ever seen a real bridge? How did it look?*
  - *What happens to the stars when the sun rises?*

- **Ask for an explanation:**
  - *How were you able to get the blocks to stand up that way?*
  - *What is the bird doing?*

- **Ask about same vs. different:**
  - *How do you know this is a triangle and that's a square?*
  - *What's the difference between the shaker and the drum?*

- **Ask to consider feelings:**
  - *How would you feel if someone knocked down your tower?*
  - *What can you do to make Marcos feel better?*

- **Ask to recall information or experiences:**
  - *What happened to the bear after he ate all of the pie?*
  - *Why did the wolf want to blow the houses down?*

- **Ask something nonsensical:**
  - *What if we all looked exactly the same?*
  - *What if there were only ten people in the entire world?*

> *"Critical thinking involves children in the learning process by allowing them to probe and question while encouraging them to analyze and process the information through reflection and evaluation"*
> **(Dewey [1910] 2008).**

Introducing Complex Language

Ask questions that encourage language development: receptive and expressive. Children begin to use and understand complex vocabulary and the language of STEM (Science, Technology, Engineering, Math) when adults inject positional and directional cues, concepts of time, STEM concepts and related terminology, and measurement words into every day discussions. Here are a few examples:

- *What do you **observe**?*
- *What would happen if you used **triangles** instead of **squares** on the **bottom**?*
- *What makes these **two pieces** fit **together**?*
- *How do you know the colors **match**?*
- *How can you fit **more** ducks **inside** of the tub?*
- *What will you do **first/next/last**?*
- *Why do you think the orange has **segments**?*
- *How can you **extend** the train track to reach the station?*
- *What do you have to do to make the road **wide** enough for the truck to fit?*
- *How will you **divide** these up so everyone gets one?*

- *How will you build the bridge **over** the water?*
- *What will it look like if you **take away** some **pieces**?*
- *How are the **two** towers the **same**?*
- *What do you think of when you see a **wavy line**?*
- *How can you draw a shape **next** to the other one?*
- *Why don't you **investigate** how it happened?*
- *What will you do with the **empty** space in **between**?*
- *How can you find out **how many** dolls will fit in the stroller?*
- *How can you make the ball roll **faster**?*
- *Can you think of a way to make them **equal**?*
- *What if she sits **down** and you stand **up**?*
- *How **long** should the butcher paper be to cover the **whole** table?*
- *What if your friend only wants **half** a cup of water?*

Prompts and Commands

Sometimes open-ended inquiry takes
the form of soft prompts and commands
that invite children to share and explain.

- *Talk to me about what you saw.*
- *Describe how you worked together.*
- *Share with us what happened.*
- *Explain how you came up with the idea.*
- *Tell me about how you made your structure.*
- *I'd like to hear what you liked about doing this.*

Pretend prompts help build a sense of
community. When asked to pretend an
event is happening or pretend to take
action, children become focused on one
task together like a group of actors.

*"Children's play helps them focus on
common problems in the format they
know best: story"* (NAEYC, 2011).

If the script is not appropriate for
whatever reason, re-write it.

"Think dramatically!"
- Vivian Gussin Paley

*"Pretend the room is filling with lava, and
we must put everything away before it
gets burned. How fast can we get the toys
onto the shelves if we work together?"*

*"How can you help the kite fly as high as
the birds?"*

*"Some of the blocks are hiding. How can
we find them all and put them in the
basket?"*

*"We support children's learning
by asking questions;
we ask questions
to evaluate children's learning"*
(Massey, Pence, Justice,
and Bowles, 2008).

BLOOM'S TAXONOMY

Benjamin Bloom developed a Taxonomy for examining the thinking process. Using questioning strategies designed for each level of Bloom's Taxonomy can help in the development of open-ended higher-level questions. Here is a general overview.

- **Identify, remember, and repeat facts.** Help children recall information.

  ◊ *How do you know what shape this is?*
  ◊ *Describe what you saw.*
  ◊ *Tell me about what happened.*
  ◊ *How do you know the caterpillar was hungry?*

- **Understand, interpret, and describe the meaning.** Help children explain ideas and concepts and process what they know.

  ◊ *Tell us how to do it.*
  ◊ *Explain why you think so. What would you do to repeat the pattern?*
  ◊ *Why do you think yours is the tallest?*

- **Apply knowledge to new situations or use it to solve problems.** Help children use what they know in a new way.

  ◊ *How would you change the ending?*
  ◊ *What can you do to fix this?*
  ◊ *How would you use a tool like this in the sandbox?*

- **Analyze, compare, and examine information.** Help children experiment with what they know and distinguish between different parts.

  ◊ *What can you do to take a closer look?*
  ◊ *What do you notice about your shadow when you move?*
  ◊ *How are these the same/different?*
  ◊ *Why do you think that happened?*
  ◊ *How can you find out more about it?*

- **Create, construct, and design elements.** Help children use knowledge to create a new product or respond to unfamiliar situations.

  ◊ *How can you build a more stable tower?*
  ◊ *How can you sort these parts differently?*
  ◊ *What would happen if you used all of the material?*

- **Evaluate, check, and make judgments based on available criteria.** Help children look at things from different perspectives, justify their opinions, and reflect on their viewpoints.

  ◊ *What would you have done differently?*
  ◊ *How do you think you can solve the problem?*
  ◊ *How would you feel if this happened to you?*

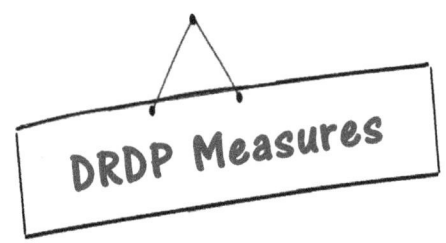

DRDP Measures

Consider referring to the **Desired Results Development Profile (DRDP)** measures when formulating questions while observing children in typical environments, activities, and routines. The DRDP assesses a child's developmental progress by measuring knowledge, skills, and behaviors.

- ## Social and Emotional Development

  ◊ *How can you work together to fix it?*
  ◊ *What can you do to help your friend?*
  ◊ *Why did you choose the pink scarf for your friend?*
  ◊ *How can you show your friend how the timer works?*
  ◊ *How do you feel when that happens?*
  ◊ *Why do you think your friend is excited about her birthday?*
  What about painting makes you happy?
  ◊ *How do you treat a baby?*
  ◊ *How can you both get a turn?*
  ◊ *How did you decide on which roles you would play?*
  ◊ *Why didn't the three little pigs befriend the wolf?*

- ## Language and Literacy Development

  ◊ *What would you do if you were the rabbit in the story?*
  ◊ *How did you know where to find the markers?*
  ◊ *Tell me what you know about planting seeds.*
  ◊ *How do you ask for something you want?*
  ◊ *Why do you need paper towels?*
  ◊ *How did you spend your day yesterday?*
  ◊ *Tell me about the people in your family photo.*
  ◊ *Describe your favorite dinosaur.*

  ◊ *Which word doesn't fit with the others? Why?*
  ◊ *How do you know that's the letter A?*
  ◊ *Describe the kind of noise the animal makes.*
  ◊ *How do you think the eggs got to be green?*
  ◊ *Tell me what you want me to write about your drawing.*

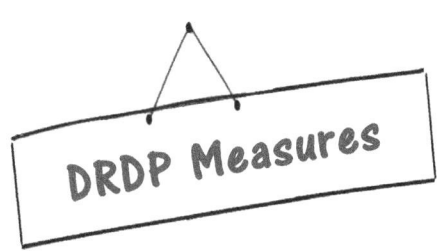

DRDP Measures

◊ How will your parents know which story is yours?
◊ What can you do to remember what your customers order?
◊ How does the fish move?
◊ How can you find something else that begins with the "S" sound?
◊ What do you like about this song/story?

- **Cognition, Including Math and Science**

◊ How can you sort/place these to make them easy to find/count?
◊ What's the difference between a rock and a pebble?
◊ How do you know these shoes are a pair?
◊ How do you know how many you have?
◊ How can you find out who has more/less?
◊ How can you make sure everyone gets a napkin?

◊ What do you have to do to make the train track longer/straighter?
◊ What can you use to transport the pieces to the station?
◊ What will you do if you need more blocks?
◊ How did you know what came next in the pattern?
◊ What if you wanted to make the same sounds?
◊ How are these shapes/pieces different/the same?
◊ How can you find the pieces that fit together?
◊ How do you know these are longer than those?
◊ Show me how you would use the string/stick/material/tool.
◊ What do you notice about the inside of the apple?
◊ How would you describe the shape of your sandwich?

NOTES

> *"Understanding a question is half an answer."*
> **- Socrates**

NOTES

Developing Open-Ended Questions

Read through the **Important Tips** on the previous pages.

Effective open-ended questions start with the following words: why, how, and what if. Open-ended prompts begin with words like: tell me, show me, I wonder if, and describe. Wording is very important.

Open-ended questions should have no set or predetermined answers, so don't have any expectations. Remember, the questions should inspire or invite children to observe, analyze, think critically, make connections to what they know, describe, explain, take more complex steps, experiment, or reflect.

Lists of open-ended questions are provided on the following pages. Children are always in the process of learning new information and making connections to what they know. Don't make the mistake of assuming they already know something. Unless you know for sure, begin with questions in their simplest form.

Select questions that are age-appropriate and also consider:

◊ the age of the child
◊ the developmental stage
◊ the level of verbal skills
◊ the language spoken
◊ the extent of vocabulary
◊ the culture
◊ the make-up of the family
◊ the level of confidence
◊ the environment
◊ the available materials
◊ the particular activity
◊ the level of participation
◊ the level of interest in the activity
◊ the actions observed by the adult

Use the questions provided to structure queries about topics that are not in the book. A question related to size, such as, *"Why are some cars big and others small?"* can be adapted for dolls, leaves, balls, bridges, seashells, etc. Prompts about how things fit can also be modified for puzzles, clothing, dramatic play, blocks, etc.

GENERAL PROMPTS

PREDICT · GUESS

1. How do you think it will work/react/respond?
2. How do you think it will feel/taste? sound/smell/look?
3. What do you think you might find/see/discover?
4. What do you think will/could happen first/next/last?
7. What do you think will/could happen when/if_____ ? Why?
8. How many do you think are inside? How can you find out?
9. What do you think will/could happen if there were/were no_____?
10. What do you think will/could happen if there were too many/not enough _____?
11. What do you think will happen if you change _____?

ANALYZE · OBSERVE
COMPARE · EXPERIMENT

1. What do/did you notice about the way this moves?
2. What else can you do while the glue dries?

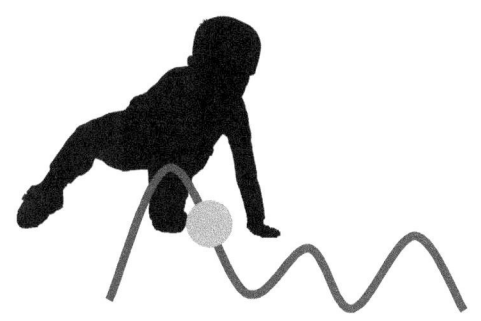

3. How did/does it feel/taste/sound/smell/look?
4. What do you think caused it to feel/taste/sound/smell/look like that?
5. What happened or didn't happen at the beginning/end/in the middle/before/after?
6. Why do you think it happened/didn't happen?
7. What's the most important thing to do? Why?
8. In what ways are these the same/different?
9. How much/many will you need? How do you know?
12. What do you think caused it to change?
13. What if you took away/took out/added/found/lost some?
14. What was the hardest/easiest thing to do? Why?
15. What did you like best/least about...?
16. How is your project coming along?
17. How did you get your idea/the material?
18. What do you think of when you paint?
19. What steps did you take?
20. What other _____ do you know?
21. How do you know it's the dullest/sharpest/brightest/darkest/smoothest/roundest/shortest/fastest/etc.?
22. How can you prove it?
23. Tell me about how you worked together.
24. Tell me about what you saw/noticed/have/did.
25. Tell me about the story/character/ending.
26. What changed since you first started?

GENERAL PROMPTS

CREATE · DESIGN · CONSTRUCT

1. What can you make?
2. How will you make it?
3. Tell me what you're thinking.
4. How are you planning to do that?
5. What will you do to prepare for it?
6. Show me what you can do with this.
7. Tell me how you would make/build/ assemble a _____.
8. How can you draw your design.
9. What materials will you need?
10. What will you do with the materials?
11. How many ways can you _____?
12. Why did you choose these instead of those?
13. How do/did you know what to do?
14. What other ideas do you have?
15. How can you organize/sort these to make your work easier?
16. Show me what you can do with what you have.

PROBLEM-SOLVE · ADAPT

1. What worked/didn't work? Why?
2. What can you do to get it to work?
3. Tell me your idea/thoughts.
4. How can you change/improve it?
7. How can you solve the problem/fix it/find a solution?
8. How can you make it better/stronger/etc.?
9. Why do you think it looks/smells/tastes/ sounds/feels like that?
10. Why do you think that happened?
11. Why do you think it doesn't fit?
12. What challenges did/do you have?
13. What can you do to figure it out?
14. How can you do this another way?
15. What can you do instead?

16. How might you do/say that differently?
17. How can I help?
18. What if you asked a friend to help?
19. How can we work together to solve this?
20. How can you make sure everyone gets one/a chance?

REFLECT

1. What made you think of that?
2. What did you learn from this?
3. What do you think this means?
6. Tell me about a time when...
7. What do you remember from...?
8. How does something like this help people/others/animals/insects/the world?
9. What have you learned that you can teach to others?
10. What do you know now that you can share with others?
12. How can you teach someone else to do it?
13. What was easy/hard for you to do?
14. What will you do differently next time?
15. How can you find out more about this?
16. Why do you think it was important to clean your hands?
17. How did you feel when you were working on it/finished it?
18. How can you use this inside/outside/over there/somewhere else/to help people?
19. How would you feel if that happened to you?
20. What do you think about the steps you took?
21. What are your options now?

NOTES

> *"I cannot teach anybody anything. I can only make them think."*
> **- Socrates**

NOTES

NOTES

NONSENSICAL · EXAGGERATED QUESTIONS

What if...

1. ...there were no books to read/movies to watch?
2. ...people had to read books upside down?
3. ...books didn't have words/pictures/pages/covers?
4. ...your toys could move and talk, like in Toy Story?
5. ...all dolls became real live babies?
6. ...you were invited to have dinner with a king or queen?
7. ...no one had a name?
8. ...you could fit in toy cars?
9. ...stories didn't have endings?
10. ...bikes/cars/scooters didn't have wheels?
11. ...everything was free?
12. ...it costs money to stand/sit/walk/play?
13. ...you could never sit/lay down/sleep?
14. ...all of your dreams became real?
15. ...you never had anything to use for writing?
16. ...people didn't have soap?
17. ...bugs/insects were bigger than people?
18. ...animals/insects/fish could talk to people?

19. ...you could make a new animal/insect?
20. ...snails could run?
21. ...birds were as big as planes?
22. ...cats barked, and dogs meowed?
23. ...humans were raised in nests?
24. ...every wish people made came true?
25. ...our shadows moved by themselves?
26. ...no one grew fruits/vegetables?
27. ...there was no food anywhere in the world?
28. ...you had to eat the same food every day?
29. ...people didn't have phones to call each other?
30. ...there were no parents/teachers/sisters/brothers?
31. ...all of the parents became children?
32. ...children never grew up?
33. ...people grew up and then got younger instead of older?
34. ...smiling/crying was against the law?
35. ...our eyes were on top of our heads?
36. ...people were 100 years old when they were born?
37. ...no one ever washed their hands/took a bath?
38. ...people had four arms/legs?
39. ...people walked on their hands instead of their feet?

NONSENSICAL · EXAGGERATED QUESTIONS

40. ...people slept all day and went to school at night?
41. ...nobody went to school?
42. ...no one ever told the truth?
43. ...no one remembered/celebrated birthdays?
44. ...all of our clothes/shoes came in one size/style?
45. ...you never cleaned your home/room/dishes/clothes?
46. ...people were as tiny as ants?
47. ...people were as big as giants/buildings?
48. ...everyone lived underground?
49. ...people lived on top of the clouds?
50. clouds were made out of Play-Doh?
51. ...people could pull stars out of the sky?
52. ...people could only see one color?
53. ...people lived forever?
54. ...people could walk on water?
55. ...planes flapped their wings?
56. ...people could climb rainbows?
57. ...rainwater had a flavor?
58. ...you could never go outside?
59. ...people were all invisible?
60. ...nobody ever slept?
61. ...people had wings and could fly?
62. ...the sky was purple/black all day long?
63. ...trees grew upside down?
64. ...grass was white/black?
65. ...the sky rained food?
66. ...the ocean was made out of Jell-O
67. ...it rained/snowed every day?
68. ...there were no cars?
69. ...people paid with candy instead of money?
70. ...there were real superheroes?

71. ...you had a superpower?
72. ...there were no community helpers?
73. ...there was no tape or glue?
74. ...there were no letters/numbers?
75. ...there were no colors except black/white?
76. ...your favorite color smelled bad?
77. ...no one ever recycled?
78. ...dinosaurs were alive and living among us?
79. ...there were no weekends?
80. ...you found a treasure in your backyard?
81. ...you could travel back in time/into the future?
82. ...you could be any character in a book?
83. ...everyone could hear your thoughts?
84. ...you could change your name?
85. ...you could change one thing about yourself?

QUESTIONS ABOUT FAVORITES

1. What does it mean to have a favorite thing?
2. What is your favorite/least favorite thing to do at school/after school/at home/at the park/on the playground/outside/inside/etc.? Why?
3. What do you like/not like about it?
4. Describe it to me.
5. How do you know so much about it?
6. Where have you seen/tasted/heard/felt/smelled it before? Tell me about that experience.

What/Who is your favorite or least favorite...

7. ...name?
8. ...letter/word?
9. ...color?
10. ...shape?
11. ...number?
12. ...poem/story/book?
13. ...character in a story/book?
14. ...joke?
15. ...toy?
16. ...puzzle/game?
17. ...sport/team?
18. ...athlete?
19. ...hobby/activity?
20. ...thing to do?
21. ...career?
22. ...chore?
23. ...piece of clothing?
24. ...costume?
25. ...pair of shoes?
26. ...hairstyle?
27. ...restaurant?
28. ...meal/food/snack/drink?
29. ...dessert/candy/ice cream?
30. ...sound/scent/flavor/texture?
31. ...fruit/vegetable?
32. ...food group?
33. ...picture/photo/poster/sign/sculpture?
34. ...photographer/artist/painter/sculptor?
35. ...movie/television show/play?
36. ...actor/actress?
37. ...streaming service?
38. ...stuffed animal?
39. ...superhero/superheroine?
40. ...superpower?
41. ...cartoon character?
42. ...song/type of music/band/singer?
43. ...dance move?
44. ...animal/insect/pet?
45. ...dinosaur?
46. ...flower/tree/rock?
47. ...time of day?
48. ...day of the week/month?
49. ...season/weather?
50. ...place to go?
51. ...town/city/state/county/country?
52. ...theme park/theme park ride?
53. ...playground?
54. ...car/vehicle/motorcycle/plane/boat?
55. ...tradition?
56. ...holiday/celebration?

GETTING TO KNOW YOU

1. Tell me everything about yourself/ your family/where you live.
2. What do you like about being ___ years old?
6. What is the worst thing about being ___ years old?
7. What do you like to do? Why?
8. How did you learn to do that?
9. What is important to you?
10. What is the easiest/most challenging thing for you to do?

....

11. What makes you happy/sad/scared/ angry/anxious/frustrated/lonely/etc.?
12. When you are sad, what cheers you up?
13. What makes you feel strong/weak/tired/ hungry/etc.?
14. How do you know when you're having fun?
15. What is the silliest thing you've ever done?
16. What is the funniest joke you've ever told/heard?
17. How do you calm yourself when you are angry/frightened/anxious/energetic?
18. What makes you a nice friend/person?
19. What do you think your friends would say about you? Why?
20. How do you help your parents/ friends/ family/teacher/community?
21. Why do you think it's important to help people/your community?
22. What have you done that makes you proud?
23. How can you tell if you're working or playing?
24. What do you think your best skill/talent is? Why?

....

25. What would you do if you could be a mom/dad/teacher/someone else for a day?
26. What would you do if you could be a queen or king for the day? Why?
27. Tell me about a story/show/movie you'd like to write.
28. What would you change if you could change anything in the world? Why?
29. Where would you go if you could go anywhere? Why?
30. What do you want to do/be when you grow up? Why?
31. If you could pick another name, what would you call yourself? Why?
32. If you could be a book/song/color, what would you be? Why?
33. What would you wish for if you had three wishes? Why?
34. What would you do if you had a billion dollars? Why?

NOTES

> *"Without a good question, a good answer has no place to go."*
> **- Clayton Christensen**

MEMORY · RECALL QUESTIONS

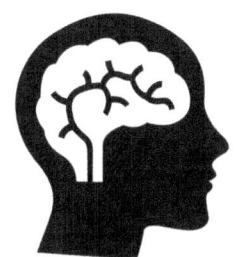

1. *Describe what happened just now/today/ yesterday.*
2. *Tell me about what you learned today.*
3. *What do you remember about today/ yesterday/the weekend/the activity/the experiment/summer break/your vacation/etc.? Tell me more.*
4. *What was your favorite/least favorite part of today/yesterday/the weekend? Why?*
5. *What was the hardest/easiest thing you did today?*
6. *What are you thankful for today? Why?*

· · · · · · · · · · ·

7. *Tell me about the games you played.*
8. *Teach me the games you like to play.*
9. *Tell me about how this works.*

· · · · · · · · · · ·

10. *What games did you play during recess*
11. *Share what you did that was fun/ exciting/hard/easy/messy/etc.*
12. *What happened that made you happy/ sad/angry/sorry/etc. today?*
13. *What are you looking forward to doing tomorrow/this weekend?*

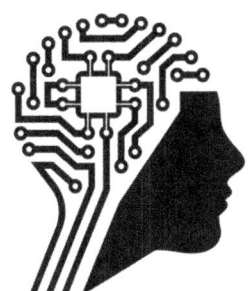

14. *How would you describe me/yourself/ your friend/your family/your pet/etc.?*
15. *Tell me about yourself/your friend/your family/your pet/etc.*

16. *How did you meet?*
17. *How did you become friends?*
18. *Tell me about what you and your friend/ family/nanny/babysitter/pet like to do together.*
19. *What did you do with your friend/family/ nanny/babysitter/teacher/pet?*
20. *What is the nicest thing a friend/family member/nanny/babysitter has ever done for you?*
21. *What does your pet like to do?*
22. *Why did you choose that type of pet?*

· · · · · · · · · · ·

23. *Did any of your friends do/say anything silly/funny/sad/? What?*
24. *Why do you think they did/said that?*
25. *What did you say when they said that?*
26. *What did you do when they did that?*
27. *How did that make you feel?*
28. *What can you do to change how you feel?*
29. *What did your teacher/friends/parents suggest?*
30. *Did you tell anyone "thank you" or "you're welcome" today? Why?*
31. *What would you do if you were me/a parent/an adult/a teacher/president for a day?*

· · · · · · · · · · ·

32. *How would you describe your room/ home/school/playground/neighborhood/ community/etc.?*

MEMORY • RECALL QUESTIONS

33. What do you like/dislike about your room/home/classroom/school/playground/neighborhood/community/etc.?
34. What if you could redesign it? What would you change/add/take away?

••••••••••••

35. How did you get here?
36. Which route did you take? Why? Show me.
37. What if you drew a map to show me?
38. Why did you come/leave?

••••••••••••

39. How did you find out about this?
40. What did you think you would do?
41. What did you expect would happen?

••••••••••••

42. What happened in the story?
43. What happened first/next/second/third/last?
44. How do you feel about the story/book/characters/setting?
45. Tell me about a song/poem/chant/story you heard today.
46. What did you like or dislike about the song/poem/chant/story?

••••••••••••

47. What do you think about when you lay down/rest/wake up?
48. What's the funniest/saddest/scariest thing you have ever seen? Why do you think so?
49. If you could change one rule, what would it be?
50. What happened in the block/kitchen/dramatic play/art/reading/playground area?

51. What happened on the playground/in the yard?
52. What happened when you played house?
53. What did you do inside/outside?
54. What happened at breakfast/circle/snack/lunch/dinner time?
55. How did you find the missing piece?
56. How did you make the discovery?
57. How did you solve the problem/fix it?
58. How am I supposed to use this piece/material?

••••••••••••

59. What could you/they have done differently?
60. What could do/say next time?
61. How can you make your day better than it has been?
62. How can you make today/tomorrow better than yesterday/today?
63. What can you do to remember how you fixed it/did it?

"HOW DO YOU...?" QUESTIONS

How do you...

1. ...play?
2. ...play that game?
3. ...solve a puzzle?
4. ...pretend you are doing something?
5. ...make a phone call/text?
6. ...get help when there is an emergency?
7. ...ask for help?
8. ...offer to help?
9. ...stay safe when there is a fire/ tornado/hurricane/storm?
10. ...cross a street?
11. ...ask for something?
12. ...say you don't want something?
13. ...share?
14. ...count?
15. ...write/draw/paint/mold clay?
16. ...mix colors?
17. ...read a book?

18. ...check out/borrow a book from the library?
19. ...write/send a postcard or letter?
20. ...pack/send a package?
21. ...help your parents/teacher/brother/ sister/others?
22. ...learn something new?
23. ...sharpen a pencil?
24. ...erase something you've written?
25. ...turn on a computer?

26. ...search for information on the computer?
27. ...Google it?
28. ...program a robot?
29. ...make friends?
30. ...keep friends?
31. ...hurt someone's feelings?
32. ...make someone feel better?
33. ...apologize?
34. ...show someone you care about them?
35. ...keep from hitting/fighting?
36. ...solve a problem?
37. ...fix a mistake?
38. ...repair something that's broken?
39. ...mend torn clothes?
40. ...do the laundry/clean your clothes?
41. ...find out how something works?
42. ...know which is the front/back?
43. ...measure something?
44. ...know it's bedtime?
45. ...get ready for bed?
46. ...turn the water on/off?
47. ...brush your teeth?
48. ...wash your hands?
49. ...take a bath/shower/dry off?

50. ...know when to wake up?
51. ...make a bed?
52. ...change the sheets?
53. ...turn the lights on/off?

"HOW DO YOU...?" QUESTIONS

54. ...dim the lights?
55. ...open/close/lock/unlock the door?
56. ...open/close/lock/unlock the window?
57. ...know which shoe goes on which foot?
58. ...button/zip your clothes?
59. ...tie/Velcro your shoes?
60. ...know if your clothes are on inside out/backward?
61. ...put on a coat/sweater?
62. ...take care of a pet?
63. ...take care of a baby?
64. ...change a diaper?
65. ...keep the bugs away?
66. ...keep from getting sunburned?
67. ...keep from getting hurt?
68. ...talk to your mom/dad/grandma/ grandpa?
69. ...play football/basketball/soccer/golf/ tennis/etc.?
70. ...hold, catch, roll, toss, kick, bat a ball?

71. ...ride a bike/roller skate/ride a skateboard?
72. ...swim in water/dive?
73. ...boogie board/ski/surf?
74. ...walk/run/hop/jump/skip/slide/ dance/balance on one foot/etc.?
75. ...balance on one foot?
76. ...jump rope?
77. ...balance/keep from falling?
78. ...know where to step?
79. ...ride a horse?
80. ...invite friends to a party?

81. ...throw a party?
82. ...make sure everyone has fun?
83. ...prepare/serve food/cook a meal?
84. ...make ice?
85. ...make ice cream?
86. ...sit properly in a car/bus/plane?
87. ...stay safe in the car/bus/plane?
88. ...buy a ticket?
89. ...travel to a faraway place?
90. ...call an elevator?
91. ...tell an elevator where to stop?
92. ...volunteer?
93. ...earn money?
94. ...save money?
95. ...pay for things?
96. ...get a job?
97. ...start a business?
98. ...fill something up/empty it?
99. ...behave in the library/hospital/classroom?
100. ...build a house/bridge/tunnel/tower/ enclosure, etc.?
101. ...fold and fly a paper plane?
102. ...make origami?
103. ...weave a basket?
104. ...mow/water the lawn?
105. ...plant a seed/garden?
106. ...recycle/compost?
107. ...save our planet?

SCIENTIFIC INQUIRY

The Scientific Process:

1) Purpose or goal
2) Hypotheses or prediction
3) Experiment or test the hypothesis
4) Analyze the data and results
5) Draw a conclusion and explain results

1. Tell me about what you are doing.
2. That's interesting. How did you do that?
3. What can you do with it?
4. What are your plans for those?
5. How do you know how to do it?
   . . . .
6. What do you know about making predictions/guessing what will happen?
7. What do you think will happen?
8. What do you expect to find?
9. What makes you think that?
10. What evidence do you have to support your prediction?
    . . . .
11. What tools/materials will help you?
12. What tool will you need? (magnifying glass, microscope, eyedropper, pipette, measuring cup, tweezers, tongs, hammer, nails, magnets, beakers, ruler, etc.)
13. What material will you use? Why? (cork, foil, plastic, wire, sponge, rubber band, paint, paperclip, water, sand, clay, tray, feather, pipe cleaners, foam, sponge, etc.)
14. How does the material/tool/equipment work?
15. What is the purpose of this tool/material?
16. How do you think this tool/material was made?

17. What would happen if you used different materials/tools?
18. What will you do with those?
19. What else can you do with the material/tool?
20. What is the same/different about these materials/tools?
21. How can you find out how many/much you need?
22. How can/did you organize/sort the material to make your work easier?
23. Why did you place those there/together/apart?
24. How do they fit/work together?
25. Why don't they fit/work together?
26. What would happen if you added more/took some out?
27. Why do you have so few/many?
28. What if you tried a different size/shape/color?
    . . . .
29. What do you know about experiments?
30. How do we learn from experiments?
31. Why do we conduct experiments?
32. What are you trying to find out?
    . . . .
33. What steps will you take?
34. What will/did you do next/before/first/after/then/next/second/last?
35. What if you observed it for a while?
36. What if you took more time?
    . . . .
37. What did you notice/observe/see/hear/smell/feel/taste when you did that?
38. How does it look/sound/smell/feel/taste?
    . . . .

SCIENTIFIC INQUIRY

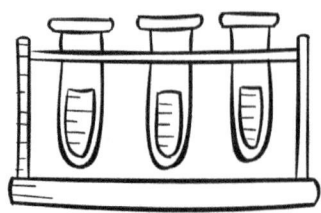

39. What happened?
40. How can you explain what happened?
41. How does/did it react or respond?
42. What is/was it doing?
43. Why do you think it does that?
44. What do you think caused that?
45. How is it doing that?
46. Why doesn't/didn't it work?
      · · · · · · · · · · ·
47. What changes do you observe?
48. How do you know it changed?
49. Why do you think it changed?
50. What changed the most/least?
51. How can you keep it from changing?
      · · · · · · · · · · ·
52. How did you figure that out?
53. How will you solve the problem?
54. What is/was the easiest/most challenging thing you did?
      · · · · · · · · · · ·
55. How does it move/work/turn/spin/fly/ roll/stop/go/etc.?
56. How can you keep it from falling/spilling/ melting/mixing/floating/splashing/ bubbling/moving/going/stopping/rolling/ mixing/freezing/dropping/flying/etc.?
57. How can you make it do that?
58. What would happen if you opened/tilted/ filled/emptied/mixed/moved/opened/ pulled/pushed/dropped/flipped/ upended/shook/lifted/rolled it?
59. What would happen if you took it apart/ separated those/put it back together/ attached this?
      · · · · · · · · · · ·

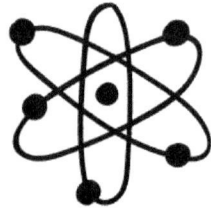

60. How can you find out more about it?
61. What might you try instead?
62. How else can you do the experiment/test it?
63. What would you do if you had more time?
64. What will you do differently next time?
      · · · · · · · · · · ·
65. How can you find out if you guessed, predicted/estimated correctly?
66. What happened that you didn't expect to happen?
67. Why do you think that happened?
68. What might have caused that to happen?
69. Why do you think you got that result?
70. How would you describe what happened?
71. How would you explain the results?
72. What did you learn from the process/ experiment?
73. What did you discover?
      · · · · · · · · · · ·
74. How can you record what you did?
75. How will you remember what happened?
76. How can you gather more information?
      · · · · · · · · · · ·
77. How could a friend help?
78. How can you work as a team?
79. How do you know which tasks you will do?
80. What if you worked with someone who has done it before?

81. How can you put it away until later/next time/tomorrow?
82. What will you do with it after you finish?

NOTES

THE HUMAN BODY

1. Tell me about your **body**/body parts.
2. How would you describe your body/body parts?
3. How do your body parts work? (head, mouth, arms, fingers, hands, legs, feet, tummy, etc.)
4. How do your fingers/wrists/arms/ shoulders/legs bend?
5. How does your body move?
6. How does your body grow?
7. What types of things help your body grow?
8. How can you tell how much you've grown?
9. How do you know how tall you are?
10. How can you find out how much you weigh?

....

11. How do you take care of your body?
12. How do you clean your body?
13. Why do feet/bodies stink sometimes?
14. Why do you take baths/showers?
15. Do you prefer to take baths or showers? Why?
16. Why do people use soap when they wash their bodies?
17. Why do people cut their fingernails/ toenails?

....

18. How does your **brain** work?
19. How do you think your brain tells your body what to do?
20. What happens when you think about something?
21. Why do you remember/forget things?
22. What can you do to remember things?
23. Why is it important to wear a helmet?

....

24. What makes your **heart** beat?
25. How can you measure your heartbeats?
26. What can you do to change the rate of your heartbeat?
27. What happens to your heartbeat when you run/exercise/get excited/get scared/ move fast/sleep/rest?
28. Why do you think your heart beats fast when you run/exercise/move quickly/get excited?
29. Why do you think your heart beats slowly when you calm down/rest/sleep?
30. What if your heart stopped beating?
31. Why do you think the heart is called the hardest-working muscle?

....

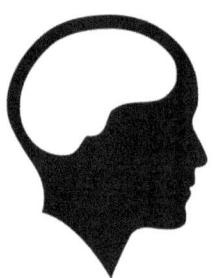

THE HUMAN BODY

32. How does your **nose** work?
33. Why do you think you have two holes in your nose?
34. Where does the air go?
35. How do you feel when you smell something bad/sweet/good/you like/you don't like? Why?
36. Why do we blow our noses?
37. Why do noses run/bleed/turn red/get sore/get congested?

. . . .

38. How do you **breathe**?
39. What organ holds the air when you breathe? How do you think it works?
40. How does air get into your **lungs**?
41. What happens to your chest/lungs when you breathe?
42. What happens if you can't breathe?
43. How do you take a deep breath vs. a shallow breath?
44. What do you have to do to hold your breath?
45. Why can't you hold it longer?
46. How do you breathe when you're excited/resting/calm/scared/walking/running/etc.?
47. Can people breathe underwater? Why? Why not?
48. What would happen if people tried to breathe underwater?
49. What happens when you breathe in smoke?

. . . .

50. What do you know about **skin**?
51. What do you notice about your skin?
52. Why does your skin cover your entire body?
53. How does skin move when you do?
54. Why do some people have hair growing on their skin, and others don't?
55. What happens if you pull/pinch/rub your skin?
56. How does your skin feel when you rub/scratch it?
57. Why do people have different skin tones/colors?
58. What do you know about melanin?
59. Does it matter what color your skin is? Why? Why not?
60. Can you tell anything about a person by their skin tone? Why? Why not?
61. How does our skin protect us?
62. How do people get a tan/get sunburned?
63. Do you think we are all the same under our skin? Why? Why not?
64. How can we prove that we are all the same under our skin?
65. Why are all skin tones beautiful?

. . . .

66. Why do people **sweat**?
67. Why do people sweat when they get hot/exercise?
68. Is it normal for a person to sweat when they exercise/work out/are hot? Why? Why not?
69. What should you do if you sweat a lot?
70. How can you replace the water you lose when you sweat?

THE HUMAN BODY

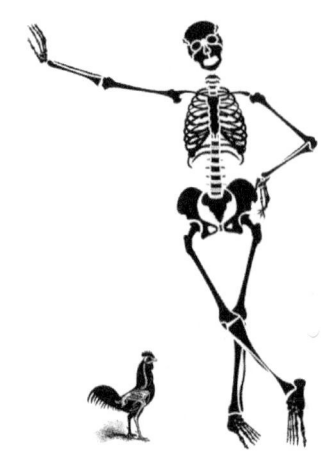

71. Why is it important to drink water when you sweat?
72. Is there such a thing as sweating too much? Tell me about it.
73. What does it mean to be dehydrated?
74. Are you healthy when you are dehydrated? Why? Why not?
75. What happens to your body if you don't drink water/hydrate?
76. Did you know your ears, lips, and nails don't sweat? Why do you think that is?

  ···········

77. What is **blood**?
78. How does blood stay in your body?
79. Why do you think human blood is red?
80. What about animals and insects? Do you think they all have red blood, too? Why? Why not?
81. How does blood move around your body?
82. What does blood do in your body?
83. How does blood deliver nutrients/oxygen to cells?
84. What does it mean to donate blood?
85. Why do people donate blood?

  ···········

86. Feel your arm/leg. What is this hard thing under your skin?
87. What do you know about **bones**?
88. Why do you think people have bones?
89. Why are the bones under your skin. Why not on top?
90. What if bones were on the outside of our bodies?

91. What if people didn't have bones?
92. How do bones/skin grow?
93. How are bones held together/ connected?
94. How do people move their bones?
95. What happens when a bone breaks?
96. How does a bone heal after it breaks?
97. How do doctors fix bones that break?
98. What is a **skeleton**?
99. How is a human skeleton different from that of an animal?

  ···········

100. How do **muscles** work?
101. How do muscles help you move?
102. Do you think we can move without our muscles? Why? Why not?
103. How do you contract/tighten/loosen a muscle?
104. How do muscles make you weak/ strong?
105. How can you tell how weak/strong a muscle is?
106. What can you do to make your muscles stronger?

  ···········

107. Why do people have **teeth**?
108. Describe your teeth.
109. What do you notice about your teeth?
110. How do your teeth help you? What is their job?

THE HUMAN BODY

111. Why do you have to chew your food?
112. What do you think would happen if you didn't chew your food before you swallow?
113. What if your teeth were soft like clay/cotton?
114. What if you didn't have any teeth?
115. What is the difference between your front teeth (incisors, canines) and your back teeth (premolars, molars, wisdom teeth)?
116. Why do you think we are born with two sets of teeth? (baby and adult)
117. What happens when your tooth falls out/gets loose?
118. Why do you think we lose our baby teeth when we are young?
119. Do you think you can get baby teeth to grow back? Why? Why not?
120. How do you get new adult teeth?
121. How do people straighten their teeth?
122. Why do people straighten their teeth

Also see Teeth > Health

··········

123. What do you know about your **eyes**?
124. Describe your eyes.
125. Why do you think eyes are different colors/shapes?
126. Do you think the colors mean anything? Why? Why not?

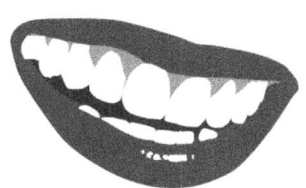

127. What if you wanted to change your eye color?
128. Why do you think the muscles in the eyes are called the busiest?
129. Why do people have eyelids/eyelashes?
130. Why do people open/blink their eyes?
131. What happens when you open/blink your eyes?
132. Why can't you see when you close your eyes?
133. Why is it dark when you close your eyes?
134. Why do your eyes produce tears when you cry?
135. Why do you think it's impolite to stare?
136. Why do some people wear corrective glasses/contact lenses?
137. Why do people wear sunglasses?
138. How do people move around if they can't see/are blind?

··········

139. How do **ears** work?
140. What do you do if you want to listen to someone/something?
141. What if sounds are too loud/quiet/soft?
142. Is it safe to stick things in your ears/ Why? Why not?
143. What happens if you damage your eardrums?
144. Do you think there is a real drum in our ear? Why? Why not?
145. How do eardrums get damaged?
146. What if you couldn't hear anything?
147. What do people do who can't hear/are deaf?

··········

THE HUMAN BODY

148. *How does your **tongue** work?*
149. *Why do you think your tongue is pink instead of another color?*
150. *What makes a tongue change color?*
151. *Does your tongue change color forever, or just for a little while? Why?*
152. *How does your tongue feel?*
153. *What are those nubs for on your tongue?*
154. *What if your food is too cold/hot?*
155. *What happens when food is sour/ sweet/salty/spicy/etc.?*
156. *How does your tongue move around?*
157. *How does your tongue help you clean your teeth?*
158. *How does your tongue help you make sounds?*
159. *What if your tongue was shorter/ longer?*

············

160. *Where does food go when you eat? How do you know?*
161. *What do you know about your **stomach**?*
162. *How does the stomach work?*
163. *What does your stomach do with the food?*
164. *Why do people get hungry?*
165. *How do you feel when you are hungry?*
166. *What happens if you eat too much food/overeat?*

167. *Why do people get stomachaches?*
168. *What would happen if you stopped eating food forever?*
169. *What causes people to burp/belch/ throw up?*
170. *How does gas/a burp come out?*

············

171. *What do you know about **hair**?*
172. *How does hair grow?*
173. *How do you take care of your hair?*
174. *What do you do to keep your hair clean?*
175. *How do you keep the knots out of your hair?*
176. *Why do people brush/comb their hair every day?*
177. *How do you get your natural hair color/texture?*
178. *What do you notice about the different textures/colors/styles of people's hair?*
179. *Why do you think there are different colors/textures/styles of hair?*
180. *What do you think makes hair curly/ wavy/straight/kinky/a certain color?*
181. *Can people change the type/style/ color of hair they have? How?*
182. *How do people use tools to cut/style their hair?*
183. *Why do you think people cut/color/ style their hair differently: short, long, buzzed, braided, messy bun, ponytail, etc.?*

THE HUMAN BODY

184. Why do some people have more hair than others?
185. Why do you think some people don't have any hair?
186. Why do people have hair on other parts of their bodies/face/arms/legs?
187. Why do people shave their hair?
188. How do people shave their hair?
189. Why do you think hair grows back after it is cut/shaved?
190. What can people do who don't have hair?

....

191. How do you take a **bath/shower**?
192. What's the difference between taking a shower and taking a bath?
193. Why do people take baths/showers?
194. How does staying clean keep you healthy?
195. Where do people wash their bodies/ hair? Why?
196. What are the steps to taking a bath/ shower?
197. How do people use materials/tools to wash and dry their bodies?
198. Why do people like to bathe in warm water?
199. Why do people stink/have body odor?
200. How do you have fun bathing/ showering?

....

201. Why do people have **belly buttons?**
202. How do people get a belly button?
203. Is everyone's belly button the same? How are they the same/different?
204. What's the difference between a belly button and a button on your clothes?
205. Why do you think a belly button is called an umbilicus?

....

206. Why do you think people go to the **bathroom/potty**?
207. Why do we use the toilet when we go to the bathroom?
208. Tell me what you do after you use the bathroom.
209. Why do people use toilet paper?
210. How does a toilet work?
211. What happens if you put too much toilet paper in the toilet?
212. Why do we flush the toilet after going to the bathroom/potty?
213. Where do you think the water goes when you flush the toilet?
214. What is sewage?
215. What is the purpose of a septic tank?
216. Why is it important to wash your hands after you use the potty?
217. What's the difference between toilet water and drinking water?
218. What if you have to go to the bathroom, but there is no toilet?

....

THE HUMAN BODY

219. What does it mean for parts of your body to fall asleep?
220. How does your body react when it gets very cold/hot?
221. Why do you shiver when you're cold?
222. Why do your teeth chatter when you get cold?

·············

223. What do you know about your **senses**?
224. What does it mean to taste/touch/see/hear/smell?
225. How can you identify something using your senses?
226. How does your body taste/touch/see/hear/smell?
227. Why do you think we have two eyes, two ears, two nostrils, and one mouth?
228. Do you think your senses help you remember things? Why? Why not?
229. How do your senses help you get through the day?
230. What if you couldn't smell/see/hear/touch/taste?
231. What do you think about this smell/sight/sound/taste/texture?

232. How do different smells/sights/sounds/tastes/textures affect you?
233. What are your favorite/least favorite smells/sights/sounds/tastes/textures?

·············

234. What questions do you have about your body?

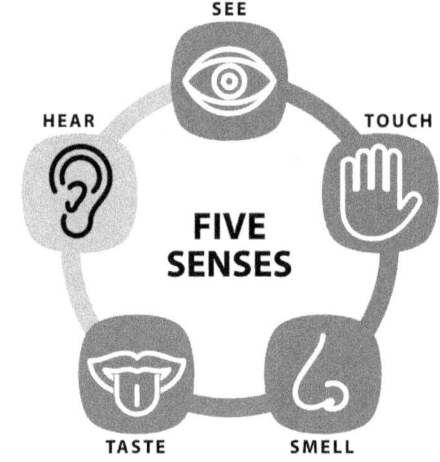

HEALTH

1. What does it mean to be **healthy**?
2. How do people stay healthy?
3. How do you know if your body is healthy?
4. How can you keep your body healthy?
5. What does it mean to have healthy habits?

·············

6. What's the difference between healthy and unhealthy **food**?
7. How does healthy/unhealthy food affect your body?
8. What can you do to feed your body healthy food?
9. Why is it important to start the day with a healthy breakfast?
10. What does "eat colorfully" or "eat a rainbow" mean?
11. How does a person eat a rainbow?
12. What is junk/processed food?
13. Why do people call food "junk food."
14. Why do people eat junk food when they know it's not healthy?
15. Is it okay to eat junk food? Why? Why not?

·············

16. What do you know about **germs**?
17. How can you keep germs away?
18. How do germs spread?
19. How can germs make us sick/affect our bodies?

20. Why do you wash your hands/body?
21. Why is it important to keep your body clean?
22. What can happen if you don't wash your hands/body?

·············

23. What happens when you get tired?
24. Why is it important to **rest/nap** when you're tired?
25. Why do people need to sleep?
26. How long do you think you should sleep every night? Why?
27. What will happen if you don't take a nap when you're tired?
28. What do you think would happen if you never slept?
29. Why is it important to get enough sleep every night?
30. How do you get ready to go to sleep?
31. Why do you think people snore/roll over/ talk/walk when they are asleep?
32. How do you wake up?
33. What if you want to wake up at a specific time?

·············

34. What does it mean to be **sick/**have an **illness**? (cold, flu, COVID, a disease)
35. How do people get sick?
36. Why do people get sick?
37. What do you know about the cold/flu/ COVID/viruses/diseases?
38. Tell me an illness/disease with which you are familiar. What do you know about it?

HEALTH

39. Where do you go when you get sick? Why?
40. How do people get better/well?
41. Does everyone eventually get better/well? Why? Why not?
42. What do people do to make others feel better when they are sick?

···········

43. What happens when people cut their skin?
44. Why do people **bleed** when they cut their skin?
45. What can you do to stop bleeding?
46. What would you do if the cut was small/really big?
47. What does the skin look like when it is healing?

···········

48. How do you think scabs/scars form on the skin?
49. Why does a scab/scar form on your skin?
50. Why does every scar look different?

···········

51. What happens when your skin gets dry/chafed/burned?
52. How does your skin feel when it's dry/chafed/burned?
53. How do you treat dry/chafed/burned skin?
54. What do you think causes a burn/rash/dry skin?

···········

55. Describe how a bruise looks?
56. Why do bruises form on your skin?
57. Why do bruises turn skin purplish/dark colors?

···········

58. What is an **allergy**?
59. Why are people allergic to things?
60. What do you think causes people to have allergies? Why?
61. Why is it important to know what you are allergic to?
62. Why is it important for people to know what allergies they have?
63. What happens if someone has an allergic reaction?

···········

64. Why do people **sneeze**?
65. What happens when you sneeze?
66. How can you keep from sneezing on other people?
67. What happens if you don't cover your mouth when you sneeze?
68. How does covering your mouth prevent the spread of germs?

···········

69. What is a **fever**?
70. Why does your body temperature rise when you're sick?
71. What can you do to bring a fever down?
72. How do you measure the temperature of your body?
73. Is a low/high body temperature a good thing or a bad thing? Why?

···········

HEALTH

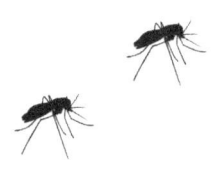

74. What happens when a **bug/insect bites** you?
75. Why do you think insects or bugs bite/pinch/sting?
76. How do people react to bites and stings?
77. Why do some people react to bug bites?
78. Why do some people itch/swell when a bug bites them?
79. How can you keep bugs from biting you?

....

80. What does it mean to **exercise**/work out/be physically active?
81. What can you do to exercise/work out?
82. Do you like to exercise? Why? Why not?
83. How do you feel when/after you exercise?
84. Why should you exercise every day?
85. Why do you think you have recess at school?
86. How would you feel if you didn't have recess at school every day?
87. What do you think would happen if you never exercised/worked out?
88. Why do you think you should rest after you exercise?

....

89. How do you clean your **teeth**?
90. What tools do you use to clean your teeth? (toothbrush, floss, Waterpik, mouthwash)
91. How do the tools help you?

92. How do your teeth feel when they are/aren't clean?
93. How often do you think you should clean your teeth? Why?
94. Why is it important to brush/floss your teeth every day?
95. What happens if you don't take care of your teeth?
96. What if you never cleaned your teeth?
97. How do sweets/sugars weaken your teeth?
98. What is a **cavity**?
99. How do you think you get a hole in your teeth?
100. What happens if you damage your teeth/get cavities/break a tooth?
101. How does a **dentist** help you?
102. Why do your teeth fall out when you are young?
103. What happens after your teeth fall out?
104. How does someone straighten their teeth?
105. What does an orthodontist do?

....

106. Why do people visit a **doctor** when they are/aren't sick?
107. Is it important to visit a doctor every year? Why? Why not?
108. Why should you have a physical?
109. What if people can't go to a doctor?
110. How does a doctor find out/know what's wrong with you?
111. What kind of tools/equipment does a doctor use? How?
112. How does a doctor see what's inside of a person's body?

HEALTH

113. *Why does a doctor swab the back of your throat/check your ears/look in your nose/take your temperature/listen to your lungs/give you shots?*

·············

114. *What is an **ambulance**?*
115. *How do you call for an ambulance to come to you?*
116. *What is a **paramedic**?*
117. *How do the paramedics driving the ambulance know where you live?*
118. *How do paramedics help you?*
119. *How do the paramedics learn how to help people?*

·············

120. *What is a **hospital**?*
121. *Why do people go to a clinic/hospital/ emergency room?*
122. *Why do people stay overnight in a hospital?*
123. *What do people do who work in a hospital?*
124. *What happens in a hospital?*
125. *What do hospitals have that you don't have at home? Why?*
126. *How does a nurse differ from a doctor?*

·············

127. *Why do people get **shots**/immunized?*
128. *What happens when you get a shot/ immunized?*

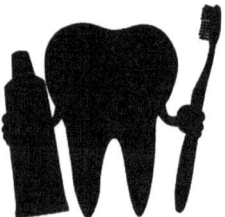

129. *How does getting shots/immunized help people?*
130. *What do you like/dislike about getting shots?*

·············

131. *What is a **prescription**?*
132. *How do you fill a prescription?*
133. *Do you fill a prescription like you fill a cup?*
134. *Why do people take **medicine**?*
135. *How do people get the medicine they need?*
136. *What is the difference between prescribed medicine and over-the-counter medicine?*
137. *Why do you have to be careful when you take medicine?*
138. *How do you know how much medicine to take?*
139. *What if you take too much medicine?*
140. *How do you know which medicine to take?*
141. *Have you ever taken medicine? Tell me about it.*
142. *What would happen if you took the wrong medicine?*
143. *What if people can't get the medicine they need to be healthy?*

MINDFULNESS · MEDITATION

1. What is mindfulness?
2. What does it mean to be mindful?
3. How can you find a happy place?

....

4. What does it mean to be **calm**?
5. What do you know about calming down/meditating/relaxing?
6. Why is it healthy for you to calm down/relax/meditate?
7. How does calming down/relaxing/meditating help you?
8. How do you calm yourself down/meditate/relax/find peace?
9. What steps do you take to relax/meditate?
10. How do you breathe when you are relaxing/meditating?
11. Describe what you picture in your mind when you relax/calm down.
12. How do you clear your mind of the things you don't want to think about?

....

13. What's the difference between a deep **breath** and a shallow breath?
14. How do you take deep/shallow breaths?
15. How can you help your body relax/**meditate**?
16. How does closing your eyes help you relax/meditate?

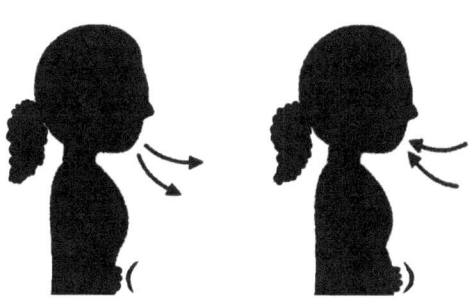

17. How does your body feel when you are relaxed/meditating? Why?
18. How do you shut out distractions/noise so you can relax/meditate?
19. Is it better to have silence or noise when you are trying to relax/meditate? Why?

....

20. Why do people sit/lay still when they relax/meditate?
21. Where is the best place to relax/meditate? Why?
22. Does where you relax/meditate make a difference? How?

....

23. How can you stay in the moment?
24. What is making you afraid/tense/fearful? Why?
25. What thoughts, beliefs, or stories are making you happy/sad/mad/anxious/scared?

....

26. When do you feel the most relaxed? Why?
27. Why do you think you are feeling that way?
28. What can you do about changing the way you feel?
29. What would you do differently if you knew nobody would judge you?

....

30. What are you the most grateful for in your life? Why?

MINDFULNESS · MEDITATION

31. What are you the proudest of in your life? Why?
32. What can you do to solve your problem/address your concern?
33. What is the one thing you can do today to make your day/life better? Why?
·············
34. What do you know about **stress**?
35. Why do you think you are stressed?
36. Do you think people can feel stress in their minds/bodies? How?
37. What can you do about the stress you feel/others feel?
38. Have you ever been stressed? Tell me about it.
39. What do you think stress does to a person?
40. How can you reduce the stress you are going through?
·············
41. Tell me about what/how you are **feeling**?
42. Why do you think you feel that way?
43. If you could label/put a name to your feelings, what would you call them? Why?

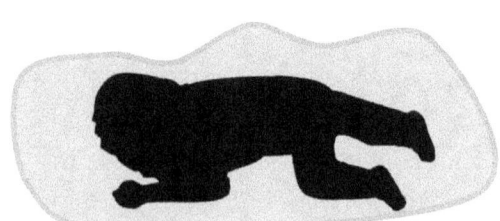

44. What makes you feel happy/sad/ anxious/angry/scared/frustrated/ disappointed/depressed/overwhelmed/ proud/excited?
45. What if you talked about your feelings with me/a friend/a relative?
46. What can you/I do to help you feel better?
47. What do you like to do when you're feeling down?
·············
48. What is a **dream**?
49. Do you have to be asleep to have a dream? Why? Why not?
50. Why do you think people dream?
51. Do you think everyone has dreams? Why? Why not?
52. Do you think your dreams are telling you something? Why? Why not?
53. What do you think your dreams mean?
54. What's the difference between a good dream and a bad/scary dream?
55. Why are some dreams scary and others not?
56. How do you calm down after having a scary dream?
57. What do people mean when they say, "Dreams can come true?"
·············

SOCIAL SKILLS ▪ CONFLICT RESOLUTION

1. What happened?
2. Tell me both sides of the story one at a time.
3. What is the problem?
4. I see that you are upset. What is bothering you?
5. I wonder if you can tell me what you did.
6. Help me understand what happened.
7. Could you expand on that with all of the facts?
8. I'm curious as to why you chose to do that.

....

9. What would you like to talk about?
10. What happens when you say/do that?
11. How did you react to that?
12. How did you/he/she/they respond when that happened?
13. Can you repeat the beginning/second part, so it is clear to me?

....

14. It's hard to understand/hear you like this. What can you do to calm down?
15. What can you do to feel better about what happened?
16. How can I/your friend help you?

....

17. Let's talk about your **feelings**.
18. You look very angry/upset/sad. Tell me why.

19. How do you feel right now?
20. How do you feel about what he/she did?
21. How do you feel about what happened?
22. How did it make you feel when …?
23. How do you feel when someone takes all of the___?
24. What can you/your friend do to make you feel better?

....

25. How do you think your friend feels now?
26. How would you feel if this happened to you?
27. How do you think he/she feels when you do that?
28. Why do you think your friend is upset/crying/yelling?
29. What can you do to make your friend feel better?

....

30. Tell me about a time when you felt this way.
31. Tell me about a time when this happened to you or someone you know.

....

32. Have you already tried to solve this problem? How?
33. What happened when you tried that solution?

SOCIAL SKILLS · CONFLICT RESOLUTION

34. *Why do you think that didn't work?*
35. *What could you have done differently?*

....

36. *Tell me what concerns you.*
37. *Tell me why that bothers you.*
38. *Tell me why you reacted that way.*

....

39. *How can you **solve** this **problem**?*
40. *What would you like to see happen?*
41. *What would it take for you to be able to move forward?*
42. *What do you think would be the best solution?*
43. *What ideas do you have that would meet both of your needs?*
44. *Why do you think your friend disagrees with your solution?*
45. *How can you both decide what will work/ is best?*
46. *How can you both agree on a solution?*
47. *How can you put your plan into place?*
48. *What materials/equipment do you need to make your plan work?*
49. *Do you both agree with this solution? Why? Why not?*
50. *What else can you try that will make both of you happy?*

51. *What do you need to do to make that happen?*

....

52. *What would happen if you each took a turn/waited/shared?*
53. *Why can't you both play at the same time?*
54. *How can you both/all play together?*
55. *What can you do to share?*
56. *What can you do while you patiently wait for your turn?*
57. *How will you know when it is time?*
58. *How will you know how long that is?*
59. *Have you considered...?*

....

60. *What will happen if you both pull on it?*
61. *What will happen if you don't treat this gently?*
62. *How will you use this if you break/twist/ drop it?*
63. *How would it feel to be building/playing/ working together?*
64. *What if someone gets hurt?*

....

65. *What was the conflict/problem in the story?*
66. *How did the characters in the story solve the problem?*
67. *If you were in the story, how would you have handled the problem?*

DISABILITY · SPECIAL NEEDS

1. What does it mean to have a **disability/ special need**?
2. Why do people have disabilities/special needs?
3. How do people become disabled?
4. What do you think it might feel like to have a disability?
5. How can you learn more about this disability/special need?
6. Why are some disabilities/special needs visible but not others? (physical, learning, sensory, psychological)
7. Why do you think there are so many different disabilities/special needs?
8. How can a disability or special need keep you from doing certain activities?
9. Why is it harder/easier to do some things when you have a disability/special need?
10. Do you know someone with a disability/ special need? Tell me about them.
      ···········
11. How can a disability affect how a person moves, sees, hears, or communicates?
12. How can someone with this disability/ special need get around/play/do their work?
13. How does a person who is deaf/mute communicate?
14. How can someone who is blind do the things you're doing?
15. How can someone missing a limb get around/play/work/do things?
      ···········
16. Tell me what you know about the tools that can help people with disabilities/ special needs.
17. What do you know about adaptive equipment/service animals?
18. How does adaptive equipment/do service animals help people with disabilities?

19. What kinds of adaptive equipment/ service animals are you familiar with? How does it work?
20. Have you ever met a service animal? Tell me about it.
      ···········
21. Are there any special abilities that people with disabilities/special needs might have?
22. What do you think are the biggest challenges for people with disabilities/ special needs?
23. Have you ever seen someone with a disability receive special services or support? What was it like?
      ···········
24. How might a person with a disability need extra support/help?
25. Why are there special parking spaces for people who have disabilities?
26. What do you think we can do to make our places/schools more accessible for people with disabilities?
27. How can you help people who have disabilities?
28. What do you think are the best ways to show respect and support to people with disabilities?
29. How can you be a good friend to someone with a disability?
30. How can we make sure that people with disabilities are included in our community?
31. What do you think we can do to make sure everyone is included and respected, regardless of abilities or special needs?

DIVERSITY · INCLUSION

1. What do you know about **diversity**? (Difference/Differences between two or more things.)
2. What does "multicultural" mean?
3. What does the word "human" mean?
4. What makes you human?

· · · · · · · · · · ·

5. What does the word "family/friend" mean?
6. What makes a **family**?
7. How would you describe your family?
8. How do you know you are family?
9. Draw a picture of your family.
10. Tell me something special about the people in your family/you live with.
11. What do you notice about other families?
12. Does everyone have the same type of family? Why? Why not?
13. Does it matter what kind of family you have? Why? Why not?
14. How are families you know the same/different from yours/other families?
15. How is the number of people in your family the same/different from other families?
16. In what ways do you look like/not look like your parents/siblings/relatives/family/friends?
17. Why do or don't you think you look like or don't look like your parents/siblings/relatives/family/friends?

18. Do all children look like their parents/siblings/relatives/family? Why? Why not?
19. Do you have to look the same to be family/relatives/friends? Why? Why not?
20. Do you think a family can include people from different cultures? Why? Why not?
21. How would you feel if someone told you that your family is strange/not a real family? Why?
22. What do you know about **traditions**?
23. How are traditions passed on from person to person?

· · · · · · · · · · ·

24. In what ways are you and I the same/different?
25. Do the differences you notice matter to you? Why? Why not?
26. Why do you think people have different hairstyles/hair color/body types/skin color/eye color/height/weight/shoe sizes?
27. How would it feel to live in a world where every person/everything is or looks exactly the same, and nothing ever changes?
28. If people looked exactly the same, how would you tell them apart?
29. Do you think we are all the same on the inside? Why? Why not? How?
30. How would you feel if there was only one style or type of food/toy/doll/clothing/shoe/action figure/car/bike/skateboard/flower/tree/etc.?
31. What do you think the term "melting pot" means?

· · · · · · · · · · ·

DIVERSITY · INCLUSION

32. Does everyone you know think/act/react the same/differently? How?
33. Should you judge an entire group by what one person does in the group? Why? Why not?
34. Why do you think people see/do/say/feel/act differently?
35. Why should you accept people who are different from you?

· · · · · · · · · · ·

36. What does the word *"tolerance"* mean?
37. How can you be more patient/tolerant?
38. Why do you think people have different opinions about things?
39. What can people do when they disagree/argue with each other?

· · · · · · · · · · ·

40. What do you know about **languages**?
41. Does everyone speak the same language? Why? Why not?
42. Why doesn't everyone speak the same language?
43. Can you tell which language someone speaks just by looking at them? Why? Why not?
44. Can you tell someone's ethnicity just by hearing them speak? Why? Why not?
45. What if a person speaks two languages?
46. How can you communicate with someone who doesn't speak your language?
47. What would you do if you couldn't understand what someone was saying?

48. How would you feel if you traveled to another country and no one could understand you?
49. What would you do to help people understand what you were saying?
50. How do you say "hello" or "friend" in other languages?
51. Please teach us how to count in your language.
52. How can you learn a new language?
53. If you could learn to speak a new language, which language would you want to learn? Why?

· · · · · · · · · · ·

54. Can you tell someone's ethnicity just by looking at them/what they wear/how they act? Why? Why not?
55. Why do you think people judge others by the way they look, speak, move, or act?
56. Do you think it is right to judge others like that? Why? Why not?
57. How would you feel if someone judged you by how you look or sound?
58. Does everyone who has the same skin color as you speak your language? Why? Why not?
59. How do our differences make where we live more interesting/a better place?

· · · · · · · · · · ·

60. What do you know about your **culture**/other cultures?
61. Do you think everyone from the same country looks/talks/dresses/eats/lives the same way? Why? Why not?
62. How can you find out more about your friend's culture?

DIVERSITY · INCLUSION

63. What makes learning about other cultures/ways of life interesting?
64. What can you learn from other cultures?

············

65. Why do you think people wear different styles of **clothing**?
66. Why do people wear traditional clothes?
67. What's the difference between clothes you wear every day and traditional clothing/garments?
68. What's the difference between every day clothes and costumes?
69. What can you teach people about your culture's traditional dress and meaning?

············

70. What do you remember about this culture/country from the **story** we read?
71. What do you notice about the characters in this story?
72. Why is it interesting/helpful to read about/explore the lives of people who are different from you?
73. How do stories/our experiences help us learn about the rest of the world?
74. How do characters help us see things from different perspectives?
75. How is the way the character lives in this story the same/different from the way you live?
76. Would you rather read about a character that is just like you or one that is different from you? Why?

77. Would you make the same choices as this character? Why? Why not?
78. Would you have solved the problem the same way as this character? Why? Why not?
79. What would you have done differently if you had the chance? Why?
80. What do you think the character would say about your choices?

············

81. What do you think makes someone a good **friend**?
82. What do you remember about visiting your friend? Going to the festival? The museum? The church? Our tour?
83. What do you remember about visiting another town/state/city/country?
84. How were you welcomed?
85. What do you think you can learn from people who are different from you?
86. Can someone be your friend when they don't look, speak, or act like you? Why? Why not?
87. What do you think when you meet someone who doesn't look, speak, or act like you?
88. If you were choosing a friend, what characteristics would you want to see in them? Why?
89. How can you make that person feel welcome?
90. What can you do if you want to cook/prepare food from another culture?

DIVERSITY · INCLUSION

91. *How can you share arts and crafts from your culture with others? - Papier Mâché maracas (Caribbean and Latin), dreamcatchers (American-Indian), origami (Japanese), or Rangoli sand art (Indian).*

....

92. *What does "**inclusion**" mean?*
93. *Why do people want to feel included?*
94. *How can you make people feel included in a group/an activity?*
95. *What if it's hard to include them?*
96. *What if the person can't do the things you can do?*
97. *What if the person has a physical challenge/mental challenge/disability?*
98. *How do you think a disabled person feels when they are excluded?*
99. *How can you find creative/different ways to play and include them?*
100. *How can you change the game/activity to include everyone?*
101. *What if you spoke to the group about including them?*
102. *What can you say to the group if they don't want to include a person?*
103. *How can you lead the group in finding a solution that will satisfy everyone?*
104. *What would you do if you couldn't find a way to include everyone?*
105. *Is it fair or unfair when children are left out because they are different? Why?*

106. *How can we redesign our classroom so that it is easier for a friend who uses a walker/wheelchair/assistive device to move around?*

....

107. *How would you feel if your friends didn't want to play with you because you look or speak differently than them?*
108. *What does it mean to be kind?*
109. *How can you be kind to someone?*
110. *What can you say to friends who aren't being kind?*
111. *What can you do if you see/hear someone being teased/made fun of/left out?*

....

112. *Think of a time when someone **teased**/made fun of/left you out because you looked or sounded different from them. How did it make you feel?*
113. *Have you ever teased/made fun of someone? What happened?*
114. *How did you feel after you teased/made fun of them?*
115. *How do you think they felt after you teased/made fun of them?*
116. *Think of a time when you said something that wasn't understood.*
117. *How did that make you feel?*

....

118. *How do your experiences shape who you are?*

DIVERSITY · INCLUSION

119. What do your experiences teach you about people?
120. How has someone helped you when you least expected it?
121. Why didn't you expect them to help?
122. How have you helped someone in a surprising way?
123. Why do you think they were surprised?

· · · · · · · · · · ·

124. What do you notice about this toy/doll/book/picture/movie/television show/game?
125. Do you think everyone would enjoy this toy/doll/book/picture/movie/television show/game? Why? Why not?
126. Why do some children think toys/clothing are made specifically for boys or girls?
127. Why is it okay for ALL children to play with dolls/action figures/kitchen toys/trucks/construction tools/blocks?
128. What difference does it make if boys and girls wear certain clothes/colors? Why?

129. Why do you think packaging and marketing attracts different people?
130. How would you redesign the package of your favorite toy so that either a boy or a girl would want to play with it?
131. If you could change something about this program/book/toy/game, what would you change? Why?

· · · · · · · · · · ·

132. Tell me about where you live.
133. Tell me about your **community**.
134. What happens in your community?
135. Do you think all communities are the same? Why? Why not?
136. What makes a community?
137. Describe the people who live/work in your community.
138. Why are people called community helpers?
139. In what ways do people help their community?
140. How can you help your community?

HOME

1. What makes a home?
2. Tell me about your home.
3. Describe where you live.
   ···········
4. What is a home/house/condo/apartment/motorhome/camper?
5. Do you think everyone lives in a house/apartment/condo/home/camper/car? Why? Why not?
6. Why do people live in houses/homes/apartments/condos/motorhomes/cars/on the street?
7. What can we do to help people who don't have a home?
   ···········
8. How is your home different from others you've seen/visited?
9. Why do you think there are different types of homes?
10. Why do you think people around the world live in different kinds of homes?
11. Why are some homes large/small/one-story/two-story/in buildings?
12. Why are most homes built on/near streets?
13. What about homes that are built in the mountains/city? How are they the same/different?
    ···········
14. What do you notice about the shape/style/size of your home?

15. How does your home look/smell/sound?
16. How do you feel when you're in your home?
17. How do you feel when you get home after school? Why?
18. Why do you think you feel that way?
19. What is your favorite/least favorite thing in your home? Why?
20. Do you think your home makes you feel that way, or is it the people inside? Why?
21. Tell me about the people with whom you live.
    ···········
22. How do you stay **safe** in your home?
23. Why do people use keys/locks/alarms/cameras/monitors?
24. How does your home protect you from what's outside/the weather?
25. What happens when it rains/snows/hails/is windy/there is a storm?
    ···········
26. What do you know about home **addresses**?
27. How do people find your home?
28. How do people send mail to your home?
29. How does the postal worker know where you live?
30. What do the numbers in an address mean?
31. How do you know which street someone lives on?
32. What is a zip code?

HOME

33. How do you find stores/hospitals/other people's homes?

·············

34. What do you know about **maps**?
35. How can you draw a map of the inside/outside of your home to show me where things are?
36. How can you draw a map to show me how to get to your home?
37. What places are near your home?

·············

38. What kinds of things or activities do you do inside/outside your home?
39. Do animals/insects live in homes like yours? Why? Why not?
40. How do you keep your **room**/home clean?
41. Why do rooms/homes get dirty/messy?
42. What type of furniture goes in a home? Why do you need it?
43. What types of rooms do you have in your home?
44. Tell me about where you sleep/eat/bathe/work/play/watch TV in your home.
45. Why do you think some homes have different rooms/areas/sections? (living room, dining room, bedroom, kitchen, bathroom, laundry room, mudroom, movie room, hallway, garage, carport, elevator, fountain, garden, Jacuzzi, swimming pool/etc.)
46. What do people do in those rooms?
47. Do people have to have those rooms in their homes? Why? Why not?

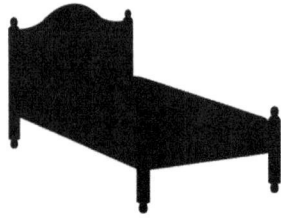

48. What if people don't have those rooms? What do they do?
49. Why do you think some homes have or don't have windows/doors/a roof/stairs/a fireplace/a chimney/carpet/rugs/walls/a sink/a toilet/a bath tub/a shower/appliances/plumbing/electricity/gas/a yard/etc.?
50. Tell me what you know about those things.
51. Why do you use those things?
52. How do you use those things?
53. How do you know what to do with those things?

·············

54. What if you wanted to **design** a home? How would you do it?
55. Which rooms do you think are the most important to have? Why?
56. What do you think you need the most/least in a home? Why?
57. How can you draw plans to **build** your home?
58. How can you learn to build a home?
59. What materials/tools would you need to build a home? Why?
60. Where can you find materials/tools to build a home? How do you know?
61. What would you have to do to build a home for yourself/an animal/an insect/a doll/a superhero/in a tree?
62. How can you make your home stronger/taller/wider/thinner?

HOME

63. How can you find out how strong/tall/ wide/thin your home is?

....

64. What does it mean to **maintain** something?
65. What happens when something in your home breaks/stops working?
66. How do people know how to **fix** things that break/stop working?
67. What happens when people don't know how to fix something that breaks/stops working?
68. Why does it cost money to fix things?
69. Why do people hire someone to fix things instead of doing it themselves?
70. What do people do with things they can't fix? Why?

....

71. Do you have to have furniture/appliances in your home? Why? Why not?
72. What if you don't have furniture/ appliances?
73. Tell me about the furniture/appliances in your home.
74. What types of things can you find inside/ outside of your home?
75. What things don't you need in a home? Why?
76. What can you do if you have too many things in your home?
77. How do you get rid of things you don't need in your home?

....

78. What is the difference between renting and buying a home?
79. How much do you think it costs to buy a home? Why do you think homes cost so much?
80. How much do you think it costs per month to rent a home?
81. What if you wanted to plant a garden/ plant a tree by your home? What would you do?

....

82. What is a **neighborhood/community**?
83. What do you notice about your neighborhood/community?
84. Describe your neighborhood/community.
85. How do you know if you live in a neighborhood/community?
86. What types of things can you find in a neighborhood/community?
87. Why do you think being part of a community is important?
88. What do you think it means when someone says, "Home is where the heart is?"

CLOTHING · SHOES

1. What do you know about clothes/shoes?
2. Why do people wear clothes/shoes?
3. What if people didn't wear clothes/shoes?
4. When is it okay not to wear clothes/shoes?
5. Does everyone have the same clothes/shoes? Why? Why not?
6. What do you have to do to get dressed?

············

7. What are the different types of clothes/shoes people wear?
8. What's the difference between your clothing and shoes?
9. How do you know what to wear every day?
10. What does it mean to wear casual clothing?
11. What does it mean to dress up?
12. Why do people dress up?
13. Why do you think clothes come in different designs/styles? (colors, fabrics, lengths, sizes, types, etc.)
14. Can you wear your parent's/caregiver's/teacher's clothes/shoes? Why? Why not?
15. How is one design/style the same or different from another?
16. Why are there clothes for different activities? (work, school, bedtime, fitness, sports, swimming, etc.)
17. Why are there shoes for different activities? (sneakers, running shoes, sandals, flip-flops, boots, cleats, flippers, house slippers, etc.)

18. What else do people wear? Why? (swimsuits, hats, coats, gloves, stockings, scarves, socks, ties, etc.)
19. What is the purpose of wearing those things?

············

20. How would you describe what you're wearing?
21. How do your clothes/shoes feel on your skin/feet?
22. Does it matter what design/style/color your clothes are? Why? Why not?
23. Describe the design/image/graphic/colors/pattern on your clothes/shoes.
24. Describe the clothes you see that have stripes/lace/fringe/studs/grommets/V-necks/crew necks/dots/patterns/holes/short sleeves/long sleeves.
25. Describe the clothes you see that have images of people/animals/insects/dinosaurs/shapes/numbers/letters/etc.
26. Describe the shoes you see that have stripes/patterns/laces/grommets/straps/lights/glitter/a design/etc.
27. How do you think the design got on the shoes/clothes?
28. What if you drew the design you see on the clothes/shoes?
29. What if you drew your own design?
30. Can you find designs/images/graphics/colors/patterns on other things that are around you?

············

CLOTHING · SHOES

31. *What do you like/dislike about the clothes/shoes you wear?*
32. *What is your favorite/least favorite piece of clothing? Why?*

....

33. *What do you know about the **sizes** of clothes/shoes?*
34. *Why do you think stores have so many different sizes?*
35. *How do you know what size clothing/ shoes you wear?*
36. *How do you know if clothes/shoes will fit before you buy them?*
37. *What if you try on clothes/shoes that don't fit?*
38. *Can you wear clothes/shoes that are too small/big? Why? Why not?*
39. *Why do you think your clothes/shoes don't fit anymore?*

....

40. *Why do people change their clothes/ shoes to do things?*
41. *If you could change your clothes right now, what would you change into?*
42. *When do people change their clothes/ shoes? Why?*
43. *Why do people layer their clothes/put some clothes over other clothes?*
44. *How do you know if clothes match/go together?*
45. *Can two people wear the same style of pants/shirt/shorts/dress/skirt/shoes? Why? Why not?*

46. *What would happen if we all wore the exact same clothes/shoes? How could you tell us apart?*
47. *What do you notice about your friend's clothes/shoes?*
48. *What's the difference between what your friend is wearing and what you are wearing?*

....

49. *How do you keep shirts/pants/shorts/ dresses closed?*
50. *Why do you think clothes have buttons/ zippers/elastic/Velcro/seams/collars/ hems/belts/pockets/long sleeves/short sleeves/etc.?*
51. *What keeps buttons/zippers/Velcro/ patches on your clothes?*
52. *What happens when buttons pop off?*
53. *What happens when zippers get stuck?*
54. *What happens when Velcro no longer sticks?*
55. *What happens when you get a hole in your clothes/shoes?*
56. *What can you do to repair the hole?*
57. *What can you do to get a knot out of your shoelaces?*
58. *What would you do if your zipper broke?*

....

CLOTHING · SHOES

59. Why do people take care of their clothes?
60. How do people take care of their clothes?
61. How do people wash/dry/hang/iron/fold/take care of their clothes?
62. Do you have to use a washer to wash clothes? A dryer to dry clothes? Why? Why not?
63. What if you don't have a washer or dryer? What do you do?
64. Can you clean your clothes while you're wearing them? Why? Why not? How?
65. What if you wore the same clothes every day and never cleaned them?
66. How do you get wrinkles/stains out of clothes?

············

67. How do you think clothes/shoes are made?
68. What if you wanted to make clothes/shoes? How would you do it?
69. What material do you think would make a good shoe? Why?
70. What does it mean to thrift shop for clothes/shoes?
71. Do you have to buy your clothes? Why? Why not?

············

72. What does it mean to **sew**?
73. How do you sew?
74. How can you practice sewing?
75. What tools/machines do people use to sew?
76. How do tools/machines help people sew?
77. How do sewing tools/machines work?
78. Is it easier to sew by hand or with a machine? Why?
79. What does a machine do that you can't do by hand?
80. How do people repair clothes/shoes?
81. How can you change the style of your clothes/shoes?
82. What can people do to change the color/design of their clothes/shoes?
83. What's the difference between sewing, knitting, and crocheting clothes?

COOKING · KITCHEN

1. What does cooking mean?
2. Why do people cook **food**?
3. How does a person cook food?
4. What do people do when they cook?
5. How can you learn to cook food?
6. Does all food have to be cooked? Why? Why not?

· · · · · · · · · · · ·

7. Tell me about the meals you know how to make.
8. How do you know how to make that meal?
9. How do you think people know how to cook/bake food?
10. Why do you think you should help prepare/cook food?
11. How do you feel when you help prepare food?

· · · · · · · · · · · ·

12. Tell me about what you made/cooked.
13. Where have you seen people cooking? What were they doing?
14. How did you make your food/meal/drink?
15. What steps did you take?
16. How do you know what to do first/second/next/last?
17. How do you make juice/a sandwich/a pizza/a salad/soup/etc.?

· · · · · · · · · · · ·

18. What do you know about **ingredients/seasoning/spices**?
19. What do you notice when you add/mix the ingredients?
20. Why do you think people add ingredients/seasoning/spices to food?
21. How do the ingredients/seasoning/spices change the flavor?
22. How do you know how much to put in/on your dish?
23. What do you think will happen if you put in more/less seasoning or spices?
24. What would happen if you left ingredients/seasoning/spices out altogether?
25. What did you use to measure the ingredients/seasoning/spices? Why?
26. How do people know what/how much seasoning to put on their food?
27. Show me how you measured.
28. How do the seasonings/spices relate to your culture?
29. Why do you think food changes when you mix in/add ingredients?
30. How does the food change when you mix in/add ingredients?
31. Why can't you see the sugar/flour/etc. anymore?
32. What did you notice when you added water/oil/vinegar/eggs/dry goods?

· · · · · · · · · · · ·

COOKING · KITCHEN

33. What is a **recipe**?
34. How can you find recipes?
35. How do you follow a recipe?
36. How do recipes help people who want to cook?
37. How do you know if you will like a recipe?
38. Can you change a recipe? How?
39. How would you write a recipe for others to follow?
40. What is your favorite/least favorite recipe? Why?

· · · · · · · · · · ·

41. What **tools/equipment/utensils** did you use to prepare/cook/bake? Why?
42. How do tools/equipment make preparing food easier?
43. How did you know how to use the tools/equipment?
44. What if you didn't have the tools/equipment you needed?
45. Tell me about the tools you know how to use in the kitchen.

· · · · · · · · · · ·

46. What do you know about **temperature**?
47. What's the difference between cold food and hot food?
48. How can you tell the temperature of food?
49. What tool do you need to measure the temperature of food?
50. What food tastes best when it's cold/hot? Why?
51. Why do you think some food has to be kept hot/cold?

52. What happens when food isn't kept hot/cold when it should be?
53. Can some food be served either hot or cold? Why? Why not?
54. Is food ever too cold or too hot to eat? Why?
55. Is it best to eat hot ice cream/pizza/French fries/salad/smoothie/hamburger/hotdog or cold? Why?
56. How does food taste when you don't serve it at the right temperature?
57.

· · · · · · · · · · ·

58. What's the difference between cooking on a grill/fire pit and cooking on a stove/in an oven?
59. How does a microwave work?
60. What's the difference between cooking food on a stove versus a microwave?

· · · · · · · · · · ·

61. What shape will your food be when you finish?
62. How will you make the shape?

· · · · · · · · · · ·

63. How do you know how much food/drink to make?
64. How do you know how many to make/cook/bake?
65. What do you have to do to split the food/drink in half (for two people)?
66. How can you make sure everyone gets one?

· · · · · · · · · · ·

COOKING · KITCHEN

67. What happens to food when you keep it/ store it too long?
68. How do you know when food is fresh/safe to eat?
69. What happens when food spoils/goes bad?
70. Why do you think food spoils/goes bad?
71. What can you do to help food stay fresh?
72. How do you know if food needs to be cooked/refrigerated?
73. How do you know where to store food before/after you cook?
74. Why is some food stored in a can and other food in a bag/box?
75. What happens when we don't store food properly?
76. When food smells good/bad, do you want to eat it? Why? Why not?
77. What would happen if you ate spoiled food?
78. Why is it important to follow the directions on food containers?
79. What do you do when food falls on the floor?

· · · · · · · · · · ·

80. How does food change when it's cooked?
81. Why do you think food looks different after it's cooked?

· · · · · · · · · · ·

82. Would you cook food you don't like? Why? Why not?
83. What happens when people avoid cooking food because they don't like it?

84. Why is it important to taste what you are cooking/preparing?

· · · · · · · · · · ·

85. How do you know which pot/pan to use when cooking?
86. How can you find lids that match these pots/pans?
87. What if we didn't have pots/pans/trays/ cookie sheets?
88. What do you notice about the dishes/ bowls/pots/pans?
89. How do you stack/organize the dishes/ bowls/pans?
90. How can you put these measuring cups in order?

· · · · · · · · · · ·

91. How do you knead/flatten the dough?
92. Why do you think dough/bread/cake rises?
93. Why do you think butter melts?

· · · · · · · · · · ·

94. What if you wanted to decorate what you cooked? How would you do it?
95. Do you think this food is made in a bakery or a factory? Why?
96. How do you think this food is made?
97. What does healthy/junk food mean?

· · · · · · · · · · ·

98. How do you stay safe when you cook/in the kitchen?
99. How do you stay safe around a stove/ grill/hot food/hot liquid?
100. How do you keep from burning yourself when you cook food?

NOTES

> *"The ability to ask the right question
> is more than half the battle of finding the answer."*
> **- Thomas J. Watson**

NOTES

MEALTIME

1. What do you know about **food**?
2. Why do people need/eat food?
3. Why do people eat different foods?
4. Why do you wash your hands before you eat?

············

5. Tell me about the food you eat every day.
6. Tell me about the food you eat for breakfast/lunch/dinner/snacks.
7. Tell me about the food you like the most/least. Why?
8. What can you do to change the way you feel about the food you don't like?
9. What do you think your friends will like/dislike about this food/meal/drink?

············

10. Where does the food come from that you eat? How do you know?
11. How did the food get here?
12. Do you think all of the food comes from the same place? Why? Why not?
13. Do you think the food you eat has feelings? Why? Why not?

············

14. What do you notice about your food?
15. What can you tell me about the food on your plate?
16. What is the same/different about your food on your plate/the table?
17. How many shapes can you find on your plate/the table? How do you know what shape that is?

············

18. What does it mean to **taste** food?
19. Why is it important to taste new food?
20. How do you think this food/meal/drink is going to taste?
21. What will happen if you choose to taste/not to taste the food?
22. How big does a taste have to be? Why?
23. What is a taste test?
24. How will you know if you like/don't like the food?
25. How do flavors/textures/colors/tastes/affect how you feel about food?
26. What did you think when you tasted the food?
27. Describe how your food/meal/drink tastes.
28. How do we use our senses when we taste food?
29. Why do you think you liked/didn't like the food before?
30. Why do you think you like/don't like the food now?
31. Tell me how the food feels in your mouth.
32. How can you make your food taste better?
33. Why do you think food tastes salty/sweet/bitter/sour/bland/spicy?
34. How does this food compare to other food you've eaten?
35. What would happen if you never tasted new foods?

············

MEALTIME

36. How do you know how much food will fit on your spoon/fork/plate/chopstick?
37. What happens if you put too much food on your spoon/fork/chopstick/plate?
38. How do you know when to stop pouring?
39. What if you only want half of a cup?
40. What would happen if you poured too little/too much into your cup?

. . . .

41. What do you know about **utensils**?
42. Do you have to use utensils to eat? Why? Why not?
43. Does everyone eat the same way? How do you know?
44. Where have you seen people eat differently than you? How did they eat?
45. How do you use a utensil/fork/knife/spoon/chopsticks?
46. Why do you have to be careful when using forks/knives/sharp utensils?
47. What foods can you eat with a fork/knife/spoon/chopsticks/your fingers?
48. What can you use besides a knife to cut food?
49. Would you use a spoon or a fork to eat soup? Why?
50. How else can you drink soup?
51. When is it okay to eat with your hands?

. . . .

52. What if you wanted to cut your food into smaller pieces? How would you do it?
53. How do you know which pieces are smaller/larger?

. . . .

54. What do you do when you get food on your hands?
55. What do you know about **napkins**?
56. How do you use a napkin?
57. Why should you place the napkin on your lap?
58. What do you notice about the shape of your napkin?
59. What can you do to change the shape of your napkin?

. . . .

60. Why is a placemat on the table?
61. What is a place setting?
62. How can you make/design a place setting?
63. How do you know how many cups/plates to put on the table?
64. How can you ensure everyone gets a fork/spoon/knife/plate/serving?

. . . .

65. What is a/the **straw**? How is it used?
66. How does the liquid get up the straw?
67. What happens when you suck/blow in a straw?
68. Why do you think that happens?
69. What if the straw gets a hole/crack in it?
70. Do you have to use a straw to drink? Why? Why not?
71. What happens to the straw when you finish using it?
72. Do you think a lot of straws get thrown away? Is that a good or a bad thing? Why?

. . . .

MEALTIME

73. How do you know when it's time to eat?
74. How do you know when you are hungry/thirsty/full?
75. How do you know when to stop eating?
76. How do you know when you have eaten too much/not enough food?
77. How do you feel when you have eaten/drank too much?

. . . .

78. Why do people sit down/stand still to eat?
79. Is it a good idea to run/play/move/laugh/sing when you are eating? Why? Why not?
80. Is it a good idea for people to sit and eat their meals together? Why? Why not?
81. What makes dining together interesting?
82. What do you enjoy the most/least about eating together? Why?

. . . .

83. What happens if you eat too many sweets/pieces of candy/treats/cookies/chips?
84. What happens to your body when you drink a lot of soda/pop?
85. What do you think would happen if you only ate sweets all day/week?
86. Why is it important to drink water instead of soda/pop/sweet drinks?
87. Why do you think water is good for everyone?
88. Does everyone have clean water to drink? How do you know?

89. Does everyone eat the same food every day? How do you know?
90. Does everyone have food to eat? How do you know?

. . . .

91. What does it mean to eat healthy food?
92. How do you know which food is healthy/unhealthy for you?
93. Why is it important to eat healthy food?
94. What does it mean to make healthy choices?
95. What is your favorite/least favorite healthy food? Why?

. . . .

96. Do you prefer to eat unhealthy or healthy food? Why?
97. How does healthy/unhealthy food make you feel after you eat it?
98. Why do some foods make you feel like slowing down/speeding up?
99. What does it mean for a food to be a "go/slow/whoa" food?
100. Which foods are "go/slow/whoa" foods? Why?
101. Why do some foods give you more energy/slow you down?
102. What food can you buy or cook fast/quickly?

. . . .

103. What does **nutrition** mean?
104. Which foods do you think are/are not nutritious? Why?
105. Why should you eat nutritious foods?
106. How do you know what is in the food you eat?
107. How does food feel when it's cold/hot/warm/frozen/wet/dry/etc.?

MEALTIME

108. What happens when you try to eat food that is too cold/hot?
109. What do you think makes food sweet/sour/tart/spoiled/salty/bland/smooth/lumpy/grainy/crispy/etc.?
110. Describe what food tastes like when it is sweet/sour/tart/spoiled/salty/bland/smooth/lumpy/grainy/crispy/etc.
111. What do you like most/least about water/fruit/vegetables/food?
112. How can we find out which food everyone likes the least/most?
113. What can we do to make a chart?
············
114. What do you know about **food groups**?
115. How can you sort foods by their food groups? (dairy, whole grains, fruit, vegetables, meats, sweets?
116. Do you have a favorite food group? Tell me about it.
············

117. Why do you think you like some foods but not others?
118. If you could only eat one thing for the rest of your life, what would it be?
············
119. Why do people ask for food to be delivered?
120. How does food get delivered?
121. How does the delivery person know where you live?
122. Does it cost more for your food to be delivered? Why? Why not?
············
123. What does it mean to have a **food allergy**?
124. How do you know if you are allergic to food?
125. How can you find out what's in the food you are about to eat?
126. Why is it important to know if you are allergic to food?
127. Why is it important to tell people about your food allergies?
128. What happens if you eat food that you're allergic to?
············
129. What can you do with your leftover food?
130. How do you know which size container to put the food in?
131. How can you find lids that match the containers?
132. What if you didn't have lids/a container for your leftovers?
133. How else can you cover the container?

COMMUNITY HELPERS · FIREFIGHTERS

1. What is a firefighter?
2. What does a firefighter do?
3. How do firefighters help the community?
4. What's the difference between a firefighter and a doctor/teacher/mail carrier/what your parents do/etc.?
5. What else do firefighters do?
6. How else do firefighters help people?
7. How do you call for help if you see a fire?
8. Have you ever met/seen a firefighter? When? Describe how the firefighter looked. What was he/she doing?
9. Have you ever visited a fire station? Tell me about your visit.
10. What do you think you have to know to be a firefighter?

· · · · · · · · · · ·

11. Why is a **firetruck** red?
12. What's the difference between a firetruck and a regular car/truck?
13. What type of tools/equipment does a firetruck have? How is it used?
14. Should everyone drive a firetruck? Why? Why not?
15. How do firefighters know how many firetrucks to take to a fire?

· · · · · · · · · · ·

16. How do firefighters get the water to the fire?
17. How do firefighters get on the roof to put the fire out?
18. Why does the fire truck have a hose/ladder?

19. How do firefighters use the hose/ladder?
20. What do you notice about the hose/ladder?
21. What would happen if firefighters didn't have a hose/ladder?
22. Do you have a hose or ladder at home?
23. How are they used?

· · · · · · · · · · ·

24. Why do firefighters turn on their **sirens**?
25. Describe how a siren sounds.
26. What happens when people hear the siren?
27. Why do you think the siren is so loud?
28. Why do firefighters wear headphones in the fire truck?

· · · · · · · · · · ·

29. What does it mean to fight a fire?
30. How do firefighters put out a fire?
31. What is a fire hose?
32. Why is the fire hose so long?
33. How is a fire hose used?

· · · · · · · · · · ·

34. How do firefighters find the **water** to fight the fire?
35. How can firefighters transport water to a fire?
36. Should you use water to put out every kind of fire? Why? Why not?
37. What would happen if firefighters ran out of water?

· · · · · · · · · · ·

38. What do firefighters wear? Why?
39. Describe a firefighter's uniform/equipment.

COMMUNITY HELPERS · FIREFIGHTERS

40. Why do you think firefighters wear hard hats/steel-toe boots/air masks/face shields/gloves/suspenders?
41. Why is a firefighter's coat so big/heavy?
42. Why does the firefighter's uniform have reflective bands?
43. Why do firefighters carry air tanks?
44. Do you think firefighters get hot when they fight a fire? Why? Why not?
45. Do you think it's comfortable carrying so many things to fight a fire? Why? Why isn't it?

············

46. How do you think firefighters communicate when they are in a burning building?
47. Why is it important for firefighters to communicate with each other?

············

48. How do people know when there is a fire?
49. What is a **fire alarm/smoke detector**?
50. Why do people install fire alarms/smoke detectors in their homes and buildings?
51. How does a smoke detector/alarm tell us there is a fire?
52. What would happen if there were no fire alarms?

············

53. What do you know about **fire drills**?
54. Why do people have fire drills?
55. What are you supposed to do if you hear a fire alarm? Why?

56. Why is it important to know where to go/where not to go if there is a fire?
57. Why are there EXIT signs in buildings?
58. If there is a fire, do you think you should take the stairs or the elevator? Why?
59. Should you walk into a burning building? Why? Why not?

············

60. What is a **fire extinguisher**?
61. Where have you seen fire extinguishers? Why are they there?
62. How does a fire extinguisher work?
63. What is the difference between a fire extinguisher and a water hose?

············

64. How do fires start?
65. How can people keep fires from starting?
66. Where do you think most fires start? Why?
67. Why shouldn't you touch or play with fire/matches/lighters/stoves/grills/fire pits?

············

68. What qualities/skills should a firefighter have?
69. Who can be a firefighter? Why?
70. How do you become a firefighter?
71. Do you think firefighters have to keep training? Why? Why not?

············

COMMUNITY HELPERS · FIREFIGHTERS

72. Why do firefighters have to be nice to each other?
73. Why do firefighters work as a team?
74. What would happen if firefighters didn't work as a team?
75. How do animals help firefighters?

· · · · · · · · · · · ·

76. What do you think firefighters see when they walk into a burning building?
77. How do firefighters keep fires from spreading?
78. Do you think fires spread faster in an open area or in one that has closed spaces?

· · · · · · · · · · · ·

79. What is an **emergency**?
80. Is a fire an emergency? Why? Why not?
81. What should you do if there is a fire/emergency?
82. How do firefighters know there is a fire?
83. How do firefighters know where to go to put the fire out?

· · · · · · · · · · · ·

84. What should you do if there is a fire?
85. Why should you crawl low to the ground under smoke?
86. How can you practice crawling low?
87. Why should you stop, drop, cover your face, and roll if you are on fire?
88. How can you practice the stop, drop, and roll technique?

· · · · · · · · · · · ·

89. Have you seen **fire hydrants** on the street? How are they used?
90. Why are there fire hydrants on the streets?
91. How do firefighters use fire hydrants?
92. Why do you think people aren't supposed to park in front of a fire hydrant?

· · · · · · · · · · · ·

93. Tell me what you know about **fire stations.**
94. Where do most firefighters eat/sleep when they are working? Why?
95. Why don't firefighters go home to their families every night?
96. What types of things do firefighters have at the fire station?
97. How do you think their children feel when they don't come home at night?
98. Do you think firefighters miss their families?
99. Would you like to become a firefighter someday? Why? Why not?

· · · · · · · · · · · ·

100. What do you think fire inspectors do?
101. Why is it important to inspect buildings?
102. What is a fire regulation/code?
103. Why do you think there are fire regulations/codes?
104. Why do you think there are limits to how many people can be in a room/building?

SCHOOL

1. What does it mean to go to school
2. Why do you think people go to school?
3. What do you think the world would be like if children never went to school?

· · · · · · · · · · ·

4. What is it like to go to school?
5. Tell me about your day.
6. What's the most interesting thing you heard/did/said/saw at school today?
7. What would you change about today if you could?

· · · · · · · · · · ·

8. How do you get to school? What's that like?
9. If you could choose any way to travel to school, how would you?
10. What rules do you have to follow on the bus/in the car/when walking?

· · · · · · · · · · ·

11. Why is it important to be on time for school?
12. What happens when you are early/late for school? Why?
13. What can you do to be on time for school?
14. How do you know where to go when you get to school?

15. What do children do when they arrive at school?
16. What do you do first/second/next/last in class?

· · · · · · · · · · ·

17. Describe your school/**classroom**/campus.
18. How is being in school the same or different from home/other places?
19. What do you do at school?
20. What types of things do you learn in school?
21. How do you learn things at school?
22. What do you want to learn at school? Why?
23. What do you enjoy the most/least about your teacher/class/school?
24. What are your favorite/least favorite things to do at school? Why?

· · · · · · · · · · ·

25. Tell me about your teacher/friends/ classroom/school/recess.
26. How do you learn/remember everyone's name?
27. Why is it important to learn/remember people's names?
28. What kinds of things does your teacher do/say/ask you?
29. How do you make friends at school?
30. Who are your friends at school? What is it you like about them?

SCHOOL

31. Who are the friends you talk to/play with most/least? Why?
32. What do you wish your teacher/friends knew about you?

    ············

33. How do you find things in your classroom?
34. How do you know where to put your coat/hat/backpack/lunch/etc.?
35. How do you know where to put toys/supplies/your things?
36. Why do you think it's important to put things away in the same place?
37. What would happen if you never put toys/supplies/games/puzzles/books back in their place?
38. Is it better to be organized or messy? Why?

    ············

39. How can you draw a picture that will help me recognize your school?
40. How can you draw a map, so I don't get lost in your school?

    ············

41. How do you think a person becomes a teacher?

42. How does a teacher help you understand subjects?
43. What would you do/say if you were the teacher for a day?
44. What would you add/take away from this school if you could?
45. What would you put in a new school that this one doesn't have? Why?

    ············

46. What kinds of **rules** do you follow in your class?
47. Why do you think your teacher/school has rules?
48. Are there any rules you like/don't like? Why?
49. How would you write the rules differently?
50. What would you do if you were a teacher and the children weren't listening/behaving in class?

    ············

51. How do you know when it's time to read/play/rest/eat/go outside/go home?
52. Tell me about a **story/**book your teacher has read at school.
53. Why do you think your teacher reads books/stories?
54. How do you feel when your teacher reads books/stories?

SCHOOL

55. *What is your favorite/least favorite story? Why?*
56. *Tell me about the stories you like.*

· · · · · · · · · · ·

57. *What do you do at school when it's time to go home?*
58. *Why do you think children go home after school?*
59. *How do you get home from school?*
60. *What if children never went home from school?*

· · · · · · · · · · ·

61. *Tell me about what happened today.*
62. *What was the best/most interesting part of your day?*
63. *What didn't go so well at school?*
64. *What are you looking forward to learning in school tomorrow/this month/this year?*
65. *What worries you about school?*
66. *How do you handle problems with peers/ friends/people at school?*
67. *How do the other children treat you at school? Let's talk about it.*
68. *How do you treat people at school? Why?*
69. *How do you control yourself when you get upset/angry/mad at school?*
70. *What can you do to remain calm when you are anxious at/about school?*
71. *Who do you turn to when you have a problem at school? Why? How do they help?*

· · · · · · · · · · ·

72. *What would you do if you could be invisible in a classroom all day?*
73. *Where would you sit if you could switch seats in your classroom? Why?*
74. *What's different/the same about this school/school year when you compare it to last year?*
75. *What would you change about your school/classroom? Why?*

· · · · · · · · · · ·

76. *What do you know that you can teach others?*
77. *What do you think you could do to help others in your class?*
78. *What can I do to help you with school/ school work?*

COLORS

1. What is color?
2. What do you think/notice about colors?
3. How do colors help us/make things interesting?
4. How do you know which color that is?
5. How can you tell the difference between this color and that color?

. . . .

6. How do you think colors are made?
7. What do you think you can use to make color?
8. What else can you use to make color?
9. How would you find/create a color that matches this one/thing/your skin?
10. What would you do first/second/next/last?
11. What is your favorite/least favorite color? Why?
12. What colors have special meaning to you? Why?
13. Why do you think there are so many different colors in the world?
14. Why do you think there are so many different colors of clothes/shoes/leaves/cars/furniture/etc.?
15. Which color did you use the most/least? How can you tell?
16. Does this color have a special meaning in your country? Tell me about it.
17. How can you find out more about colors?

. . . .

18. How can you change the color of things?
19. What does mixing colors mean?
20. How do you **mix** colors?
21. What happens when you mix colors?
22. What colors do you think will mix the easiest/best/hardest/worst?
23. What made you think of putting these colors together?
24. What would you do if you wanted to make a new color that no one has seen?
25. What colors do you think you should mix to make green/orange/purple/grey/etc.
26. What would happen if you tried to take a color out of the mix?
27. What would happen if you added another color/black/white?
28. What do you know about primary colors (red, yellow, blue)?

. . . .

29. What do you notice about the colors of the rainbow?
30. What do you notice about the colors in this book/painting/photo?
31. Why do you think the artist used this color/these colors?
32. Which do you like better, light colors or dark? Why?
33. How do you know if a color is lighter/darker/brighter/duller/redder/greener/etc.?
34. Why do you think the color got lighter/darker/brighter/duller/redder/greener/etc.?
35. How do you make a color lighter (tint)/brighter/darker (shade)?

COLORS

36. How do you make a color redder/greener/etc.?
37. What would you have to do to match one color to another?

. . . .

38. What do you think of when you see this color?
39. How do you feel when you see this color?
40. What color do you think of when you are happy/mad/sad/excited/etc.? Why?
41. What color do you think of when something is cold/hot/dark/light/bright/etc.?

. . . .

42. What do you notice about these reds/greens/blues/etc.?
43. How can you sort/match/organize these according to their color/shade/tint?
44. How can you line them up according to their color/shade/tint?
45. Show me what you can do with this color.
46. What would happen if you combined different brushes/crayons/markers/implements to make colors?
47. What colors do you think go well together?

48. What makes something change colors?
49. Why do some animals/insects change color?

. . . .

50. Which color do you think you'll see the most/least when you are outside/inside? Why?
51. Why do you think grass/dirt/the sky/the moon/etc. is that color?
52. Why do you think the sky changes colors?
53. Why do you think it's dark at night and light in the day?
54. What colors do you think of when you think of summer/winter/love/something scary? Why?

. . . .

55. How do you think we get the color of our skin/eyes?
56. How do people change their hair/nail/skin color?
57. Can people change the color of their skin forever? Why? Why not? How?
58. Can everyone see color? Why? Why not?

. . . .

59. Which color tells us to stop/go/yield/wait? How?
60. Do you think you can figure out someone's favorite color if they don't tell you? How?
61. How can we play/make games using colors?
62. How can you use these colors to make a pattern?

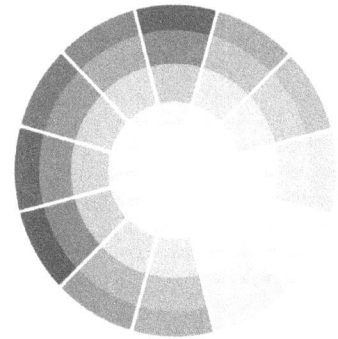

NOTES

> *"A wise man doesn't give the right answers. He poses the right questions."*
> **- Claude Levi-Strauss**

NOTES

BALLS

1. What do you know about balls?
2. How do you know this is a ball?
3. What do you think of when you see a ball?
4. Describe the ball.
5. What do you notice about the ball?
6. What do you notice about the texture/ print/design/size of the ball?
7. How does your ball feel when you hold/ squeeze it/hug it?
8. Where else have you seen/played with a ball? What were you doing?

· · · · · · · · · · ·

9. Why do you think the ball is round/ shaped like a circle?
10. Are all balls round? How do you know?
11. What if your ball wasn't round?
12. What if your ball was in the shape of a square?
13. What shape do you think makes the best ball?

· · · · · · · · · · ·

14. What can you do with your ball?
15. How do you know you can do that?
16. Tell me about when/where you have done this before.
17. What else can you do with your ball?
18. What would happen if you let go/didn't let go of the ball?
19. What if you let go of the ball sooner/ later?
20. How would you hold/carry two/three balls?

21. How else can you get your ball from here to there?

· · · · · · · · · · ·

22. What do you think is inside of a/this ball?
23. How do you think this ball was made?
24. Do you think all balls are made the same? Why? Why not?
25. What do you think we would have to do to find out how this ball was made?
26. What if your ball was made out of stone/ rock/snow/water/foam/paper/yarn/etc.?
27. What if you wanted to make a ball? How would you design it?
28. How can you draw a picture of your ball?

· · · · · · · · · · ·

29. What if your ball had a hole in it?
30. What does it mean to inflate/deflate a ball?
31. How can you inflate/deflate a ball?
32. What happens when you pump air into a ball?
33. What tool/equipment do you have to use to inflate a ball?

· · · · · · · · · · ·

34. What's the difference between these balls? (beach ball, basketball, football, baseball, tennis ball, wiffle ball, etc.)
35. How can you tell which ball is smaller/ bigger/harder/softer/lighter/heavier?
36. Is your head/hand bigger or smaller than this ball? How can you tell?
37. What if your ball was hard/soft/flat/ squishy/small/large/heavy/light?
38. Why do you think your ball is hard/soft/ flat/squishy/small/large/heavy/light?
39. Does being hard/soft/flat/squishy/small/ large/heavy/light make a difference in how the ball moves?

· · · · · · · · · · ·

BALLS

40. How can you sort these balls according to their color/size/texture/type/design/weight?
41. What if you organized these balls by what they can do?
42. How can you tell which ball weighs more/less?
43. How can you tell which ball is smaller/bigger?
44. How can you organize/sort these balls according to the way they move/roll/bounce?
45. Where is the best place to store the balls? Why?

. . . .

46. Which size ball do you like best/least? Why?
47. Which type of ball do you like most/least? Why?
48. What's your favorite/least favorite thing to do with a ball? Why?

. . . .

49. How does your ball move?
50. Why do you think your ball is/isn't moving?
51. What can you do to make your ball move?
52. Why do you think your ball does that?
53. What else do you think makes balls move?
54. What do you hear/see when your ball moves? Why?

55. How can you make your ball move differently?
56. What was different about the way the ball moved this time?
57. Why do you think your ball moves differently each time?
58. What's the difference between how these balls move?
59. How can you make your ball move faster/slower/farther/shorter/higher/lower?
60. Which ball makes the most noise when it moves? Why?

. . . .

61. How do you pass/roll/bounce/push/tap/drop/toss/throw/catch/kick/dribble the ball?
62. What happens when you pass/roll/bounce/push/tap/drop/toss/throw/catch/kick/dribble the ball?
63. What do you have to do to pass/roll/bounce/push/tap/drop/toss/throw/catch/kick/dribble the ball?
64. Show me how to pass/roll/bounce/push/tap/drop/toss/throw/catch/kick/dribble the ball?
65. Why do you think your ball rolls/doesn't roll?
66. Which ball rolls the slowest/fastest? Why?
67. How can you tell which ball rolls faster/slower/farther?
68. Why do you think your ball bounces/doesn't bounce?
69. Do all balls roll/bounce? Why? Why not?
70. Which ball bounces the least/most? Why?
71. Why do some balls bounce higher than other balls?

BALLS

72. *How do you know how high the ball can go/bounce?*
73. *Why does your ball stop rolling/bouncing?*
74. *How can you make your ball stop rolling/bouncing?*

....

75. *What happens when your ball rolls/bounces into things?*
76. *What happens when your ball hits a wall/something?*
77. *How do you keep that from happening?*

....

78. *How can you get the ball to bounce or launch lower/higher?*
79. *What would happen if you dropped your ball from somewhere lower/higher?*
80. *What if you toss/kick/hit the ball harder/softer/with more force?*
81. *What would happen if you rolled/tossed/threw/kicked/batted the ball softer/harder?*
82. *What makes your ball go up/come down after you toss/throw it?*
83. *Why do you think your ball went in that direction/curved/flew away?*
84. *How do you know how far the ball rolled/flew?*
85. *What would happen if you rolled/bounced the ball on different surfaces? (gravel/rocks, sand, grass, water, concrete, etc.)*
86. *Which ball is better for dribbling/tossing/catching/throwing/kicking? Why?*

87. *How can you move/pass/roll/bounce/toss/catch the ball without using your hands?*
88. *Why type of equipment can you use to hit/bat the ball?*

....

89. *How do you catch a ball?*
90. *What if the ball was lighter/heavier/smaller/larger?*
91. *What would happen if you used one/both hands?*
92. *How can you catch a ball without using your hands?*
93. *What other things can you use to catch a ball?*
94. *How would you do that?*

....

95. *What can you do to get the ball in the receptacle/basket/bin/container/hole?*
96. *Why do you think the ball didn't go into the receptacle?*
97. *How can you fix that?*
98. *What do you have to do to hit the target with your ball?*
99. *What can you do if the ball doesn't hit the target?*
100. *What would happen if you moved your target/receptacle closer/farther away?*
101. *What would happen if you raised/lowered/tilted/turned your target/receptacle?*
102. *What would happen if you made your target/receptacle smaller/bigger?*
103. *How many balls do you think are in the receptacle/hit the target? How can you find out?*

BALLS

104. What do you have to do to get the ball through the ring/target?
105. What do you have to do to get the ball over the net?
106. How would you redesign your target/receptacle?

....

107. How can you control where the ball goes?
108. How can you use the ball to knock something over?
109. What happens when the wind blows the ball?
110. Why do you think your ball moves when the wind blows?
111. How would this ball move on water/different surfaces?
112. How can you make your ball change directions?

....

113. Show me how you can make your body into a ball.
114. Show me how you can move like a ball.

....

115. What games can you play with your ball?
116. How can you play ball with a friend/with friends?
117. Tell me about the sports that use balls.
118. Have you ever seen an animal play with a ball? What did they do?

....

119. What does **juggling** mean?
120. How do people juggle balls?
121. What do you have to do to keep the balls in the air?
122. How do you know how many balls you can juggle?
123. What if you wanted to juggle 100 balls?

....

124. What is a **ramp**?
125. Describe a ramp.
126. How do ramps help us?
127. Why do you think ramps are called simple machines?
128. How does a ramp affect the way the ball moves?
129. How can you build a ramp for your ball?
130. How can you use these materials to build a ramp?
131. How can you connect one ramp to the other?
132. What would happen if you rolled a ball down/up a ramp?
133. How can you change what happens when the ball gets to the end of the ramp?
134. Which ball rolls down a playground slide/ramp the fastest? Why?
135. What would happen if you changed the surface of the ramp?

....

136. What is a **Rube Goldberg** device?
137. What if you drew plans for a ramp/Rube Goldberg device?
138. What do you have to do to keep the ball rolling through the device?
139. How can you fix the device so that it works better?

NOTES

BOXES

1. What is a box?
2. What can you do with a box/boxes?
3. How else can you use a box?
4. Why do people use boxes?
5. How are boxes helpful?
6. What jobs do you know of that involve boxes?
7. Have you ever used a box before? What did you do with it?

    • • • • • • • • • • •

8. What do you notice about this box?
9. Describe the box to me.
10. What do you think the picture/words mean on this box?
11. How do you think this box is used?
12. Do boxes have to have a base/sides/lid? What happens if they don't?
13. Do boxes have to be square or rectangular? Why? Why not?
14. Why do boxes come in different sizes/shapes/materials?
15. How do you think a box is made?
16. Does a box have to be made with hard material? Why? Why not?

17. What would you like to do with this box/these boxes? Why?
18. How can you make that happen?

    • • • • • • • • • • •

19. How do you flatten/collapse a box?
20. How do you fold/close/open/unfold a box?
21. What do you have to do to take a box apart?
22. How can you put the box back together?
23. What can you use to secure the bottom of the box before you put something inside?
24. How do you open a box that is taped?
25. How can you fix the damaged box?

    • • • • • • • • • • •

26. How can you find out how many sides your box has?
27. How can you find out what size this box is? How tall/long/wide/deep?
28. How can you tell which box is larger/smaller/thinner/wider/taller/shorter/longer/flatter/lighter/heavier?
29. How are these boxes the same/different?
30. Are all of the sides the same size? How can you tell?
31. What do you have to do to measure the box?
32. How do you know which box you should use?
33. How can you find out how much each box weighs?

    • • • • • • • • • • •

34. What do you think is inside of the box? Why?
35. What do you wish was inside of the box? Why?
36. What if you tried to put one box inside of another?

    • • • • • • • • • • •

37. How do you know what will fit in the box?
38. Can you fit inside the box? Why? Why not?
39. How do you know when the box is full/empty?
40. How do you know how much/many you can put in the box?
41. How can you rearrange the things inside the box to make more room?
42. How can you use the box to catch/store something?

BOXES

43. Do you think you need a different shaped box? Why? Why not?
44. How can you mark the box, so you know what's inside?

···········

45. Is it dark inside the box? What can you do to add light in there?
46. What would happen if you put holes in the box?
47. What do you think would happen if you sat/stepped on the box? Why?
48. Should you put wet things in boxes? Why? Why not?
49. What do you think would happen if the box got wet?

···········

50. How can you make a box?
51. What materials would you use to make a box? Why?
52. Why are you making a box?
53. How can you play pretend/make-believe with a box?
54. What if you wanted to decorate the box? How would you do it?
55. What materials would you use to decorate the box? Why?

···········

56. What can you **build** with boxes?
57. How many boxes do you think you'll need? How can you find out?
58. How can you use this box to make a quiet space/car/garage/rocket/stove/refrigerator/bridge/ramp/television/puppet theater/etc.?

59. What if you wanted to climb through the box, like a tunnel?
60. You made a house out of the box? How can you add doors or windows?
61. You made a rocket out of the boxes? How can you see where you're going?
62. You made a bridge out of the box? How can you tell how strong it is?
63. You made a robot out of the boxes? Tell me about your robot.

···········

64. How would the boxes look if you lined them up?
65. How can you line up the boxes by size/shape/color/type?
66. What if you wanted to stack the boxes? How would you do it?
67. How can you put one box inside of the other/s?
68. How can you use the boxes to sort/organize things by size/shape/color/weight?

···········

69. What do you know about **recycling**?
70. How can you recycle a box?
71. Why would you want to recycle a box?
72. How can you use this box in a new and different way?
73. What does the phrase "reduce, reuse, and recycle" mean?
74. Why should people recycle different materials? (paper, glass, metal, and plastic)
75. How does recycling help the environment/world?

NOTES

"Children do not come into the world with the capacity for abstract thought. Instead, children must construct abstract concepts through their interactions with concrete objects in the environment" (McNeil & Jarvin, 2007).

NOTES

NOTES

MANIPULATIVES

1. Tell me about what you have.
2. How would you describe what you have?
3. What made you choose those?
4. What do you think it will look like when you're finished?
5. What will you do with it?
6. How does it work?
. . . .
7. How fun! What do you plan to do with them?
8. How will you use your manipulatives to create/build something?
9. What if you draw a plan first? How would that help?
10. What steps will you take to make it?
11. How do you know how to make it?
. . . .
12. How do you know how many you need/have?
13. How will you know if you need more/fewer of them?
14. What if you want to add more/take some away?
15. How can you find out what else you need?

16. What else can you use? How will you use it/them?
. . . .
17. How are they the same/different?
18. How can you tell which piece is the smallest/biggest/shortest/tallest/longest/etc.?
19. What can you do to measure it?
20. How can you make it smaller/bigger/shorter/longer/taller/thinner/wider/etc.?
21. How can you sort/organize these?
22. How can you arrange them by how they look?
23. How can you arrange them by size/color/shape/weight?
. . . .
24. What kind of design would you like to make? What made you think of that?
25. How can you make that happen?
26. How would you make a straight/curved/wavy/zigzag line?
27. How would you make different shapes/letters/numbers out of them?
28. How can you make a picture out of them?
. . . .
29. What do you notice when you do that?
30. What happened when you did that?
31. What do you think caused that to happen?
32. How can you do it another way?
. . . .

MANIPULATIVES

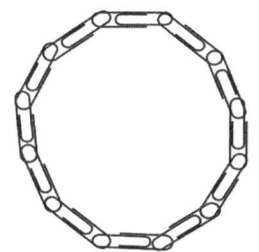

33. *How can you lift/move/carry them?*
34. *How can you keep it from falling/leaning/ breaking/tearing?*
35. *How can you connect them/take them apart?*
36. *How can you make it stand up/lay flat/ lean at an angle?*
37. *How can you make it fit in/under/on top of/around/through here?*
38. *What do you have to do to make it reach the other side/the top?*

....

39. *How do you know which pieces to put on the top/bottom/side?*
40. *How do you know which pieces won't work?*
41. *What are your favorite/least favorite pieces to use? Why?*

....

42. *How do those materials work/fit together?*
43. *Why do you think those materials work/ fit together?*

44. *How can you figure it out/fix it/solve the problem?*
45. *How do you keep them clean?*
46. *Why do you think you should clean them?*
47. *What will happen if they get dirty/ broken/damaged?*
48. *How do you keep from breaking them?*

....

49. *What if you couldn't use your hands?*
50. *How can you use something else?*
51. *What if you used a tool?*

....

52. *What if you asked a friend to help you?*
53. *What can I do to help you?*

....

54. *What if you want to change your design?*
55. *What would you do differently next time?*
56. *What would happen if you left them outside?*
57. *How can you leave them neat and organized for the next person who wants to play with them?*

MAGNETS

 CAUTION: When a child swallows two or more magnets, the magnets can damage the digestive system. A magnet in one loop of the bowel is attracted to a magnet in another loop of the bowel, causing digestive tissue to be trapped between them, which can result in severe injury or death.

1. What do you know about magnets/ magnetism?
2. How do you think magnets work?
3. How do magnets help us? How are they useful?
4. How do you think magnets are made?
5. Why do people use magnets?
6. Tell me some things you can do with magnets.

· · · · · · · · · · ·

7. Tell me about where you have you seen magnets before.
8. How can you test a magnet to see if it works?
9. How can you find out if an object is attracted to a magnet?
10. Why do you think magnets are attracted to other magnets?

· · · · · · · · · · ·

11. How can you test different metals to see if they are magnetic?
12. Tell me about things that are attracted to magnets.
13. What happens if you hold a magnet against an object that isn't magnetic?
14. What happens if you hold a magnet next to plastic/water/paper/clay/coins/cans/ wire/a paper clip/tacks/nails/nuts & bolts/rubber/stones/sticks/etc.?

15. What types of things are/aren't attracted to magnets? How do you know?
16. Tell me about things that are attracted to magnets.
17. Why do you think magnets are attracted to some objects but not others?
18. How can you sort/organize objects, so you will know which are magnetic and which are not?

· · · · · · · · · · ·

19. What do you know about **metal**?
20. Describe what happens when a magnet meets metals. (coins, brass, copper, aluminum cans, aluminum foil, steel can)
21. Why do you think magnets are attracted to metals?

· · · · · · · · · · ·

22. Why would the ends of two magnets repel each other instead of attracting each other?
23. Why can't you see magnets attract each other (magnetism), but you can see what it does?
24. Does it matter what shape/size/color the magnet is? Why? Why not?

· · · · · · · · · · ·

MAGNETS

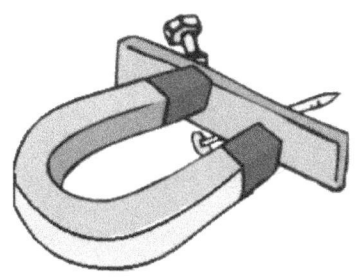

25. How close do magnets have to be for a magnet to work?
26. What do you notice when you hold magnets near each other?
27. What happens when you move the magnet closer/away?
28. What happens when you flip over one of the magnets?
29. What materials will a magnet go through to move an object?
30. What if you put something between the magnet and an object? (fabric, paper, wood, clay, your hand)
31. How does a magnet work with different objects?
32. What if you put something between the magnet and another magnet?
33. What if you put a magnet/objects in water/oil/sand/dirt/etc.?
34. Does it matter if you hold a magnet over/under another object? Why? Why not?
··········
35. How do you think you can pick up/move something with a magnet?
36. How can you use magnets to keep things from moving?
37. What else can you do with magnets?
38. Are some magnets stronger than others? How do you know?
39. What do you think might affect a magnet's strength?
40. How do you think you can test the force of magnetism?

41. How can you tell if one magnet is stronger than another?
42. How does the strength of a magnet affect the distance it will attract an object?
43. How can you tell how many objects a magnet will hold?
··········
44. What if you use more than one magnet?
45. What happens if you stack magnets?
46. Do you think magnets wear out over time? Why? Why not?
··········
47. What toys do you have that use magnets? How do you know?
48. What can you do with toys that have magnets?
49. How do you think magnets help drawers/doors close?
50. How can you use magnets to make art?
··········
51. How can magnets be dangerous for humans/people?
52. Why do you think it is dangerous to swallow a magnet?
53. How do you think magnets can damage objects? (watch, clock, computer, cell phone, etc.)

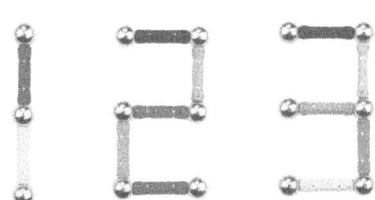

NOTES

PUZZLES

1. What is a puzzle?
2. What makes this a puzzle?
3. What do you do with a puzzle?
4. How do you solve a puzzle?
5. Tell me about the puzzles you have seen.
6. Do all puzzles lay flat/stack/look the same?
7. How do the pieces feel in your hands?

....

8. Are puzzles supposed to be easy or hard/ challenging? Why?
9. Why are there so many puzzle pieces?
10. What do you do with all of the pieces?
11. How do you know how to put a puzzle together?
12. Why do you have to be patient when solving a puzzle?
13. Why do you need time to complete a puzzle?

....

14. How do you begin to solve a puzzle?
15. How do you know how the puzzle should look?
16. What do you have to do to solve the puzzle?
17. How do you know which pieces go/don't go with this puzzle?
18. How do you know what will work there?

19. Why aren't you using your feet instead of your hands to put the puzzle together?

....

20. How do you put the pieces in order?
21. What do you have to do to put the pieces in order?
22. What if the pieces aren't in order?

....

23. How do you know the pieces will fit?
24. How do you find pieces that fit?
25. What do you do if a piece doesn't fit?

....

26. What would happen if you turned the piece/flipped it?
27. What if the piece was smaller/bigger/ thicker/thinner/wider?
28. What if the piece is too small/big?
29. How can you make a piece that will fit?

....

30. What do you notice about your finished puzzle?
31. What do you think of when you see the finished puzzle?
32. Tell me about the puzzle's picture/ shape/image.
33. How is this puzzle different from that one?

....

34. What if you wanted to create a puzzle? How would you do it?

PUZZLES

35. How did you get that idea?
36. What materials can you use to make a puzzle? Why would you choose those?
37. What do you like about working with the material?
38. What tools do you need to make a puzzle?
39. Why do you need the tools?
40. How will you use the tools?
41. How do you think the puzzle will look when you're finished?
42. When you make another puzzle, what will you do differently?

....

43. How many puzzle pieces do you think there are? How can you know for sure?
44. How can you organize these puzzles?
45. Why do you think we have to keep puzzle pieces together?

46. What would happen if these puzzle pieces got mixed with other puzzle pieces?
47. What would happen if you lost/were missing/broke a puzzle piece?

....

48. What is your favorite/least favorite puzzle? Why?
49. What kind of puzzles do you like to put together? Why?
50. What do you like/dislike about puzzles?
51. Do you like puzzles with lots of pieces or only a few? Why? Why not?

....

52. How can you work with a friend to complete the puzzle?
53. How can I help you?

MATH · NUMBER SENSE

1. What is math?
2. How does math help us do things/solve problems?
3. How do you practice math?
   ···········
4. What is a **number/numeral**?
5. What do you know about numbers?
6. How do numbers help us?
7. Tell me how/where you can find numbers.
8. How do you know that's a number?
9. Describe how the number looks/is shaped.
10. How can you tell which number it is?
11. How do you know the names of the numbers?
12. How are these numbers similar/different?
13. How do you know which numbers are the same/identical/match?
14. How do you know if a number is even/odd?
    ···········
15. What if you don't know how many things/objects there are? What can you do?
16. How did you figure out how many you have/need?
17. How do you **count**?
18. How can you use your fingers to count?
19. Why/How do people count things?
20. Which number do you start with when you count? Why?
21. How do you know which number goes first/next/last?
22. How do you know what order the numbers go in when you count?
23. Why can't you say the same number twice when you count?
24. What's a good way to keep from missing objects when you count?

25. Why can't you count two things as one?
26. When you count, do you think the next number is bigger or smaller? Why? Why not?
27. How do you know when to stop counting?
28. What does the last number tell you when you finish counting?
29. What does the word total mean?
30. How do you know what the total is?
31. How did you get that answer?
32. What would happen if you added more/took some away?
    ···········
33. How did you get that number/amount?
34. Why does it help to count out loud?
35. How do you know which objects you are counting?
36. What can you do to make it easier to count?
37. How can you count using cubes/sticks/pebbles/coins/etc.?
38. How can you show me this number/quantity/amount differently? (pips, dice, hashtags, fingers, movement, etc.)
    ···········
39. What if you counted while you moved/clapped/stomped/etc.?
40. How can you count in a fun way?
    ···········
41. How many items are missing? How do you know?
42. How can you find out if you have enough for everyone?
43. How can you make sure everyone gets one?
44. Which number is missing? How do you know?

MATH · NUMBER SENSE

45. How can you find the missing items/ number?

46. Why are there only two chairs/pencils/ cups/etc. here?

• • • • • • • • • •

47. How can you **sort/**organize/arrange them?

48. Tell me how/why you sorted those.

49. How do you know these are alike/ different?

50. How do you put these in order by size/ quantity/weight/etc.?

51. How can you tell (or describe) the difference between these sets/groups?

52. What happens if you put the groups together/mix them up and count again?

• • • • • • • • • •

53. What do you notice when you compare these groups/objects?

54. Which group has more/less? How do you know?

55. Is the number of objects in this group greater than/less than/equal to the number of objects in that group? How do you know?

56. How can you find out which one is shorter/longer/taller/faster/slower/ wider/thinner/lighter/heavier/more full/ higher?

57. How can you find out how short/long/ tall/fast/slow/wide/thin/heavy/high/ low it is?

58. What would happen if you split the group in half/ separated them?

59. How can you sit so that others fit in this space?

60. How many do you need if you want to share with friends/a friend?

• • • • • • • • • •

61. How can you decorate your number?

62. What made you think of doing that?

63. How would you describe what you did/ you're doing?

64. What if you wanted to use more/fewer materials/colors in your design?

65. What can you do to fix it?

• • • • • • • • • •

66. How do you know this is the whole piece/ a group/a set?

67. How can you separate this into pieces/ groups/sets?

68. How can you cut this in half/thirds/ quarters?

• • • • • • • • • •

69. What's your favorite/least favorite number? Why?

70. What do you mean when you say you are _____ years old?

71. The answer is five; what might the question be?

• • • • • • • • • •

72. How can you have fun with numbers?

73. Make up a story/song about your favorite number.

74. What if you made a drawing to show how many there are?

75. What kinds of games can you play with numbers?

• • • • • • • • • •

76. What does it mean to add/subtract/ multiply/divide numbers or things?

77. Why would people need to add/subtract/ multiply/divide numbers or things?

78. How do you add/subtract/multiply/ divide?

79. Show me what to do/you did.

80. How can tools help you add/subtract/ multiply/divide?

81. Show me how this tool works.

NOTES

MATH · GEOMETRIC SHAPES

1. What do you know about shapes?
2. How do you know that's a rectangle/square/circle/etc.?
3. Why do you think this shape is called a rectangle/square/circle/etc.?
4. Describe this shape.
5. Describe a square/triangle/circle/oval/rectangle/etc.
6. What is the difference between a circle and a square/rectangle/octagon/etc.?
7. What do you think of when you see this shape?
8. Is the shape the same if you turn/rotate it? Why? Why not?
9. What if you flip the shape over/fold it in half?

··········

10. How can you find a shape that matches this one?
11. What's the difference between these shapes?

··········

12. What does it mean when we say something is round/square/oval/etc.?
13. How do you know when things are round/square/rectangular/oval/etc.?
14. Do all objects have to be in the shape of a square/triangle/circle/oval/rectangle/etc.? Why? Why not?

··········

15. How do shapes help us?
16. What can you do with shapes?

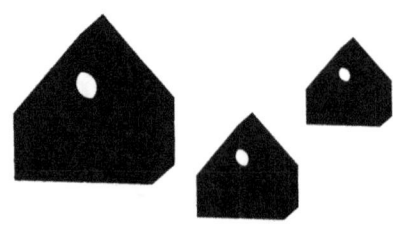

17. How do we use shapes to tell us where to go?
18. Why do you think we make signs out of different shapes?

··········

19. What is a **side/angle**?
20. What can you tell me about the sides/angles of shapes?
21. How many sides/angles does this shape have? How do you know?
22. How can you discover which shapes are the same/symmetrical on both sides/halves?
23. Show me the different sides of your body.
24. Show me how your body/body parts can bend at an angle.

··········

25. Is a book the shape of a circle or a square/rectangle? How do you know?
26. What if you looked for shapes in this book/magazine? How many do you think you can find?
27. What shapes can you find inside/outside/in nature?

··········

28. How can you measure your shape?
29. How can you tell (or find out) which shape is smaller/bigger/thinner/thicker/wider/shorter/longer/brighter/darker?
30. What if you want to find out how many of each shape you have?
31. Does it matter what color the shape is when you count? Why? Why not?

MATH · GEOMETRIC SHAPES

32. *What do you have to do to put these shapes into those holes?*
33. *What can you do to put one shape inside of another?*
34. *What if the shapes don't fit inside of each other?*
35. *How many of these objects do you think will fit on top of/around your shape? How can you check to see if you're right?*

· · · · · · · · · · ·

36. *How can you organize these shapes by size/color/type/number of sides/angles?*
37. *What would the shapes look like if you lined them up?*
38. *Which group has more/less/the most/the least/the same amount? How can you find out?*

· · · · · · · · · · ·

39. *What can you use to make shapes?*
40. *How can you use tools/pencils/crayons/paint to make shapes?*
41. *How can you make shapes with wooden blocks/play dough/geoboards/rubber bands/popsicle sticks/pipe cleaners/yarn/laces/wire/tubes/pattern blocks/cardboard/a scarf/etc.*
42. *How can you scrape shapes into sand/clay/dirt/shaving cream/foam/etc.?*
43. *How can you draw shapes with crayons/markers/paint/water/etc.?*

44. *How can you use your body to make shapes?*

· · · · · · · · · · ·

45. *How many different ways can you make the same shape?*
46. *How can you make this shape into a different shape?*
47. *How can you make your shape smaller/bigger/thinner/thicker/wider/shorter/longer/brighter/darker?*
48. *What happened when you folded/molded your shape?*
49. *How did the shape change?*
50. *Why do you think the shape changed?*
51. *What if you folded your shape in half? Why?*
52. *How would your square/rectangle/triangle/circle change if you folded it?*
53. *What would your shape look like if you changed it/added sides/added angles/removed sides/took out angles/cut it in half?*

· · · · · · · · · · ·

54. *How can you make your image/**pattern** look the same on the other side (symmetrical)?*
55. *Describe the patterns you see in this shape.*
56. *Tell me about the shapes you see in this pattern.*
57. *What do you think comes next? Why?*
58. *How would you extend the pattern?*

· · · · · · · · · · ·

MATH · GEOMETRIC SHAPES

59. How can you use shapes to make a map of your home/room/school/street/neighborhood?
60. What if you drew around/cut out the shapes you like?
61. How can you piece the shapes back together?

....

62. How can you use these shapes to make something/art?
63. Tell me about what you'd like to make.
64. What's the story behind what you made?
65. Tell me about what these shapes represent.
66. How did you know how many shapes you needed?
67. How did you know which shapes to use?
68. What can you do to change the color of the shape?
69. How would the shape look if you cut/tore/folded it?
70. What if you worked with a friend to create something?

....

71. What if you used shapes to create a **puzzle**?
72. How can you take your shape apart and put it back together?
73. How can you take your shape apart and make a different shape?

74. How do these shapes fit together?
75. Why don't these shapes fit together?
76. How can you tell if the shapes fit/don't fit?
77. How can you tell if this is a flat/**2-dimensional** shape?
78. How can you tell if this is a solid/**3-dimensional** shape?
79. How can you find objects that match this 3-D shape?

....

80. What is your favorite shape? Why?
81. How can you play a game using shapes?
82. What if there were no shapes anywhere?

....

83. What is a point?
84. Describe a point.
85. What is a **vertex**/are vertices (points where two or more lines meet)?
86. What can you tell me about the vertices (points) on these shapes?

....

87. What is a **tangram**?
88. Tell me about the seven tans of a tangram.
89. How do you play with a tangram?
90. How can you form shapes/images using the tans/pieces?

NOTES

> *"Telling creates resistance. Asking creates relationships."*
> **- Andrew Sobel**

NOTES

MATH · PATTERNS

1. What is a pattern?
2. How can you tell if something is/has a pattern?
3. What can you tell me about patterns?
4. Why do you think we have patterns?
5. What can you do with a pattern?
6. How can you find patterns in real life/outside/inside/in here/on this?

....

7. What does the word repeat mean?
8. How do you know when something repeats?
9. How do patterns repeat?

....

10. What do you notice about this pattern?
11. Describe the pattern.
12. What do you think of when you see this pattern?
13. What can you do to see the pattern better/more clearly?

....

14. How can you continue/extend the pattern?
15. How do you know what to do?
16. How do you know what comes next?
17. How can you tell the difference between these shapes/lines/markings/tiles/colors/etc.?
18. How does the pattern change?

....

19. How can you make a pattern?
20. What will you do to make a pattern of your own?
21. What can you use to make a pattern?
22. What else can you use to make a pattern?
23. How will you find things/materials to make a pattern?
24. What would a pattern look like if you made it out of colors/paper/letters/words/numbers/blocks/trucks/leaves/rocks/toys/clay/shapes/etc.?
25. How can you organize/sort the material to make your work easier?
26. How can you make different patterns?
27. What if you wanted to make your pattern shorter/longer/bigger/wider/thinner/etc.?

....

28. How can/did you make an image using the pattern blocks?
29. How can you make a pattern using your name?
30. How can you use sounds/words to make a pattern?

MATH · PATTERNS

31. What if you wanted to make music/a song that has a pattern? How would you do it?
32. Is there a way to hear/smell/feel/taste a pattern? How?
33. How can you use movement/your body to make a pattern?
34. What is a sequence?
35. How can you use a sequence of events to make a pattern?
36. Why are patterns fun to make?

············

37. Why did you select those materials?
38. Describe the materials you are using.
39. How did you know where to find the materials to use?
40. How are the materials the same/different?

41. What would the pattern look like if you changed the material?

············

42. What would your pattern look like if you changed it/added more/took something away?
43. What if you run out of things to make your pattern?
44. How would you fix that?
45. What can you do to solve that problem?
46. What if you run out of room to make your pattern?
47. How do you know when to stop making a pattern?

············

48. Why do you think our clothes have patterns? What about leaves/seashells/snowflakes/animals/tiles/food/etc.?

············

49. Which pattern do you like the most/least? What do you like/dislike about it?
50. What can you do to remember your pattern on another day?

MATH · MEASUREMENT
Length · Width · Height

- **Height:** measured from bottom to top
- **Length:** measured from end to end
- **Width:** measured from side to side
- **Standard tools:** rulers, measuring cups, measuring tape, yard stick, and scales
- **Nonstandard tools:** use of a single object such as, string, hands or feet, paperclips, chain links, sticky notes, etc.

1. What is a measurement?
2. How do you measure something?
3. Why would you want to measure something?
4. Have you ever seen anyone measure something? How did they do it?
5. What types of things can you measure? Why?
6. How do you know what tools to use when you measure?
7. Can you measure something by just looking at it? How? Why not?
8. How can you find out how long/high/short/tall/wide something is?
9. How long/short/tall/wide/high/low do you think it is?
10. What's the difference between something long and something short? Thin vs. wide? Short vs. tall? High vs. low?

···········

11. How would you compare these two objects?
12. How can you use a _____ to measure a _____?
13. Where do you have to place them to measure accurately? Why?
14. What if you move/turn/flip/rotate/lift/lower/the object and re-measure it? Do you think the measurement will be different? Why? Why not?

15. What's the difference between this measurement and that one?
16. Compare _____ to _____. What do you notice?
17. How would this look if it was longer/shorter/taller/wider/higher/lower?
18. How can you tell which one is bigger/smaller/longer/shorter/taller/wider/higher/lower?
19. How can you put them in order from shortest to tallest/smallest to biggest/thinnest to widest/highest to lowest?
20. How can you tell if these are equal/the same size?
21. Do you have to measure the same way to compare? Why?
22. What do you have to do to find something that is the same length/height/width/size as this?
23. How can you make a new one that is the same length/width/size?
24. How can you find things that are as short/tall/thin/wide as that?
25. How can you find other things that are shorter/taller/thinner/wider than that?

···········

MATH • MEASUREMENT
Length • Width • Height

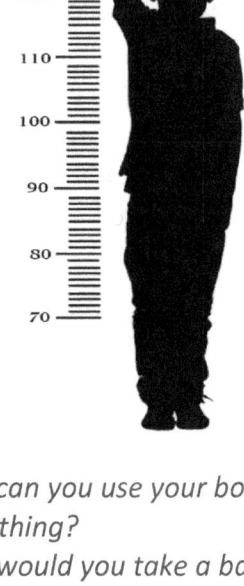

26. You left a lot of room between the _____ and the _____. Why did you do that?
27. How can you re-measure and check one more time?
28. Why does the _____ look like it is longer than the _____?
29. What if you showed me with your hands/ body?
30. What if you put them side-by-side? End-to-end? Next to each other?
31. What would happen if you added more/ took some away?
32. How do you know how much to put in/ add/take away?

· · · · · · · · · · ·

33. How will you remember this?
34. How might it help to draw a picture?
35. What if you show me what that looks like on paper?
36. How will you remember the measurement?

· · · · · · · · · · ·

37. How can you make the object longer/ shorter/taller/wider/bigger/smaller/ higher/lower?
38. What will happen if the object is too long/short/tall/wide/high/low for the _____?
39. How will you know how much to add/ take away/use/cut-off/leave?

· · · · · · · · · · ·

40. How can you use your body to measure something?
41. How would you take a baby step/giant step?
42. How can you tell how many baby/giant steps it will take to get there?
43. What things are shorter/taller/thinner/ wider than you? Why do you think so?
44. Is something taller or shorter than you if you have to look up/down at it? Why?

· · · · · · · · · · ·

45. How can a friend help you measure?
46. How would you show a friend how to measure something?

· · · · · · · · · · ·

47. How long do you think the fabric/butcher paper should be to cover the whole table?
48. How many drawings do you think will fit on the wall if we hang them end to end?

MATH · MEASUREMENT
Ruler

1. *What do you know about rulers?*
2. *Why do people use rulers?*
3. *How do people use rulers?*
    ···········
4. *When you look at a ruler, what do you notice?*
5. *Which side of the ruler will you use to measure? Why? Why not?*
6. *Why do you think a ruler is flat?*
7. *Why do you think numbers/lines are on a ruler?*
8. *Where is the zero? How do you know?*
9. *Why do you think the numbers go up/in sequential order on a ruler?*
    ···········
10. *How do you know how long a ruler is?*
11. *How can you find out how long an inch/a centimeter is?*
    ···········
12. *Why do you think we use rulers to measure?*
13. *What types of things can you measure with a ruler? Show me.*
    ···········
14. *Which end of the ruler should you start with when you measure something? Why would you start there?*
15. *How do you know which end of the ruler is the beginning?*

16. *How do you know where to put the beginning/end of the ruler when you measure?*
17. *Would it be easier to measure an object if you set it next to the ruler? Why? Why not?*
    ···········
18. *How do you know if an object is longer than the ruler?*
19. *Why would you want to know where the ruler ends when you measure?*
20. *What steps do you take to measure an object that is longer than the ruler?*
21. *What do you do next?*
22. *How can you draw a line/an object that is shorter/longer than the ruler?*
23. *What do you think the result would be if you measured again and again?*
24. *How can you remember the measurement?*
    ···········
25. *What if you wanted to make a ruler? How could you do it?*
26. *What other things can you use to measure? How would they work?*
27. *How can you use parts of your body to measure things?*

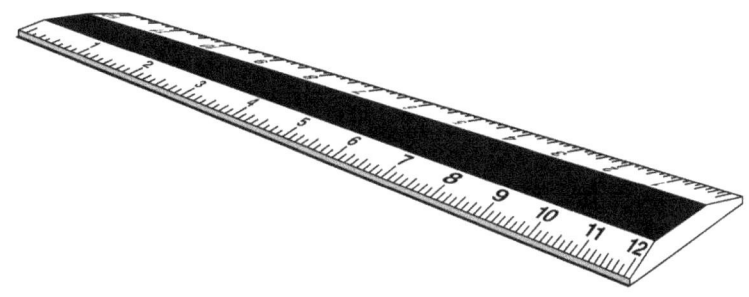

MATH · MEASUREMENT
Mass · Weight · Capacity · Volume

1. How do you know that's a container/basket/bin/cup/bucket?
2. What do you notice about the container/basket/bin/cup/bucket?
3. Describe what you see.
4. What's the difference between a _____ and a _____?
5. Why do we use different types of containers?
6. Why do you think containers come in different sizes/shapes/styles?
7. How do you know which container to use?

....

8. Why do we use containers/baskets/bins/cups/buckets?
9. What types of objects will fit in the container? How do you know?
10. How would you put/fit _____ in the container?

....

11. How much do you think the container will hold?
12. How can you make a container that will hold these?
13. How can you tell how much you can put in the container?
14. What would happen if you put too much in the container?

15. What if the _____ doesn't fit in the container? What will you do?
16. How do you keep objects from falling/spilling out of a container?
17. How do you know if you need more space?
18. What do you have to do to make space?
19. If you move things around, what do you think will happen?
20. What do you have to do to transfer contents from one container to another?

....

21. What will you do with the leftover objects?
22. Does it matter which container you use for the leftovers? Why? Why not?
23. Which container do you think will work best? Why?
24. Do you need a smaller/bigger container than you had when you started? Why? Why not?
25. What if you don't use a container at all?

....

26. What if you use different/more/fewer containers?
27. What do you think will happen if you switch containers? Why?
28. Why do you think that happened?
29. How do you know which container holds more/less?

MATH · MEASUREMENT
Mass · Weight · Capacity · Volume

30. What if you put one container inside of another?
31. How do you know which container fits inside the other?

· · · · · · · · · · ·

32. What does it mean for a container to be heavy/light/empty/full/large/small mean?
33. How does the container feel when it is empty/full/heavy/light/small/large?
34. What are the differences/similarities between the way they feel?
35. How do you know when the container is empty/full/too big/too small/too heavy?
36. How do you know if a container is light/heavy/lighter/heavier/smaller/larger than another?
37. Which container do you think is lighter/heavier? How can you tell?
38. Why do you think one container is lighter/heavier than the other?

· · · · · · · · · · ·

39. What do you have to do to pick up/move/lift/carry an object that is light/heavy/full/empty?
40. What would happen if you didn't
41. How can you find other objects that feel that way?
42. How can you find other objects that weigh that much?

43. How can you find other objects that take up that much space?

· · · · · · · · · · ·

44. How can your friends help you?
45. How can you work together?
46. How would you show a friend how to weigh something?

· · · · · · · · · · ·

47. How can you find out how much something weighs?
48. How can you tell which object weighs more/less?
49. Why would you want to know how much something weighs/holds?
50. How can you put the containers/objects in order by weight?
51. How can you put the containers/objects in order by how much they weigh?
52. How can you put the containers/objects in order by how much they hold?
53. What if you add more/take some away?
54. Do you think something big/full is always heavy? Why? Why not?
55. Do you think something small/empty is always light? Why? Why not?

· · · · · · · · · · ·

56. What do you know about **scales**?
57. Why do you think we use scales?
58. How do you think a scale works?

MATH · MEASUREMENT
Mass · Weight · Capacity · Volume

59. Have you ever used a scale to weigh something? What happened?
60. What do you think will happen if you press down on the scale?
61. What will happen if you take something off a scale?
62. Which part of a scale moves/changes when you weigh something? Why?
63. Why do you think there are numbers/lines on the scale?
64. What if the object doesn't fit on/in the scale?
65. How will you know how much to put in/put on/take out/take off the scale?

66. What happens when the object hangs off of the scale?
67. What happens if you let go/don't let go of what you are weighing?
....
68. Do you think the object will weigh the same tomorrow? Why? Why not?
69. How can you find things that weigh the same/are heavier/are lighter?

MATH · MEASUREMENT
Distance · Speed

1. What does it mean when an object moves fast/slowly?
2. Describe what happened.
3. What did you notice?

....

4. How can you tell which object travels faster/slower?
5. What do you think makes one object move faster/slower than another?
6. How can you get an object to move faster/slower?
7. How can you tell how fast/slow an object is traveling?

....

8. How do you think the object got where it is?
9. What does it mean when something is close/far away?
10. How do you know when something is close/far away from you?
11. How do you know how close/far away an object is?
12. How do you know how close/far away an object is from another object?
13. How can you bring an object closer to/farther away from you?
14. How can you tell how far the object traveled?

....

15. How can you get your object to move
16. What would happen if you used more/less force?
17. How can you get your object to move without touching it?
18. What tools/equipment can you use to move your object? How would that work?

....

19. Why do you think the object moved/didn't move?
20. Do you think the weight of something makes a difference in how fast/slow it moves? Why? Why not?
21. What would happen if you added more weight/reduced the weight?
22. What else can you do to make the object move/travel?

....

23. What happens when an object stops?
24. How can you make the object stop?
25. What if you wanted to stop the object before it got there/to the end?
26. What do you do if the object doesn't go where you want it to go?
27. What do you do if the object changes direction before it gets to the end?
28. How do you keep the object from hitting something/turning/swerving/ flying off/ falling/tumbling?

....

MATH · MEASUREMENT
Distance · Speed

29. What if you were to build a ramp/ bridge?
30. What do you think will happen if you put this object on the ramp/bridge? Why?
31. What is the same/difference between the way these objects moved?
32. What do you think makes the object roll, slide, or stay put?
33. How would you explain what happened?
34. What can you do to help the object roll/ slide/stay put?
35. What kinds of things are good rollers/ sliders? Why?
36. Do you think the shape of an object makes a difference? Why? Why not?
37. What kinds of things don't move at all? Why?
38. What would happen if you laid the ramp flat on the ground/table?
39. How can you tell which direction the object will go when it gets to the end?

· · · · · · · · · · ·

40. Which material works best for the ramp? Why?
41. What if the surface was flat/rough/ bumpy/smooth/at an angle?

42. How can you change the surface to be flat/rough/bumpy/smooth/at an angle?

· · · · · · · · · · ·

43. What's the difference between a _____ and a _____? (Bus, train, boat, plane, scooter, bike, skateboard, motorcycle, horse)
44. Do you think you would get somewhere faster on a horse or in a car?
45. Do you think the wheels help things move faster/slower/farther? Why? Why not?

· · · · · · · · · · ·

46. How does your body move fast/slow?
47. What do you have to do to speed up/ slow down?
48. What do you have to do to race against someone?
49. Why would people want to slow down/ speed up?
50. What would happen if you walked/ran/ jumped/hopped/etc.?
51. How do you know when to stop/go?
52. What happens when people stop?

· · · · · · · · · · ·

53. Why do you think people/animals/insects move in different ways?
54. Why do you think people/animals/insects move at different speeds?
55. What if we all moved at the same pace?

MATH · MEASUREMENT
Time

1. Explain what you know about time.
2. How do you know when it's time to do something?
3. How do we know what time it is?
4. How can you tell how much time has passed/something takes?

    ··············

5. What do we use to tell time? How does it work?
6. Explain how people use tools to keep time. (watches, clocks, timers, hourglasses)
7. How do timekeeping tools help us?
8. Who else uses timekeeping tools? Why?
9. How do timekeeping tools work?
10. What else can you use to keep time?

    ··············

11. How long do you think it will take to do that project/job? How can you find out?
12. How do you know how long the project/activity will take to complete?
13. Why do you think it will take that much time?
14. What do you think you can do in that amount of time?
15. What if it takes more/less time?
16. How can you tell how long something will take to complete?

    ··············

17. What does it mean to do something slowly/quickly?
18. Which activity do you think will take longer? How can you find out?
19. Why do you think the activity will take a long/short period of time?
20. What would happen if you did something too slowly/quickly?
21. Have you done this before? How does that help you do it now?

    ··············

22. How do you know when it's time to wake up/go to bed?
23. What do you notice when you wake up/go to bed?
24. How do you know when it is time to go to school/play/nap/snack/eat/use the restroom/go home/take a bath/sleep?
25. How do you know when the day begins/is over?

    ··············

26. What's the difference between the morning/afternoon/evening?
27. What's the difference between night and day?
28. Tell me about what you do in the morning/in the afternoon/at night/during the day.
29. Tell me what happened before/just now/after/today/this morning/last night/yesterday.

MATH · MEASUREMENT
Time

30. What can you do now/at this moment/later? Why?
31. What's the difference between yesterday, today, and tomorrow?
32. What kinds of activities do you do during the day/at night? Why?
33. How do you remember what you did/will do?

....

34. What does it mean to be early/late/on time for something?
35. Why is it important to be on time for school/activities?
36. How can you make sure you are on time?
37. If you had to go somewhere, when would you want to get ready/prepared?
38. What's the difference between getting ready slowly vs. quickly?
39. If you had a big project to work on, when do you think would be a good time to start?

....

40. What do you know about minutes/hours/days/months/a year?
41. What kinds of things can happen in a minute/hour/day/week/month?

....

42. How does night turn to day and day turn to night?
43. How does the sun/moon get in the sky to start and end each day?
44. What if the sun never came rose/set?
45. How does the sun/moon end each day?

....

46. How do people know which day/month/year it is?
47. Why do people care which day/month/year it is?

....

48. How do you know how old you are?
49. What does it mean to have a birthday?
50. How do you know when it's your birthday?
51. Why do you keep having birthdays?
52. What if you didn't know when you were born?
53. Do you think animals/insects celebrate birthdays? Why? Why not?

NOTES

"*When given an object, children are more likely to engage in creative explorations of that object when they are provided with more open-ended guidance versus when they are given specific information about what the object was designed to do.*" - NAEYC

NOTES

CARS · VEHICLES

When playing with cars, children can learn concepts like engineering and design, wheels and axles, positions in space, force and motion, speed, friction, and ramps.

1. What are cars/**trucks**?
2. What do you know about cars/trucks?
3. How do you know so much about cars?

············

4. What do you notice about your car?
5. Describe your car/truck. How does it look?
6. Do all cars look like that? How do you know?
7. How is this car the same/different from the others?
8. What kind of sound can a car/truck/bus make?
9. What's the difference between a car and a truck/bus/bike/scooter/bus/train/plane/tractors/motorhome?

············

10. Why did you choose that car/truck?
11. What do you like/not like about your car?
12. What would you change about your car? Why?

············

13. Tell me about the parts of your car. (steering wheel/wheels/doors/door handles/hood/roof/windows/ engine/ windshield wipers/etc.).
14. How do you think this part works/moves?
15. Why do you think this part was invented?
16. What other things have parts like these?
17. If you were going to invent a part for a car, what would it be? Why?

············

18. How can you organize the cars?
19. How would you line the cars up/park them?

············

20. How do cars or trucks work/move?
21. What makes your car move like that?
22. How are you making the car move?
23. Where else have you seen something that moves this way? Tell me about it.
24. What other things can your car do?
25. What happens before/when/after you let go?
26. How can you make the car roll faster/ slower?
27. Why do you think the car slows down/ speeds up?
28. How else can you make the car move?
29. Why do you think the car moves that way?

············

30. Why do you think the car stopped/ turned/got stuck/flipped/crashed/rolled off?
31. What can you do to keep that from happening?
32. What do you think will happen if the car keeps crashing/rolling off?

CARS · VEHICLES

33. *Is there a car that would work better? Why do you think so?*
34. *How can you tell how far your car traveled/rolled?*
35. *Why does your car go far sometimes but not other times?*
36. *How do you know which car rolled farther?*
37. *What did you do differently?*
38. *Why do you think the car changes direction?*
39. *How can you get your car to turn/ change direction?*

....

40. *What type of car/vehicle is best/worst for carrying/transporting things?*
41. *How can your car/truck help you transport things?*
42. *Which car/vehicle would hold more/ less? How do you know?*
43. *How much do you think your car will hold? How can you find out?*
44. *What types of objects will fit/won't fit in your car? Why?*
45. *What happens when you add a load to the car? Why?*
46. *How can you get the car to carry more?*
47. *What other things can you use to transport objects?*

....

48. *What do you know about **ramps**?*
49. *How can you build a ramp for your car?*
50. *What if you rolled your car on/off/up/ down a ramp?*
51. *How can you get the car to roll up to the top?*
52. *What if you rolled a car up/down the stairs?*
53. *What happens when your car gets to the bottom?*
54. *How can you change what happens when your car gets to the bottom?*
55. *What would happen if you lifted/lowered the ramp?*
56. *How can you roll your car to the next level/floor?*
57. *What if you rolled your car on a surface that is flat/smooth/rough/wet/soft/hard/ bumpy?*
58. *How can you make your car roll faster/ slower down the ramp?*

....

59. *How can you get your car/truck to pull/ tow another car/truck?*
60. *What do you need to pull/tow the car? Why?*
61. *What do you have to do to get the car/ truck to move?*
62. *What if you used a different car/vehicle?*

....

63. *Why do people park in spaces/driveways/ garages/carports/on the street?*
64. *What would happen if there were no places to park?*
65. *How do you know which cars to park in the stalls?*

CARS · VEHICLES

66. What can you do to give each car a special spot to park?
67. Why do people build roads/bridges for their cars?
68. Why do people drive cars on roads/streets/bridges?

············

69. How can you build/**design** something that rolls?
70. How would your rolling object be used?
71. Show me how you would design a new car.
72. How would your new car look?
73. What materials would you use to make a car? Why?
74. If you gave your car a name, what would it be? Why?
75. Who would use/drive the car you design/make? Why?

············

76. What do you notice when you're in a real car?
77. What kinds of things can you do in a real car?
78. What do you do to stay safe in a real car?
79. Can children drive real cars like grown-ups? Why? Why not?

············

80. Why do you think there are so many different kinds of cars?
81. What do real cars need to keep working?
82. How do real cars get the energy to move?

83. What's the difference between a gas car and an electric/hybrid car?
84. Why do people charge/put gas in cars?
85. How do people fix real cars?

············

86. What does **remote control** mean?
87. How does a remote control work?
88. How do you get a remote control car to move/turn/stop/go/back up/slow down/speed up?
89. What do people do with remote control cars?
90. How do you keep the remote control working?

············

91. Does everyone travel in cars? Why? Why not?
92. Do people have to drive cars? Why? Why not?
93. How else can people get around?
94. What if there were no cars in the world?

············

95. What if you wanted to **build** a garage/road/bridge for your car? How would you do it?
96. What materials would you use to build your structure?
97. Why do you think those materials would work the best?
98. Which materials wouldn't work well for building a car? Why?

WHEELS and AXLES

1. What is a wheel/axle?
2. Describe a wheel/axle.
3. How can you tell that something is a wheel/axle?
4. What do you notice about the wheel/axle?
5. What are some things you already know about wheels and axles?
6. How do you think a wheel/axle works?
7. What would you like to find out about wheels and axles?
8. Why do you think a wheel is round/in the shape of a circle?
9. What would happen if a wheel was another shape?
10. What pattern do you notice on the wheel?

....

11. How do wheels help us?
12. How do wheels make work easier?
13. What is a **simple machine?**
14. Why is a wheel and axle a simple machine?
15. What would happen if we didn't have wheels?
16. Can something roll if it doesn't have wheels? Why? Why not? How?
17. Does it matter what size a wheel is? Why? Why not?
18. Are all wheels look the same? Why? Why not?

19. Why are some wheels smaller/larger than others?

....

20. How does a wheel move/roll?
21. Do all wheels roll? How do you know?
22. What makes a wheel spin/turn/roll?
23. How does an axle help a wheel roll?
24. How can you make a wheel move faster/slower?
25. What makes a wheel stop spinning/turning/rolling? How?
26. What would happen if something was in front of/behind the wheel?
27. How do you think wheels would roll on a smooth/bumpy/sticky surface?
28. What would happen if you pressed against the wheel?
29. Where else can you find things with parts that roll/spin around? How do they work? (shopping cart, doorknob, chair, fan blade, can opener, dolly, steering wheel, hoist/pulley, Ferris wheel, pizza cutter, rolling pin, lawnmower, windmill, luggage, etc.)
30. What if you laid the wheel flat/sideways?

....

31. Why are there wheels on cars/buses/motorcycles/bicycles/chairs/wagons/wheelbarrows/planes?
32. Where else can you find wheels? Describe how they are used.

WHEELS and AXLES

33. Why don't you see wheels on boats/hot air balloons/ski mobiles?

....

34. What happens if a wheel/tire is flat?
35. Can you roll a flat tire? Why? Why not?
36. How do you fix a flat tire?
37. How does a horse and buggy use wheels?
38. Tell me about other things that use wheels.

....

39. How can you find out what holds the wheel in place?
40. How does the wheel attach to the body of the object?
41. What's the difference between a wheel and a tube?
42. What's the difference between a wheel on a car/truck and a wheel on a bike/scooter?

....

43. What helps the wheel spin? How?
44. Why does a wheel need an **axle** to work?
45. Why do you think the axle is positioned there/in the center?
46. Why do you think some axles are thicker or thinner than others?
47. How does the axle help the wheel spin/turn/roll?
48. Show me how the wheel spins around the axle.
49. Let's look for other objects that might have a wheel and axle.

50. Tell me about other things that use spinning or turning parts like axles.
51. What if a wheel didn't have an axle?
52. What else can you use as an axle? How will it work?
53. What if the axle was square instead of round?
54. What if there was no axle?

....

55. What if a car didn't have any wheels?
56. What if a car only had one/two/three wheels?
57. How does a wheelbarrow work on one wheel?

....

58. What if you wanted to build/draw/trace a wheel? How would you do it?
59. What materials can you use to make a wheel?
60. How can you make a picture collage of things with wheels?
61. How can you use the wheels when you paint/mold clay?
62. How can you use a wheel to make tracks?
63. How can you make a crayon rubbing of a wheel?

....

64. How can you make your body roll?
65. Do you need an axel to roll? Why? Why not?
66. How can you move your body around in circles? (arms/legs/hips/shoulders, etc.)

....

67. How can you safely play with/around wheels?

SCALE and STRUCTURE

1. What do you know about building/constructing/designing things?
2. What do you notice about the buildings/structures you see?

∙∙∙∙∙∙∙∙∙∙

3. Before you create your structure, how can you put your design ideas on paper?
4. Why is/was it important/necessary to draw your design first?
5. Before you created your structure, what did you do?
6. How can/did you use paper to plan/design your structure?
7. Did you follow your plan/design? Why? Why not?
8. How is your structure the same/different from the plans you drew?

∙∙∙∙∙∙∙∙∙∙

9. Tell me about what you are building.
10. How would you describe your structure?
11. It looks interesting. Why did you decide to build this?
12. Where have you seen a structure like this before? What were you doing?
13. What made you think of building it that way?
14. How did you **build** your structure? What steps did you take?
15. What did you do first/second/third/next/last?
16. What do you think of when you look at your structure?

17. How do/will you use your structure?
18. Why did you build this many (quantity) structures?

∙∙∙∙∙∙∙∙∙∙

19. Why did you add or not add windows/doors/walls/stories/a roof/stairs/floors/a balcony/etc.?
20. Why did you pick those colors/shapes/sizes for your structure?
21. What made you think of putting this block on the top/bottom/inside/outside/between these two?
22. What made you think of adding this piece to your structure?
23. How did you make the walls/doors/windows/base/top/etc.?
24. How did/can you get the roof to slant?
25. How did/can you get the walls to stay up?
26. What would be a good thing/shape to use for the roof/base/side/arch/etc.?
27. If you were building a real house, what materials/tools would you need?
28. What do you have to do to put a bend in the road?
29. What can you build to get the animals over the water?

∙∙∙∙∙∙∙∙∙∙

30. What made you choose these pieces?
31. How do you know how many pieces you used?
32. What would happen if you kept building?
33. What will you do if you run out of pieces?
34. What else can you use?

∙∙∙∙∙∙∙∙∙∙

SCALE and STRUCTURE

35. How will you reach the top?
36. How did you decide to put the blocks together/on the bottom/on the top/in the middle?
37. What can you add to/take away from your structure to make it look different?
38. What would happen if you added more/ took away material?
39. What would happen if you added or took away pieces from the top/bottom/side?
40. What would it look like if you decorated your structure?

....

41. How can you tell which structure has more or fewer blocks/pieces?
42. What patterns do you notice in the structure?
43. How do/did you know how tall/high/ wide/short/long/thin to make your structure?
44. What can you do to measure your structure? (long, short, tall, high, wide, thin, round, circumference)
45. How do you think you could make your structure taller/higher/wider/shorter/ longer/thinner?
46. How can you make or change a structure to fit in/on/under/over this?
47. How can you build your structure to reach the wall?
48. How do you know what will fit under or over the structure/tunnel?

49. How can you create a structure that is big enough to fit them all?
50. What will happen if they don't fit?
51. What is more important to you, the height or the width? Why?
52. If both structures have the same number of blocks/pieces, what makes this one taller/wider/longer/etc.?

....

53. What do you know about using **materials/tools** to build?
54. Why do people use materials/tools to build?
55. How do tools help people build?
56. What made you think of using those materials/tools to make your structure?
57. Can you tell me how/why you used those materials/tools?
58. How will/did you know how much material to use?
59. How can you tell the difference between the materials you used?
60. How can/did you organize the materials/ tools to make them easier to find/put away?
61. What's the difference between the materials/tools you used and the ones you didn't?
62. What's the difference between how you built your structure and the others here?
63. What if you added rocks/sticks/clay/ Legos/etc.?
64. What are you going to do with the leftover material?

....

SCALE and STRUCTURE

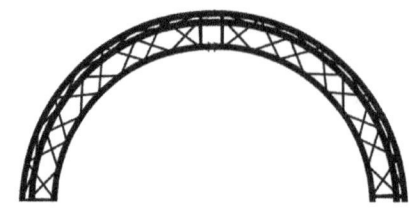

65. What would you change about your structure if you could?
66. What can you do to solve the problem/fix it?
67. How else can you do it?

· · · · · · · · · · ·

68. How can you keep your structure from falling down?
69. What would happen if you moved your structure?
70. What will happen if your structure falls?
71. Why do you think your structure fell?
72. How much can you add to/put on your structure before it breaks/falls?
73. How can you make your structure stronger/sturdier?
74. I wonder if using a different material would help.
75. What will happen to your structure if it rains/snows/gets windy/is left outside/there is an earthquake?
76. What can you do to keep the wind from blowing your structure down?
77. Which structure do you think is the weakest/strongest? Why?
78. Why do you think that one is the weakest/strongest?
79. How will heat/cold affect your structure?
80. Is it better to build your structure outside/inside? Why?

81. Is it better to build your structure on the floor/a platform/a table/a tray? Why?

· · · · · · · · · · ·

82. What if you added animals/people to your structure?
83. What will the people/animals/insects do in your structure?
84. How can you make sure the animals/insects don't escape?
85. What can you do to help the people/animals inside stay warm/dry/safe?
86. What can you bring light inside of your structure so the people/animals can see?
87. How can you build things for the animals/people to use inside your structure? (chair, bed, table, etc.)

· · · · · · · · · · ·

88. Describe what a **construction worker** does.
89. Do all construction workers work on the same job/project/task? How do you know?
90. What kinds of clothes does a construction worker wear?
91. Why do construction workers wear special clothes? (hard hats, yellow vests, gloves, steel toe boots)
92. Tell me about a time you saw construction workers.
93. How do construction workers keep their area safe?
94. Why do construction workers place cones/rope/tape around where they work?

· · · · · · · · · · ·

95. If I wanted to make a structure like yours, what would I need to do?
96. How can you remember what you built?

BRIDGES

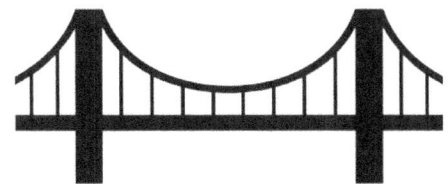

1. What do you know about bridges?
2. Why do people build bridges?
3. How do people use bridges?
4. How do bridges help people?
5. What makes a good bridge?
6. Where have you seen a bridge? Describe what you saw.
7. Have you ever crossed a bridge? What was it like?

. . . .

8. Why do we need bridges in some places but not in others?
9. What would happen if there were no bridges anywhere?
10. How do people know when they need to build a bridge?
11. Do you think animals like raccoons and squirrels use bridges to get from one place to another? Why? Why not?
12. How do bridges connect people/animals to places?

. . . .

13. Do all bridges look the same? How do you know?
14. How are bridges the same/different?
15. What do you know about the structure of different types of bridges? (beam, arch, suspension, cable-stayed, and cantilever)

16. What type of bridge would you like to build? Why?

. . . .

17. What do you have to do to **build** a bridge?
18. What if you draw plans before you start building?
19. How can you design/draw a plan for building a bridge?
20. How will your bridge be used?
21. How will you know how short/long/low/high/thin/wide to make your bridge?
22. What will happen if the bridge is too short/long/low/high/thin/wide?

. . . .

23. What materials/tools will you need to build the bridge?
24. How can you find materials/tools to build the bridge?

. . . .

25. Who/what will be crossing over your bridge? Why? What's its purpose?
26. How do you know what size and shape your materials should be?
27. What materials do you think will make a strong bridge? Why?
28. How will you know how strong/high to make your bridge?
29. Why do you think a bridge has to be strong/high?
30. What can you do to make your bridge stronger/higher?

BRIDGES

31. What will you do if you run out of material?

•••••••••••

32. How can you test your bridge to see how much load/weight it will hold?
33. Now that you have tested your bridge, what can you do now/next?

•••••••••••

34. What will you name your bridge? Why?
35. What would you do differently next time?
36. What did you learn about bridges while you were building one?

•••••••••••

37. What is a dead/live load?
38. What's the difference between a dead load and a live load?
39. Why do you think people use the words "dead" and "live" to describe the loads?

•••••••••••

40. What do you know about suspension/tension/compression?
41. What do you think would happen if a bridge was weak/wobbly/shaky?
42. What do you think would happen if a bridge wasn't built correctly?
43. How can wind/shaking affect a bridge?
44. How would you feel crossing a weak/damaged bridge?
45. Why do we have to inspect/maintain our bridges?

46. Have you ever seen a bridge that goes up in the middle to let boats pass underneath? How do you think that works?
47. What is a fixed/movable bridge?
48. What is the difference between a fixed and a movable bridge?
49. What do you know about drawbridges?
50. How do drawbridges move/open/rise/close?
51. Have you ever seen a drawbridge move/open/rise/close? Tell me about it.
52. Why do you think people build drawbridges/movable bridges?
53. What would happen if bridges didn't move when there are tall ships?

•••••••••••

54. What can you do if your bridge doesn't reach the other side?
55. How do people and cars get from one side of a river/valley/road to the other without a bridge?

•••••••••••

56. How can you find bridges near you?
57. How will you know/remember how many bridges you found?
58. What if you drew pictures of the bridges you saw/found?

•••••••••••

59. What do you notice about the bridge in this picture? (columns, beams, nuts, bolts, trusses, cables, etc.)
60. What's the difference between building a bridge over water and building a bridge on land?
61. If you could talk to a bridge, what questions would you ask it?

NOTES

"When young children are curious, interested, and confident about discovering the answers to their questions, they are best able to benefit from learning opportunities" **(Ross Thompson, 2002).**

NOTES

RAMPS · INCLINE PLANES

1. Tell me what you know about ramps/ incline planes.
2. What does "incline" mean?
3. How do you know if something is inclined?
4. How do you know that is a ramp/incline plane?
5. Where have you seen ramps/incline planes? How were they being used?
6. What do you notice about your ramp?
7. Describe a ramp/incline plane.
8. Why do we use ramps/incline planes?

············

9. What can you do to design your ramp before you build it?
10. How do you make/build/adjust a ramp?
11. Why did you choose those materials to build your ramp?
12. What will you do with your ramp?
13. How can you connect the ramps?
14. How can you have fun with a ramp?

············

15. What is a **simple machine?**
16. Why is an incline plane a simple machine?
17. Do you think a ramp makes work easier to do? How?
18. How does a ramp/incline plane help move an object?

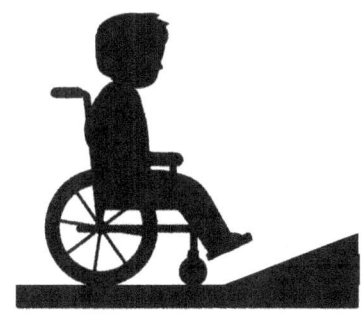

19. Why do you think we use ramps to move things?
20. What would happen if we didn't have ramps?

············

21. What do you think will happen when you put this on the ramp?
22. What would happen if you rolled something up/down the ramp?
23. What did it do?
24. What objects can move up/down the ramp? Why?
25. Why do you think some objects don't or can't move up/down the ramp?
26. Is it easier to move something up a ramp or down a ramp? Why?
27. Why do you think some objects move slower/faster down the ramp?
28. Which do you think will roll faster, the object on the flat plane or the object on the ramp/incline plane? Why?

············

29. How would you compare these ramps?
30. How is this ramp the same/different from that ramp?

············

31. Tell me what you know about planes/ angles/slopes.
32. What would happen if you raised one end of the plane?

RAMPS · INCLINE PLANES

33. What happens when the ramp is flat/ steep/too steep?

34. How can you change the ramp/angle/ slope to make things move faster/ slower?

35. How can you make the ramp flatter/ steeper/higher/lower?

36. How do you know which end of the plane to raise?

37. How can you support one end of the plane, so it becomes a ramp?

38. Why does the ramp keep falling?

39. How can you stabilize the ramp?

• • • • • • • • • • •

40. What happens when objects get to the bottom/end of the ramp?

41. What can you do to change what happens?

42. How can you get the object to stop/turn?

43. Why do you think the object didn't make it down the ramp/to the end?

44. Why do you think objects are falling off your ramp?

45. How can you keep objects from falling off the side of the ramp?

• • • • • • • • • • •

46. What's the difference between an object that rolls down a ramp and one that doesn't?

47. How can you change that?

• • • • • • • • • • •

48. How can you tell how far the object travels?

49. Which object do you think will move the fastest/slowest down the ramp? Why?

50. What can you do to find out which object travels the farthest/fastest/slowest?

51. Why do you think the object moved faster/slower?

52. How can you get the object to travel farther/faster/slower?

53. What if you tried using a different object?

54. What about that object makes you think it will act differently?

55. What if you used an object that was lighter/heavier/smaller/bigger/shorter/ longer?

• • • • • • • • • • •

56. What do you notice about the surface of the ramp?

57. What would happen if you used a different texture/material on the ramp?

58. Which texture/material makes the object go slower/faster? Why?

59. How does friction affect how the object moves?

NOTES

FORCE and MOTION

1. How does the object move?
2. How do you know if an object is moving or staying still?
3. What objects would be easy/difficult to move? Why?
4. What types of things can/can't be moved? Why? Why not?

....

5. How can/did you make the object move?
6. How can/did you move it?
7. Is it easier to move an object when you are weak or strong? Why?
8. What materials/tools/equipment can you use to help you move the object?

....

9. How would you design an object that will travel far/fast?
10. Show me the different ways this object can move. (ball, box, car, wagon, balloon, bubble, bike, skateboard, crayon, boat, person, animal, insect, etc.)
11. How can you make the object move a different way/more than one way?
12. Compare how these objects move.
13. What else can you use to make an object move?
14. How do you keep an object from moving?

....

15. What do you know about force/motion?
16. How does force/motion work?
17. Can you always see forces/motion? Why? Why not?
18. What do you think causes motion?
19. How does something in motion look?
20. Describe different types of force/motion.
21. What kind of force do you think will work the best/worst? Why?
22. How is this force/motion different/the same as that force/motion?
23. Why do you think this force/motion is the same/different?

....

24. What does it mean to put force on something?
25. What force do you use to kick a ball/pull a wagon/lift a box/push a cart/swing a rope/ride a tricycle/move a wagon/open a door/push a skateboard/push a scooter/mow a lawn/etc.?
26. How do you increase/decrease force?
27. What does it mean to push/pull something?
28. Why do people push/pull things?
29. How do people push/pull things?
30. When you push/pull something, how does it move? Why?
31. Do objects move away from you or come toward you when you push/pull them? Why?

FORCE and MOTION

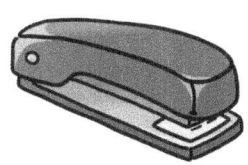

32. What objects work with a pushing/pulling motion? How? (stapler, staple remover, tape, tweezers, remote control, keypad, Post-it note, clothespin, hole punch, scissors, etc.)
33. How do you push/pull/swing/twist/turn/roll/press/squeeze/spin/bounce an object?
34. What would help you push/pull/swing/twist/turn/roll/press/squeeze/spin/bounce an object?
35. Why would you push/pull/swing/twist/turn/roll/press/squeeze/spin/bounce objects?
36. What objects change shape when you push/pull/swing/twist/turn/roll/press/squeeze/bounce them? Why do you think that happens?
37. What happened when you pushed/pulled/swung/twisted/turned/rolled/pressed/squeezed/bounced the object?
38. How can you test your theory?

39. How do some motions repeat/move in a pattern? (swing, waves, steps, bounces, etc.)
40. Why do some motions repeat/move in a pattern? (swing, waves, feet, ball, etc.)
41. How can you make a pattern of movement?

. . . .

42. What makes an object change direction? Why?
43. How can you make an object change direction?

. . . .

44. What do you notice?
45. Why is/isn't the object moving?
46. Why does the object stop/go?
47. What makes the object go back and forth/straight/in a line/around?
48. What would happen if you put the object inside/outside/on top/on the bottom?
49. How could you sort/group these according to what can be pushed/pulled/swung/twisted/turned/rolled/pressed/squeezed/spun/bounced?
50. How can you make an object move farther/closer/up/down/around/over/under?

. . . .

51. What do you know about speed?
52. How can you tell how slow/fast something is moving?
53. How can you make an object move slower/faster?
54. How do you increase/decrease the speed of an object?
55. How is fast motion different from slow motion?

. . . .

56. What kind of push will make the object go _____ inches/feet?
57. How can you tell how far an object has traveled?
58. What if the object was lighter/heavier?

. . . .

FORCE and MOTION

59. How can you knock an object over?
60. What can you use to knock an object over?
61. Why does the object fall over?
62. Why does/doesn't an object break when it falls?
63. What can you do differently to make an object fall over?

···········

64. How does the wind move an object?
65. How can you use the wind to make the object move?
66. Why does the wind move things?
67. Why doesn't everything outside move on a windy day?
68. What can you do to make wind?
69. What would happen if you blew on an object?
70. What can you do to see which objects will move in the wind?
71. Why do some objects move when you blow on them, and others don't?

···········

72. What can you build to help you move an object?
73. Draw a picture of how it will work.

···········

74. How does your body move?

75. How do you get your body to move faster/slower/sideways/up/down/around/etc.?
76. How do you make your body move?
77. Does your body need force to move? Why? Why not?
78. What kind of force can move/stop your body?
79. What if your body couldn't move?
80. How do parts inside of our body move? (eyes, blood, heartbeat, muscles, etc.)
81. Why do you think some people can't move?
82. Why do some people move faster/slower than others?

···········

83. How do animals/insects move?
84. How does the movement of one animal or insect the same/different from another?

···········

85. Would you rather push/pull a heavy object or a light one? Why?
86. What would happen if you lightened the load/added more items?
87. Would you rather push/pull a big object or a tiny one? Why?
88. What would happen if you had to push/pull an object for a long time?
89. What would happen if you had to push/pull an object up/downhill?

···········

FORCE and MOTION

90. What happens when you play tug-of-war?
91. What if you only had one person to play tug-of-war?
92. Why do you need more than one person to play tug-of-war?
93. Why do some people fall when they play tug-of-war?

. . . .

94. What do you know about **friction**?
95. What does it mean for objects to slide?
96. Why do objects slide?
97. What can you do to keep objects from sliding?
98. What happens when two objects rub together when they move?
99. How does friction affect objects that move?
100. How can you use friction to slow something down/speed it up?
101. What types of things add friction? Why?
102. How is this friction different/the same?
103. What would happen if you add/take away the friction?

. . . .

104. What do you know about **gravity**?
105. Why is there gravity?
106. How does gravity help objects move?

107. What happens when you drop an object?
108. When you drop an object, why doesn't it float up?
109. Why do you fall down and not up?
110. When you fall, why don't you fall up instead of down?
111. Can people make gravity? Why? Why not?
112. What if there was no gravity?
113. Do you think a heavy/larger object will hit the ground faster than a lighter/smaller object? Why? Why not?

. . . .

114. What is a **simple machine**?
115. How do simple machines help us move things?
116. How can you build a simple machine that will help you move something?

. . . .

117. What is a **catapult**?
118. How does a catapult work?
119. How do you know which objects a catapult will launch?
120. What if you wanted to build a catapult? How would you do it?
121. How can you test your catapult to see if it works?

. . . .

122. What are forces in nature? (landslide, mudslide, tornado, hurricane, avalanche, etc.)

LIGHT · SHADOWS

1. What is light/a shadow?
2. How do you think shadows are made?
3. How does light help make shadows?
4. Describe how the shadow looks.
5. Why do you think shadows look like they do?
6. Where have you seen shadows before? Tell me about it.

....

7. How do you know what/who is making the shadows?
8. Does everything cast a shadow? Why? Why not?

....

9. What do you notice about the color/shades of shadows?
10. Why do you think shadows are lighter/darker/that color?

....

11. This shadow looks like something I've seen before. Why do you think that is?
12. Let's compare shadows/light sources. What do you notice?
13. How is your shadow the same/different from his/her shadow?
14. Why do you think some shadows look different than others?
15. How can/did you make your shadow change?

16. What do you think will happen if we turn down/off the lights?
17. What do you think will happen if you use this light source instead of that one? (flashlight/candle/desk lamp/the sun/fireflies/lantern/light table)
18. What if we use a colored/black/neon light?

....

19. How does your shadow change when you move around/stop moving? (shape, size, and position)
20. What do you notice about your shadow when you do that?
21. What happens to your shadow when you move farther away/closer to the wall?
22. I see that the shadow got bigger/smaller/thinner/wider/etc. Why do you think that happened?

....

23. What do you think you can do to make your shadow bigger/smaller/longer/shorter/taller/clearer/wider/move faster/move slower?
24. How can you tell which shadow is bigger/smaller/longer/shorter/ etc.?
25. How can you tell how much bigger/smaller/longer/etc. this shadow is compared to that one?
26. How can you tell which light source is stronger/brighter?
27. Does it matter where the light source is located? Why? Why not?

....

LIGHT · SHADOWS

28. *What if you shine the light in front of/ beside/over/under/behind/next to/closer to/farther from the object?*
29. *What would happen if you shined the light in a different direction?*
30. *What if you shined the light through tissue/paper/wood/colored glass/lace/ magna-tiles/wax paper/foil/etc.?*
31. *What if you shine the light through something transparent/translucent/ opaque?*
32. *What if you shine the light while standing in front of a mirror?*

············

33. *How do the shadows look different today/this time?*
34. *Why do you think the shadows look different now/today from the ones you saw last time?*
35. *Why can't you see shadows today?*
36. *Why do you think there is a pattern in the shadow?*

············

37. *Why do you think you see shadows when you're out in the sun?*
38. *What happens to shadows when the sun moves?*
39. *How do shadows look at different times of the day?*

40. *Why do you think shadows change throughout the day?*
41. *How does your shadow change when you stand in the shade?*
42. *How can you tell how much a shadow changes/has changed?*
43. *Where do shadows go when the light source/sun goes away? How do you know?*

············

44. *How can your friends help you make shadows?*
45. *How would the shadow look if you added more people?*
46. *How would the shadow change if you stepped apart/raised your hands/spread your legs/etc.?*

············

47. *Can you catch a shadow? How? Why not?*
48. *Can shadows move by themselves? Why? Why not?*
49. *Do you think shadows can think/talk/ play/feel/hear/see/smell/sing? Why? Why not?*

············

50. *What can you do to remember how the shadow looked?*
51. *How can you tell a story using your shadow?*
52. *How can you make a shadow puppet show?*

············

53. *How can you make letters/numbers/ shapes/images using shadows?*
54. *How can you tell a story using shadows?*

WATER

1. What is water?
2. What do you know about water?
3. Tell me how water looks/feels/tastes/ sounds/smells.
4. Is all water the same? How do you know?
5. If you need water, how can you get it?

············

6. How does water sound when it moves/ falls/drips/flows?
7. How does water taste/smell/look?
8. How does the water feel on your hands/ feet/body/clothes?
9. How can you change the way water looks?
10. What can you add to the water to make it look different?

············

11. How can you find water?
12. How does the water get here/there?
13. Draw a map to where you found water.
14. Where have you seen water? Tell me about it.

············

15. How does water help us?
16. Why do we need water?
17. How does water help people/plants/ animals/insects?
18. What kinds of animals live around/in water?

19. What's the difference between water in the ocean and water in the sink/house/ lake/river/stream/puddle/aquarium?
20. Why do you think ocean water is salty?
21. Should people drink ocean water? Why? Why not?
22. Can we get the salt out of ocean water? Why? Why not? How?
23. What if there was no water anywhere?

············

24. How does water move/flow?
25. Why do you think water moves/flows like that?
26. Where can we see water flow in one direction? Why does it do that?
27. What makes water move/flow/rise/fall/ stay still?
28. How can you make water move/rise/fall/ stay still?
29. How can you make water move faster/ slower?
30. How can you stop water from moving/ flowing?
31. How can you redirect the water?
32. How can you make water stay still?

············

33. What is a waterfall?
34. What happens to the water after it falls?
35. How does the water get to the top of a waterfall?

WATER

36. *What happens to water when it moves downhill?*
37. *What can you do to make water move uphill?*
38. *How can you make/build a waterfall?*

· · · · · · · · · · ·

39. *How can you move/transport water?*
40. *What if there is too much water to transport/carry?*
41. *What can you use to help you move/transport the water? How would it work?*
42. *What would happen if you transported water in something that has a hole?*
43. *What would happen if it was cracked/broken?*

· · · · · · · · · · ·

44. *What happens when water gets to the very top of something?*
45. *Why does water spill/drip/fall?*
46. *Describe what happens when water spills/drips/falls/sprays.*
47. *How can you keep water from spilling/dripping/falling?*
48. *What do you do when you spill water?*

49. *How can you pick up/clean up spilled water?*
50. *What's the fastest/cleanest/easiest way to clean up the spill?*

· · · · · · · · · · ·

51. *What happens when water is poured on concrete/on carpet/on paper/in a tray/in sand/in dirt/in the grass/on fabric/on foil/on a sponge/on tissue?*
52. *What happened to the water?*

· · · · · · · · · · ·

53. *How can you tell how much water you have?*
54. *What can you do to **measure** the water?*
55. *Do your cups/pitchers hold the same amount of water? How can you tell?*
56. *Which container holds the most/least water? How do you know?*
57. *What would happen if you poured some water out/added more?*
58. *What happens when you put an object in the water?*
59. *How can you make an object move with/on the water?*
60. *What happens when you drop things into the water?*
61. *Why do some things move/stay still/float/sink in the water?*

· · · · · · · · · · ·

62. *How do people play in/with water?*
63. *What can people do in water?*
64. *What happens when you jump into the water?*

WATER

65. Why do you have to be careful around water?
66. How do you stay safe around water?

· · · · · · · · · · ·

67. Who are the people who work around water? What kinds of jobs do they have?

· · · · · · · · · · ·

68. What is a splash/ripple/wave?
69. Describe what happens when water splashes/ripples/makes waves.
70. What do you think makes water splash/ripple/make a wave?
71. How do you make water splash/ripple/make a wave?
72. How do you make a splash or wave higher/bigger/smaller/wider/etc.?
73. How do you make a ripple bigger/smaller/ wider/longer/shorter?
74. How do you think puddles form?
75. Why doesn't water spread beyond the puddle?

· · · · · · · · · · ·

76. How does a filter/strainer/funnel work?
77. How does the water move through a filter/strainer/funnel?
78. Why do you think a filter/strainer/funnel is shaped like that?
79. What happens when water pours through a filter/strainer/funnel?

80. What happens when you add dirt/sand/flour/sugar/oil/salt/paint/ice/snow/soap/food coloring to water?
81. How can you get the dirt/sand/oil/sugar/salt/soap/color/etc. out of the water?
82. How did the water change when you added _____?
83. Why do you think the water looks like that?
84. Why do some things disappear when you put them in water?
85. Why do some powders/liquids separate from the water?

· · · · · · · · · · ·

86. Why do we drink water?
87. Why do people use cups/containers for drinking water?
88. Why do you think it's important to drink water?
89. Is it safe to drink water from anywhere? Why?
90. How can you find water when you need it?
91. How does water keep us clean?
92. What makes water clean/dirty? How can you tell?
93. Does everyone have access to clean water? Why? Why not?
94. What if people don't have clean water to drink?
95. How can we help people who don't have clean water to drink?

WATER

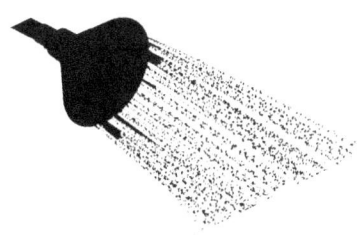

96. What can you do to clean dirty water?

············

97. What types of things can you do with water?
98. How can you use water to paint?
99. How can you use water to make lines/patterns/shapes/numbers/letters on paper/the ground.
100. How can you use water to exercise?

············

101. How do you get water into a balloon?
102. How do you get water to stay in the balloon?
103. What happens when you drop/toss a water balloon? Why?

············

104. How does water get into your home?
105. How else can you get water when you need it?
106. What is a faucet/spigot/hose/pipe?
107. How does a faucet/spigot/hose/pipe work?
108. What happens when you turn on/off a faucet?
109. What happens if the faucet/spigot/hose/pipe breaks?
110. What if you don't turn off a faucet/spigot?
111. Why do you think we use faucets/spigots/hoses/pipes for water?

112. Can you drink from faucets/spigots/hoses/pipes? Why? Why not?

············

113. What is a waterwheel?
114. What happens when you pour water into a waterwheel?
115. How does water make a waterwheel turn?
116. What makes a waterwheel turn faster/slower?
117. Why do people use waterwheels?

············

118. How do you find water in the ground/plants?
119. How do you get water out of the ground/plants?

············

120. What happens when water is left outside/sitting for a long time?
121. Where does the water go when it disappears? How do you know?
122. How did the water get there if it didn't rain?

············

123. What happens when water gets very hot/boils?
124. How do you know how the temperature of the water?
125. Why do you think water bubbles when it gets very hot/boils?
126. Do you think hot/boiling water can burn your skin? Why? Why not?

············

127. What is **steam/vapor**?
128. Describe steam/vapor.

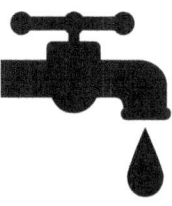

WATER

129. *How is steam/vapor made?*

130. *How is steam/vapor different from the water you drink?*

131. *How/When do people use steam/vapor?*

132. *How does steam/vapor help us?*

133. *Do you think steam/vapor can burn your skin? Why? Why not?*

134. *What is humidity?*

135. *How do you feel when the air is humid?*

....

136. *Tell me what you know about the **water/hydrologic cycle** (evaporation, condensation, precipitation, collection).*

137. *Explain what you know about the water cycle.*

138. *What happens when the sun warms water in oceans, rivers, and lakes? (evaporation)*

139. *What happens when vapors cool up in the sky? (condensation)*

140. *Why does water evaporate/condense?*

141. *What happens when water evaporates/condenses/precipitates/vaporizes/humidifies?*

142. *How does water turn from gas/steam/vapor to liquid?*

143. *Why does it rain?*

144. *Why does it rain on gray cloudy days but not clear days?*

....

145. *What is a water **well**?*

146. *How does a water well work?*

147. *How does a water well help people?*

148. *How do you dig a hole/water well?*

149. *How can you get water out of a hole/water well?*

150. *What is groundwater?*

151. *Why is there water in the ground?*

152. *How can you find water in the ground?*

....

153. *What does **conservation** mean?*

154. *Why should people conserve water?*

155. *How can you conserve water?*

156. *How do people waste water?*

157. *How do you keep from wasting water when you shower/wash dishes/water the lawn?*

158. *Have you ever wasted water? Tell me about it.*

159. *What do you think can happen if people keep wasting water?*

160. *What if there was no more water left in the rivers/bay/lakes/ocean/world?*

161. *How can you use/collect/store rainwater?*

162. *What other things should people conserve?*

ICE ▪ FREEZE ▪ MELT

1. What do you know about ice?
2. How does ice feel/smell/taste/look/ sound?
3. Is ice hard or soft? Why?
4. What can/do people do with ice?
5. What's the difference between water and ice?

....

6. How do you think ice is made?
7. How does water turn to ice?
8. How do you make water very cold?
9. What happens when water gets really cold?
10. What happens when you put water in a refrigerator/freezer?
11. Why do you think water freezes/turns into ice when it gets cold?
12. How do people get ice when they want it?
13. Can you freeze an object in ice? How? Why not?
14. How can you find the frozen object in the ice?

....

15. What happens when you put things on ice?
33. How can you tell the temperature of ice water?
34. Is it safe for you to eat ice? Why? Why not?
35. Why do people put ice in their drinks/ice chests/coolers?
36. What happens when you put ice in water/ a drink/an ice chest/a cooler?
37. Does the ice stay the same over time when it's in a drink/ice chest/cooler? Why? Why not?

38. How does a drink taste/feel that has ice in it?
39. What happens to a drink after the ice melts?

....

40. What does **melt** mean?
41. What do you think makes ice melt?
42. What happens when the ice melts?
43. How can you keep the ice from melting?
44. How can you make the ice melt slower/ faster?

....

45. What happens when you pour water on ice?
46. What would happen if you poured warm/cold water on ice?\
47. What would happen if you left the ice out for a long time?

....

48. What would happen if you chipped away at the ice?
49. What can you use to chip the ice? Why?
50. What would happen if you tried to stack ice cubes?
51. How can you change ice to a different color?
52. What happens when you drop paint on ice?
53. What if you wanted to use ice to make art/paint? How would you do it?

- Also see WEATHER

NOTES

> *"If you do not know how to ask the right question, you discover nothing."*
> - W. Edwards Deming

NOTES

BUBBLES

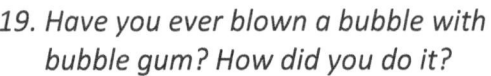

1. What is a bubble?
2. Describe a bubble.
3. What do you know about bubbles?
4. How did you find out about bubbles?
5. Where can you find bubbles? How do you know?

....

6. What do you notice about the bubble's shape?
7. What things are shaped like bubbles?
8. Why are bubbles in the shape of a sphere/round?
9. How are bubbles like balls?

....

10. Why are bubbles hollow/shiny?
11. Why do bubbles grow bigger?
12. How do bubbles grow larger?
13. Why do you think some bubbles have rainbows in them?

....

14. Tell me about a time when you've seen/played with bubbles.
15. Why are bubbles so fun?
16. How can/did you make bubbles?
17. How can you make more bubbles?
18. What else can you use to make bubbles? (besides soap and water)

19. Have you ever blown a bubble with bubble gum? How did you do it?
20. What happens when you blow?
21. What if you don't blow at all?
22. What if you blew into the water?
23. What can you do to make bubbles bigger/smaller?
24. What happens when you blow softer/harder?
25. What would happen if your solution had no soap in it?
26. What would happen if you added soap/more soap/too much soap to the water?

....

27. What tools can you use to make bubbles? (straw, whisk, syringe, wand, egg beater, bicycle pump, etc.)
28. How do you think that tool will help?

....

29. What's the difference between bubbles that float/drift in the air and bubbles that don't?
30. What happened to the bubbles when they floated/drifted away?
31. Why do you think bubbles float/drift in the air?

....

32. How do you catch/pop a bubble?
33. What happens when you catch/pop bubbles?
34. Why do you have to be gentle with bubbles?
35. How do your hands feel when/after they touch the bubbles?
36. Why do bubbles pop?

BUBBLES

37. *Where do bubbles go when they pop? Why?*
38. *What do you think makes bubbles pop?*
39. *What happens when bubbles pop?*
40. *Would you rather blow bubbles or pop them? Why?*
41. *Would you rather pop big bubbles or tiny ones? Why?*
42. *How do bubbles taste if you get them in your mouth?*
43. *What if bubbles never popped?*
....
44. *Why do you think some bubbles float/ rest on water?*
45. *How long do you think a bubble will float/rest there? How can you tell?*
46. *How can you make more bubbles?*
....
47. *How does a bubble wand work?*
48. *What if you wave the wand around?*
49. *What if you wave the wand faster/ slower/stronger/gentler?*
50. *What's the difference between these two bubble wands?*
51. *What do you think makes a good bubble wand?*
52. *Which bubble wand makes the most bubbles? Why?*
....
53. *Do you think you can measure the size of the bubbles you blow? Why? Why not?*
54. *Use your hands/body and show me the smallest/biggest bubble you have ever blown. How did you do it?*
....
55. *What is your favorite/least favorite thing about bubbles?*
56. *Do you get wet when you play with bubbles? Why? Why not?*
....

57. *Why do some drinks have bubbles (carbonated/fizzy)?*
58. *What's the difference between drinking water with bubbles and drinking water (carbonated/fizzy) without bubbles (flat)?*
59. *Tell me how a carbonated/fizzy drink feels/looks/tastes/sounds.*
60. *Do you like the taste of flat water or carbonated/fizzy water? Why? Why not?*
61. *What happens if you shake carbonated/ fizzy water right before opening the bottle/can? Why?*
62. *Do you think there is soap in fizzy water? Why? Why not?*
63. *Do you think it's safe to drink soapy water? Why? Why not?*
....
64. *What is bubble wrap?*
65. *Why do people use bubble wrap?*
66. *Describe how bubble wrap looks.*
67. *How do you think bubble wrap is made?*
68. *What happens when you step on/squeeze bubble wrap?*
69. *Can you blow bubble wrap back up? Why? Why not?*

FLOAT vs. SINK

1. What does float/sink mean?
2. How do you know if something is floating/sinking?
3. Why do you think an object floats/sinks?
4. Where do objects go when they float/ sink? Why?
5. Tell me about a time you've seen something float/sink.
6. How do objects that float help/hurt our people?

. . . .

7. Do you think something sinking can float? Why? Why not?
8. Do you think something floating can sink? Why? Why not?

. . . .

9. How can you find out if something will float/sink?
10. Why do you think it's best to set objects gently in the water/liquid?

. . . .

11. What do you think will happen if you put this in the water/liquid?
12. Do you think this will float on top of the water or sink to the bottom? Why?
13. Which objects do you think will float/sink in the water/liquid? Why?
14. What happened when you put the object in water/liquid?

. . . .

15. What do you notice about the objects that float/sink?
16. Why do you think some objects float/sink in water and some do not?
17. How are these objects the same/ different?
18. What do the sinking/floating objects have in common?
19. What's the difference between the object that sank and the one that floated?
20. Look at the water line. What do you notice?

. . . .

21. Does it matter how much water/liquid there is? Why? Why not?
22. Do you think size/weight/appearance makes a difference? Why? Why not?
23. What will happen if you put lighter/heavy things in the water?
24. What if you add more/take away objects?
25. Do you think the way an object is made/ shaped makes a difference? Why? Why not?

. . . .

26. What will happen if you take the object out of the water/liquid?
27. What will happen if you leave the object in the water overnight?
28. What do you think will happen if you try it again?

. . . .

29. Why do you think these objects float in the water but not in the air?

FLOAT vs. SINK

30. Why do you think heavy objects don't keep sinking right through the bottom of the bin to the floor?
31. How can you help sinking objects float? Floating objects sink?
32. What can you do to keep objects from floating/sinking?
33. What is the difference between the water in the bin and the water in the ocean/lake/river/bath/pool?

....

34. How do floating/sunken objects move on/in the water?
35. How can you move faster/slower in the water?
36. What would happen if you put things in the cup/bowl/boat?
37. What would happen if you put more things in the boat?
38. Why do you have to be careful when putting things in the cup/bowl/boat?
39. Why do you think the cup/bowl/boat sits lower in the water than before?
40. How can you help the cup/bowl/boat sit lower/higher in the water?

....

41. What would happen if you combined water with dirt/sand/oil/etc.?
42. Why do you think that happened?
43. What will you try next?

44. What might you try instead?
45. Is there anything else you can test? Why?

....

46. What do you notice about your toys when you take a bath?
47. Do fish float/sink in the water? Why? Why not?
48. What kinds of animals float/sink in water? Why?
49. Do people float/sink in water? Why? Why not?
50. What types of objects help people float or sink? How do they work?

....

51. What kinds of objects float/sink in the air? Why?
52. Why do you think bubbles/balloons/etc. float/sink in the air?
53. How is floating/sinking in air different from objects floating/sinking in water?

....

54. How can you find out how long something floats in the air?
55. What can you do to help the object keep from floating/sinking?
56. Why do some balloons float in the air and others don't?+
57. Does it matter how small/big the object is? Why? Why not?
58. What happens when floating balloons lose air/get a hole?

SPONGES

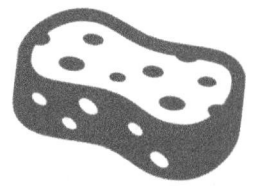

1. What is a sponge?
2. Describe the sponge.
3. How does a sponge feel/smell/look?
4. Why do you think a sponge has holes/is pliable/flexible?

············

5. Why do people use sponges?
6. What can you do with a sponge? How do you know?
7. How does a sponge help you clean?

············

8. How do you think sponges are made? Why?
9. Why do you think sponges come in different shapes/sizes/styles?
10. How is this sponge the same as/different from that sponge?
11. What can you do with a large sponge that you can't do with a small sponge?
12. Why do you think some sponges are hard on one side and soft on the other?

············

13. What do you have to do to wet a sponge?
14. What happens when you drip water on a sponge?
15. What happened to the water?
16. What happens when you dip a sponge in water?
17. What do you notice about a sponge when it's dry/wet?
18. How does a sponge feel when it is dry vs. when it's wet?

············

19. Why is the sponge dripping?
20. How can you keep the water from dripping?
21. How can you find out how much water a sponge will hold?
22. How do you get the water out of a sponge?
23. Does one sponge weigh more than the other? Why? Why not?
24. How can you find out if a dry sponge weighs more than a wet sponge?

············

25. How do you squeeze a sponge?
26. What happens when you squeeze/press on/pound on a dry/wet sponge?
27. Where do you think you should squeeze a wet sponge? Why?
28. How can you get water into the bowl using a sponge?

············

29. What other substances can a sponge **absorb**? Why?
30. What would happen if you added soap?
31. Why do you think there's a sponge by the art table?
32. What can you do with the sponge/water when you are finished playing?

············

33. What happens if you put a dry/wet sponge in the refrigerator/**freezer**?
34. Why do you think the sponge feels that way?
35. How is a frozen sponge different than one that isn't?
36. How does the sponge change/feel when it is frozen/cold?

OUTSIDE · OUTDOORS

1. What does it mean to go outside/ outdoors?
2. Describe what you see/hear/smell/feel.
3. What's the difference between outside and inside?
4. How do you know you are outside?
5. Why do you think we go/are outside?
6. What do you notice out here?
7. What can you do outside that you can't do inside?
8. What's your favorite/least favorite thing to do outside? Why?
9. What do you think of when you're outside? Why?

· · · · · · · · · · ·

10. What do you plan to do outside?
11. What games are better for playing outside?
12. What if you wanted to make up a game to play outside. How would you do it?
13. What toys/materials would you use? How? Why?
14. What can you do with things you find outside? How would you do that?
15. How can you keep the outside clean?

· · · · · · · · · · ·

16. Tell me about what you found outside.
17. How can you take a closer look?
18. How about if you used binoculars/a magnifying glass/a glass jar?
19. What if you moved/turned/lifted it?
20. How did you find that/those?

21. What can you do with that/those? How would you do it?
22. How can you examine it?

· · · · · · · · · · ·

23. Tell me about your outside voice.
24. How does an outside voice differ from an inside voice?
25. Why can you use your outside voice here?

· · · · · · · · · · ·

26. How is being outside today different from yesterday?
27. What do you see/hear/smell/feel that you didn't see yesterday?
28. How do you think this will look tomorrow?
29. Why didn't you see this before/last time/in the summer/etc.?

· · · · · · · · · · ·

30. What do you think is making that sound? Why?
31. How do you think that sound is made?
32. What can you do to copy the sound you hear?
33. Where have you heard that sound before? What was happening?

· · · · · · · · · · ·

34. How does the air feel?
35. How does the sky look?
36. How does the ground feel beneath your feet?
37. Why is the sky blue/grey/dark/light/ different colors?
38. What do you think makes the sky blue/ grey/dark/light/different colors?

OUTSIDE · OUTDOORS

39. Why is the sky blue/grass green/snow white/dirt brown or red/etc.

40. What do you think makes the air smell like that?

41. How does the ground feel/smell/look when it is dry/wet/snowing?

42. What do you notice about the ground/ soil/dirt/grass/weeds/plants/water/ rocks/flowers/trees/water/snow?

43. How are the plants different/the same?

44. Why is there water/dirt/a sky/clouds/ land/a sun/concrete/grass/concrete outside but not inside?

45. What's the difference between concrete and grass/dirt?

46. Why are so many things growing out of the ground?

47. Why don't plants grow from the sky?

48. Why are there flowers/clouds/weeds/ trees/birds/insects/buildings/roads/ cables/signs/train tracks?

49. What would happen if we didn't have those things?

50. What's the difference between flowers and weeds?

51. How can you tell one thing from another out here?

52. Who do you think put those signs/tracks/ roads there? Why?

53. How do the signs help us?

54. What do you notice about the structure/ building/bridge/tower/cave?

55. How are these structures similar/ different?

56. How do you think these were built/ constructed?

57. What do you wonder about that structure?

58. How do you think that structure stays up?

59. Do you think structures like that can grow like trees? Why? Why not?

60. How can you plan/design/construct something using things you found outside?

61. Tell me about what you made.

62. Show me how you made it.

63. What made you think of that?

64. How will your structure be used?

65. How did you balance the pieces/ materials?

66. Why do you think it fell down?

67. What else could you try?

68. Can you think of another way to make the pieces/materials stay together?

69. What can you do to keep your structure dry inside?

70. What's the difference between the city and the country?

71. What does the country have that the city doesn't?

OCEANS

1. What do you know about oceans?
2. How do you find an ocean?
3. What can you find in an ocean?
4. Describe an ocean you have seen.
5. Why are oceans important to us/our world?
6. Where does the water come from in an ocean? How do you know?
7. Why do you think there are oceans on our planet?

. . . .

9. What do you notice about the color of ocean water?
10. Why is ocean water different colors?
11. Why do you think the sky reflects off of the ocean?

. . . .

12. Why do you find sand/seashells by the ocean?
13. How does sand get on the beach/in the ocean?

. . . .

14. How is ocean water different from water everywhere else?
15. What's the difference between an ocean and a puddle/river/lake/stream/pond/aqueduct?

. . . .

16. How do you think ocean water tastes/smells/looks/feels/sounds?
17. Why do you think ocean water tastes/smells/feels/sounds that way?
18. Why do you think ocean water is salty?

. . . .

19. Is the water in the ocean clean or dirty? What makes you say that?
20. Why is there trash/glass/oil/etc. on the beach/in the ocean?
21. What would happen if the ocean was full of trash/glass/oil/etc. ?
22. Why is it important to keep our oceans clean?
23. How can we keep our oceans clean?

. . . .

24. Should people drink ocean water? Why? Why not?
25. What do you think would happen if you drank ocean water?

. . . .

26. How does water move in an ocean?
27. What do you think makes water move in the ocean?
28. How can you find out more about how water moves in an ocean?

. . . .

29. How does wind affect the water?
30. What is a wave/ripple/tide/swell/current/undertow?
31. What makes waves/ripple/tides/swells/currents/undertows in the ocean?
32. Why are waves/tides high sometimes and low other times?
33. Why do you think waves/tides are always different/changing?
34. Why are some waves/ripples/tides/swells/currents big and others small?
35. Why are currents/undertows stronger than others?

. . . .

36. Can people breathe water? Why? How? Why not?
37. How do people dress for swimming in the ocean?

OCEANS

38. What kinds of things do people do in the ocean?
39. How do people travel on/across the ocean?
40. How do people dive/explore deep in the ocean?
41. Why do you think people dive/explore deep in the ocean?
42. Can we all live in the ocean? Why? How? Why not?

....

43. When is an ocean safe/dangerous? How do you know?
44. How can people stay safe in and around an ocean?
45. Why shouldn't you swim in an ocean when it is rough/there is a storm?

....

46. Does the ocean have a place where it begins/ends? How do you know?
47. Why can't you see where the ocean begins and ends?
48. What happens when the ocean meets land?
49. What if there was no land?
40. Would you rather swim in the ocean or use a boat? Why?

....

41. How can we tell how deep the ocean is?
42. Why do you think we can see to the bottom of the ocean in some places but not others?

43. Can you fit all of the ocean water in a bucket/pond/lake/swimming pool? Why? Why not?

....

44. Why does some ocean water turn to ice?
45. Why doesn't the entire ocean freeze?
46. How do plants grow under so much water?
47. How do plants that are deep in the ocean grow without sunlight?

....

48. What is coral/a **coral reef**?
49. Describe how a coral reef looks.
50. Why do you think there are so many different kinds of coral?
51. What types of sea creatures live near coral reefs?
52. How does the coral reef protect the sea creatures?
53. Why do you think fish like to live near coral reefs?
54. How do you think coral reefs get damaged?
55. What if there were no more coral reefs in the world?

....

56. Tell me about animals that live in the ocean.
57. How do you think they breathe underwater?
58. How do they move in the water?
59. Why don't they live on land?

FISH

1. What is a fish?
2. How do you know that's a fish?
3. Describe a/the fish.
4. Why do fish have fins/gills/scales/tails?
5. How are their fins/gills/scales/tails used?
6. Why don't fish wear clothes?

·············

7. Have you ever seen a real fish? Tell me about how the fish looked/sounded/ smelled/felt.
8. What were you doing when you saw the fish?
9. Did the fish see you? How do you know?
10. What did the fish do when they saw you? Why do you think they did that?
11. Why won't fish let you pet them?

·············

12. Why do fish live in water?
13. What would happen if you took a fish out of the water?
14. What do you think fish do all day?
15. What do you think fish think about all day?
16. Do you think fish keep their families together? Why? How? Why not?
17. What do you think fish learn from their parents?

·············

18. What do you think it's like to be a fish?
19. How do fish breathe underwater?
20. How do fish find food?
21. How do fish learn to swim?
22. How do fish swim/move in water?
23. Why can't fish walk/move the way people can?
24. Do you think fish ever get tired? Why? Why not?
25. How do you think fish sleep?
26. What do fish do when they have to go potty?

·············

27. How do fish communicate/talk to each other?
28. How do you think fish find/become friends?
29. How do fish make sounds?
30. Why do you think fish make sounds?
31. What do you think a fish would say if it could talk to us?

·············

32. Do you think fish have feelings? Why? Why not?
33. Do you think fish are happy/sad/mad/ scared/curious/mean/nice? Why? Why not?
34. Why do some fish have to hide/protect themselves?
35. How do fish protect themselves from people/predators?

·············

FISH

36. How do you feel about fish/fishing?
37. Have you ever gone fishing? How was that experience?
38. How do you catch a fish?
39. Why do people go fishing?
40. What supplies/tools do you need to catch a fish?
41. How do you use the supplies/tools?
42. What do you know about fishing poles/ fishing line/nets/hooks/bait?
43. Why do people use bait to catch fish?
44. What kind of bait will attract a fish? Why?
45. What do you do with the bait?
46. What happens if the fish don't like your bait?
47. Does every fish like the same bait? Why? Why not? How do you know?
48. What do you like most/least about fish/ fishing?
49. What is it like to catch a fish?
50. Is it easy or hard to catch a fish? Why?
51. What steps did you have to take to catch a fish?
52. How do you know where to find fish?
53. I've heard that you should be quiet/ patient when you're fishing. Why do you think that is?

54. What do you think fish feel like when you touch them?
55. Why do some people catch fish and then release them back into the water?
....
56. How are fish the same/different?
57. Why are some fish wide/thin/long/ short/small/big/thick/flat?
58. Why are some fish shiny/dark/light/ bright/spotted/striped/rough/smooth/ etc.?
59. What do you notice about their stripes/ spots/markings?
60. Why do you think fish are that color/ different colors?
61. What designs/patterns do you see on fish?
62. Why are there so many different kinds/ sizes of fish?
63. How can you tell how big a fish/whale/ shark is?
....
64. What is a school of fish?
65. Why do you think a group of fish is called a school?
66. Why do some fish swim together in schools and others don't?
....
67. Do fish swim the way people do? How do they swim the same/differently?
68. Do you think fish get cold in the ocean the way people do? Why? Why not?
....

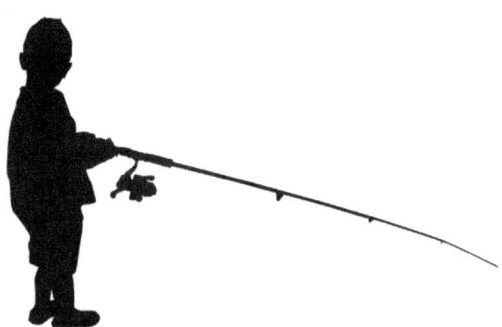

FISH

69. *Why are fish so important to the world?*
70. *What do you think would happen if ocean water froze/was too hot?*
71. *What would happen if our oceans/rivers/ lakes were too dirty for the fish to live?*
72. *Why/How does trash in the ocean/rivers/ lakes hurt fish and other sea creatures?*
73. *How can we keep our oceans/rivers/lakes clean?*

. . . .

74. *What if we lived in the ocean, and fish lived on land?*
75. *What if there weren't any fish anywhere?*

. . . .

76. *Do fish make good pets? Why? Why not?*
77. *Why can't you hold a fish like you can a hamster/dog/cat?*
78. *How would you take care of a fish?*

. . . .

79. *What is an* **aquarium***?*
80. *Why do people use aquariums?*
81. *What do you know about aquariums?*
82. *Why do people keep fish in aquariums?*
83. *How do you think fish feel when they are put in aquariums?*
84. *What about the fish's family? What must they be thinking?*
85. *What do you think would happen if you tried to teach fish tricks?*

86. *What if your pet fish grew too big for the bowl/aquarium?*
87. *How do you think fish feel when we put them in bowls and aquariums?*
88. *What if fish lived in houses/trees instead of the ocean/lakes/rivers/bowls/ aquariums?*
89. *What other animals live in water?*

. . . .

90. *How do you know how much food to feed the fish in an aquarium?*
91. *How can you make sure all of the fish get some food?*
92. *What will happen if you forget to feed the fish?*

NOTES

"*It's not the answer that enlightens, but the question.*"
- Eugene Jonesco

NOTES

SEASHELLS

1. What is a seashell?
2. How do you know it is a seashell?
3. How would you describe a seashell?
4. What do you notice about this seashell?

....

5. How do you think seashells are made?
6. How do seashells end up on the beach/in stores?
7. How do you think this seashell got here?
8. What do you think happened to the other half of the shell?

....

9. How do seashells move around in the water/on the beach?
10. How does water move seashells?
11. Tell me about the seashells you've seen/found/purchased.

....

12. Why do some animals live in seashells?
13. What do you think once lived in this seashell? Why?
16. How do you think animals get into the shells?
17. Why do you think this seashell is empty now?
18. Why do you think there are so many empty seashells?

19. What would happen if there were no seashells in the sea?
20. How do you think oysters/clams/snails/mollusks make their shells?
21. Why do you think mollusks/hermit crabs/young fish leave their shells?
22. What happens after mollusks/hermit crabs/young fish leave their shells?

....

23. How is this seashell different from/the same as that one?
24. Why do seashells come in many different shapes/sizes/colors?
25. Why do you think some shells are whole and others are broken?
26. Why are some seashells shiny/smooth/rough/bumpy/thin/wide/long/short/etc.?
27. Why do you think this seashell is shaped/looks like this?
28. Do you see a pattern on the seashell? Describe it to me.

....

29. Why do some seashells sound like the ocean when you hold them up to your ear?
30. How do you think this seashell would feel if you touched/held it?

....

31. Why do you think people like to collect seashells?
32. Do you think people should take seashells from the beach? Why? Why not?

SAND

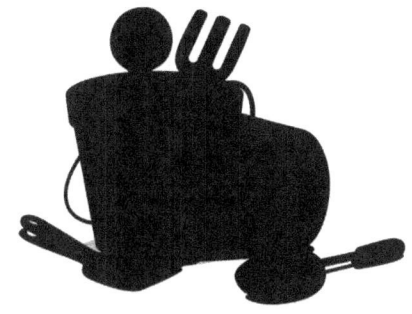

1. What is sand?
2. What do you know about sand?
3. What do you notice when you examine the sand?
4. How can you discover what sand looks like up close?
5. What do you notice when you use tools to examine the sand?
6. How would you describe sand to someone who has never seen it?
7. Where else can you find sand? How do you know?
8. How do you think sand is made?
9. How did the sand get here?
10. Have you seen sand somewhere else? Tell me about it.

....

11. How does wet/dry sand feel/smell/look/sound?
12. How does the sand feel when you sit/pat/stand/walk/stomp on it?
13. What happens when you pick up sand with your hands?
14. How can you keep sand from falling through your fingers?

....

15. Why do you think sand stays in the sandbox?
16. What if there wasn't a sandbox to hold the sand?
17. How can you keep the sand from falling out of the sandbox?

....

18. How is this sand different from that sand?
19. What's the difference between sand and pebbles/rocks?

....

20. What can you do with sand?
21. What do you notice when you dig/pour/sprinkle/sift/scoop/press/squeeze the sand?
22. What happens when you sift/press/hold/carry/squeeze/dump sand?
23. How can you make the sand flat/level/bumpy/wavy/into something?

....

24. How will you get the sand in the bucket/strainer/scooper/shovel/container/dump truck?
25. How do you know how much sand to put in the bucket/strainer/scooper/shovel/container/dump truck?
26. How many cups/scoops of sand do you think it will take to fill the bucket? How can you find out if you are right?

SAND

27. What would happen if you put too much sand in the bucket/strainer/scooper/ shovel/container/dump truck?
28. How can you get the sand from this container into the other container?
29. What will happen if you pour the sand into a different container?
30. What if you didn't have a shovel/ scooper/bucket/container?
31. What's the difference between filling the shovel & filling the pail?
32. Which shovel/container/scooper/cup/ bucket holds the most/least amount of sand? How do you can you find out?

....

33. What would happen if you tried to count all the grains of sand?
34. How can you tell how much sand you have?

....

35. What will happen if you pour sand through the strainer/funnel?
36. Why do you think sand falls through the strainer/funnel?

37. Why do you think people use strainers/ funnels?
38. Why do you think some things are still left in/don't fall through the strainer?

....

39. What happens when you pour **water** into the sand?
40. Where do you think the water went? Why?
41. What happens to sand when you pour/ put it in water?
42. How does the sand feel when it's wet?
43. What is the difference between wet sand and dry sand?
44. What if you add a little/a lot more water to the sand?

....

45. Tell me about what you made.
46. How did you make that out of sand?
47. How did you get that idea?
48. Describe what you used to make it.
49. What did you do before/first/second/ next/last?
50. What else can you do with sand? Tell me about it.
51. How can you make a road/tunnel/tower/ city/castle/house/river/bridge/etc. out of sand?

....

52. What happened to the shape you made out of sand?
53. Why do you think your sand structure held/didn't hold its shape?

SAND

54. *Why do you think your structure fell apart?*
55. *Do you think your structure will last until tomorrow/next week? Why? Why not?*
56. *How can you fix/rebuild what you made and make it stronger?*
57. *How can you make your structure bigger/ smaller/wider/thinner/longer/shorter/ taller?*

....

58. *What happened to your toys/things? Why can't you see them?*
59. *What can you do to find the toys you can't see?*
60. *What do you think you'll find if you keep digging in the sand?*
61. *How far down do you think you will have to dig? Why?*
62. *What do you notice when you scoop the sand out? Why?*
63. *What toys should be kept out of the sand? Why?*

....

64. *What can you do to get the sand from here to there?*
65. *How can you move/lift/carry sand without spilling it?*
66. *How can you get the sand that is stuck on the ramp?*

....

67. *What makes the sand warm/cold?*
68. *Why do you think the sand is warm here and cold there?*

....

69. *How can you draw letters/numbers/ shapes in the sand?*
70. *What happens if you drag your fingers/ other things through the sand?*
71. *How can you make tracks in the sand?*
72. *How can you make a pattern in the sand?*
73. *How can you use sand to make art?*
74. *What would happen if you added color to sand?*
75. *How would you add color to the sand?*

....

76. *How do you think you can keep sand clean?*
77. *Why should you wash your hands/feet after playing in the sand?*

....

78. *How can a friend help?*
79. *What do you think you should do when you both want to use the same bucket?*
80. *Why do you think you should not throw sand?*
81. *What happens when you get sand in your eyes/mouth?*

....

82. *Tell me about animals that live in/near sand.*

ROCKS

The following unique pages differ from the standard format of the book. There are 22 rock activities, and each activity is matched with open-ended questions in more detail.

Gather rocks and invent new and unique ways to transport them.

1. Where can you find rocks? Why?
2. Why are you looking for rocks outside instead of inside?
3. What do you have there?
4. Why do you think the rocks are here?
5. How do you think the rocks got here?
6. Why do you think the big rocks are hard to lift/carry?
7. What is the easiest way to carry/move your rocks?
8. How can you move the most rocks at one time?
9. How did you think of that?

Examine rocks. Add a magnifying glass.

10. How do you know that's a rock?
11. What do you know about rocks?
12. What else do you notice about your rocks?
13. Why do you think your rocks look like that?
14. What are those specs/lines/shiny things in the rock?
15. What other things can you think of that look shiny?
16. Why do you think the rocks are jagged/smooth?
17. How do the rocks feel in your hands?
18. What happens when you squeeze a rock?
19. Which rock is your favorite/least favorite? Why?

20. Why do you think rocks are hard?
21. Why do you think rocks have cracks/chips/things stuck to them?
22. Can you tell if the rock is old or new? How?
23. What is a fossil?
24. Why do you think there is a fossil in the rock?
25. How do you think the fossil got there?

Compare rocks to each other and to other things.

26. Why does this rock look like that rock?
27. How do your rocks differ from each other? How are they the same?
28. Why do you think the rocks look different/the same?
29. Why do some rocks feel rough and others smooth?
30. Why are some rocks small and others large?
31. Why are some rocks warm and others cold?

ROCKS

Sort and classify rocks by their characteristics: shape, composition, color, length, width, condition, etc.

32. *Why did you put those rocks together?*
33. *How do you know those rocks go together?*
34. *How else can you match/sort the rocks?*
35. *How can you put the rocks in order by size/shape/color/their feature?*
36. *How do you know which one goes first/ next/last?*
37. *How can you store them after they are sorted?*

Scratch rocks using different objects to test their hardness.

38. *Why do you think rocks feel like that?*
39. *How do you know what hard/soft means?*
40. *What happens when you rub two rocks together?*
41. *Why do you think one object scratches your rock and another doesn't?*
42. *What else do you think you can use to scratch a rock?*
43. *What do you hear when you scratch the rocks together?*
44. *Why do some rocks break apart easily, and others don't?*
45. *What do you have to do to break the rock apart?*
46. *What tools can you use to break a rock? Why?*
47. *What do you think you would find if you broke a rock open?*

Use rocks to scratch different surfaces: concrete, other rocks, wood, etc.

48. *Why do you think the rock left a mark?*
49. *Why do you think one rock scratches more than the other?*
50. *How can you draw something using your rock?*

Toss rocks into a puddle/pond/bucket of water and see the effects they cause.

51. *What happened to the rock?*
52. *What happens when your rocks hit the water?*
53. *How can you make the splash smaller/ bigger?*
54. *Why do you think your rocks sank to the bottom/floated on top (pumice)?*
55. *Why does the water rise after you drop in the rock?*
56. *What do you think will happen after you take your rocks out of the water?*
57. *Why do you think you see bubbles when some rocks submerge in the water?*
58. *Why do you think you can still see the rock in the water? Or not?*
59. *Why is your rock sticking out of the water? Covered by water?*
60. *How can you make the water cover your rock?*
61. *How can you keep from getting wet?*

ROCKS

Wash, polish, or paint rocks.

62. Why are your rocks dirty?
63. What can you use to clean/polish/paint your rocks?
64. What happens when you spray water on your rock?
65. What came off of your rocks when you cleaned them?
66. Why do your rocks look different when they are wet versus dry?
67. Why are some rocks shiny when they are wet and others dull?
68. Why do you think you should clean your rocks before you paint them?
69. Is it best to paint rocks when they are wet or dry? Why?
70. What made you choose those colors to paint?
71. Tell me about your design.

Use rocks to recognize and extend patterns.

72. What **patterns** do you see on the rocks?
73. What can you use to copy/extend the pattern?
74. How can you use your rocks to make a pattern?
75. What do you think comes next?
76. How can you change your pattern, so it looks different?

Line up rocks and count them.

77. How can you organize your rocks to make them easier to count?
78. How do you know how many rocks there are?

79. How do you know which group of rocks has more/less?
80. What if you added more/took away rocks?
81. What if you only counted the ones that look alike/different?
82. How can you make sure you don't miss a rock?
83. If you mix up/move the rocks around, do you think your count would change? Why? Why not?
84. How can you find out if your count is different or the same as before?

See if any of your rocks will slide, roll, bounce, or skip.

85. What would happen if you dropped the rock?
86. Why do you think some rocks do or don't slide/roll/bounce/skip?
87. How can you make your rocks roll/slide/bounce/skip?
88. What happens after your rock rolls/slides/bounces/skips?
89. Why do you think your rocks don't slide/roll up?
90. How can you make your rock skip across the water?
91. What happens when your rock stops skipping across the water?

ROCKS

92. Why do you think your rock doesn't come back to you on its own?
93. Which rock slides/rolls/skips/sinks the fastest/slowest/easiest? How do you know?
94. Why do you think this rock is the fastest/slowest?

Make rubbings using the texture of various rocks.

95. Why do you think your paper looks like that?
96. What happens if you press harder/softer?
97. Why do you think that rubbing looks different/the same?
98. What if you rub with something else?

Weigh rocks on a balance scale.

99. What is a **balance scale/scale**?
100. How does a balance scale/scale work?
101. How can you find out how much something weighs?
102. How can you tell if something is heavy or light?
103. Why are some rocks heavy and others light?
104. How do you know how many rocks to put on each side of the scale?
105. What else can you put on the other side of the scale?
106. How can you make each side of the scale level/even?
107. What can you do to make one side of the scale go down lower/come up higher?

108. What does it mean when one side of the scale drops lower/rises higher than the other?

Stack and balance rocks to make a cairn.

109. What is a **cairn**?
110. What does **balance** mean?
111. Which rocks stack the best? Why?
112. How do you know which rocks to put on the bottom/top?
113. What do you have to do to keep the rocks from falling?
114. How high do you think you can stack your cairn?
115. What other things can you stack and balance?
116. How can you balance your body on one foot?
117. How can you keep from falling over?

Cover/Wrap a rock with clay, foil, plastic, paper, fabric, tape, sand, or other material.

118. What do you have to do to get the material around the rock?
119. Which material covers rocks the best? Why?
120. What else can you use to cover a rock?
121. Why do you think that material worked/didn't work?

ROCKS

Paint or draw a design/number/letter/line on the rocks. You can also print a design and tape it on with clear tape.

122. *What can you do/make with these beautiful rocks? How?*
123. *How can you match the painted rocks? (upper and lower case letters, colors, pips/dots, numerals, lines, etc.)*
124. *How can you make a map using rocks?*

Mold rocks out of clay or press rocks into clay.

125. *How did you know what size rock to make?*
126. *How did you know what shape to make your rock?*
127. *Why do you think the clay looks like that?*
128. *What happened?*
129. *Why do you think some clay stuck to your rock?*
130. *How will you get the clay off of your rock?*

Use rocks to design and construct habitats for animals/insects/toys or structures like a cave, arroyo, bridge, tunnel, or different lines and pathways.

131. *Describe what you made.*
132. *How do you know how high/wide to make the wall/bridge?*
133. *How do you know this animal/insect/toy will fit in your structure?*
134. *What other material can help you build your rock structure? Why?*

135. *What things can you think of that are made of stone? Describe it/them.*
136. *How can you redirect water using rocks?*
137. *How does the water move around the rocks?*

Use rocks to trace a drawing or build something in our world: animal, insect, shape, letter, number, face, body, house, car, etc. Find natural shapes in stone.

138. *How did you figure out what you wanted to make?*
139. *Tell me about what you made.*
140. *Tell me about how you made it.*
141. *How did you trace/draw around the rock?*
142. *How did you get the rocks to fit/stay together?*
143. *What would happen if you took some rocks out/added more rocks?*
144. *What would you have to do to make your structure bigger/smaller/longer/shorter/wider/sturdier?*
145. *What materials can you add to your structure? Why? How?*

ROCKS

Look under rocks.

146. *What do you think you'll find under the rock? Why?*
147. *Tell me about what you found.*
148. *Why do you think that is/those are under the rock?*
149. *What kinds of insects live under rocks? How do you know?*
150. *Why do you think insects like to live under rocks?*
151. *Why don't you find things like that when you move rocks around in the basket?*

Make a rock

152. *If you wanted to make a rock, how would you do it?*
153. *What supplies do you think you need to make a rock?*
154. *Do you think the rock you make will look like the ones you found? Why? Why not?*
155. *Do you think the rock you make will be as hard as the ones you found? Why? Why not?*

Rock climbing

156. *What is rock **climbing**?*
157. *Why do people climb rocks?*
158. *Have you ever climbed a rock? Tell me about it.*
159. *Are these real rocks or pretend rocks? How do you know?*
160. *What do you do with your hands and feet when you climb rocks?*
161. *How do you know where to put your hands and feet?*
162. *Have you ever seen someone climb a rock? Tell me about what you saw.*
163. *What kinds of rocks are easy/hard to climb? Why?*
164. *What kind of equipment do people need to climb rocks?*
165. *Do you have to practice climbing rocks before you climb?*
166. *How high do you think people can go when they climb rocks?*
167. *Do you think rock climbing is a safe sport? Why? Why not?*

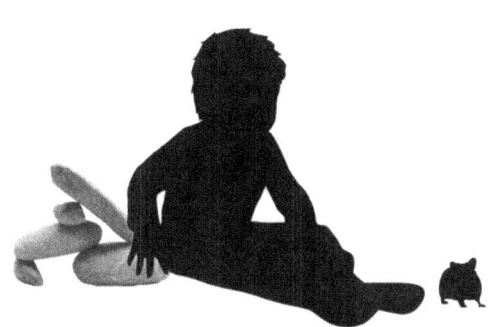

NOTES

> *"Ninety percent of asking questions is about listening to answers."*
> **- Lee Child**

NOTES

TREES

1. What is a tree?
2. What do you know about trees?
3. How do you know that's a tree?
4. Describe what you see/hear/smell/feel when you examine a tree.
5. What do you notice about the tree?
6. Why do you think trees look the way they do?
7. Tell me what you know about the different parts of a tree. (trunk, branch, leaf, pinecone, acorn, flower, twig, root)
8. How would you describe the parts of a tree?
9. How do the different parts help the tree?
....
10. Why do people need trees?
11. What are some things you can do with trees?
12. How do people use trees to have fun?
....
13. How do trees grow?
14. What makes a tree grow?
15. What is the **lifecycle** of a tree?
16. How do trees get water/nutrients?
17. What if trees have no water/dirt/sun/care?
18. How can people help trees grow?
19. How can you tell how much a tree has grown?
20. What do the rings on a piece of wood mean?

21. How can you tell how old a tree is by examining its growth rings?
22. How would it look if you drew circles within circles/concentric circles?
23. What if you made the lines thicker/thinner?
24. Why do some trees grow bigger/smaller/wider/thinner/thicker/heavier/lighter/darker/longer/shorter than others?
....
25. Why do trees grow to be different sizes/shapes/colors/textures?
26. What do you notice about the sizes/shapes/colors/textures of the trees?
27. Why do trees grow at different rates?
28. What do you notice about how the branches grow?
29. How does this tree differ from that tree?
30. How can you tell which part of the tree is bigger/smaller/wider/thinner/thicker/heavier/lighter/darker/longer/shorter?
31. How does the bottom of the tree differ from the top?
32. What do you notice about where the branches grow on the tree?
33. How are these trees the same/different from trees/shrubs/grass/plants/bushes?
34. Do you think big/tall trees are stronger than small ones? Why? Why not?
35. What happens when the wind blows a tree?
....
36. Can trees grow as big inside as they do outside? Why? Why not?
37. How would you plant a tree inside vs. outside?

TREES

38. How do you care for a tree inside vs. outside?
39. What's the difference between a tree planted in a pot and a tree planted in the ground?
40. Is it easy to pick up and move a tree? Why? Why not?

············

41. What do you think is on the inside of a branch/trunk/acorn/seed/nut/pinecone? How can you find out?
42. How can you find out what is inside the branch/trunk/acorn/seed/nut/pinecone?
43. What do you think is under the bark? Why?
44. How can you find out what is under the bark?
45. Why do trees have roots/branches/ leaves/bark/flowers/pinecones/acorns/ needles/seeds/nuts/sap/rings in the trunk?

············

46. What are tree **roots**?
47. How do roots grow?
48. How do roots help trees?
49. How do roots help hold trees in the ground?
50. How do roots absorb water and nutrients from the ground?

51. What does the ground feel like around the bottom of the tree? Why?
52. Why do some tree roots stick out of the ground and others don't?

············

53. What happens to trees when it rains/ snows/storms?
54. What animals or insects climb/live in trees? Why?
55. What animals or insects live in trees? Why?
56. How do trees help people/animals/ insects?
57. What would happen to animals/insects if someone cut down the trees?
58. Why do children like to climb trees?
59. How do children get down from trees?
60. What would see if you climbed to the top of the tree?
61. Can people live in trees? Why? Why not?

············

62. What is **sap/bark**?
63. Describe how sap/bark looks, feels, and smells.
64. What do you notice about sap/bark?
65. Why do you think trees have sap/bark?
66. What other things can you think of that are sticky?

············

67. What is **moss**?
68. How would you describe moss?
69. Why is there moss on the side of the tree?
70. What do you notice about the way moss grows?

TREES

71. Why don't you see stems, leaves, or roots on moss?
72. How does moss help prevent erosion?
73. How do animals use moss?
74. How can moss be used as a bandage?

· · · · · · · · · · ·

75. Why do some trees grow fruit and others don't?
76. What happens to the fruit if no one picks it?
77. How do people pick/reach the fruit at the very top of the tree?

· · · · · · · · · · ·

78. Why don't people grow like trees?
79. Why do you think trees can't move the way people do? (walk, run, jump)
80. What if you wanted to move like a tree? How would you do it?

· · · · · · · · · · ·

81. What types of things do people make out of trees? How do you know?
82. How do people make things out of trees?
83. What is **wood**?
84. How do you know that is wood?
85. How is wood used?
86. Why do people sand wood?
87. How do people make materials/tools/ objects/toys/paper out of wood?

· · · · · · · · · · ·

88. How do trees die?
89. Why do you think trees die?
90. Do you think trees are starting to die when their leaves fall? Why? Why not?
91. What happens to trees when they die?
92. Do you think people should cut down trees to make things? Why? Why not?
93. What would the world be like if there were no trees?
94. Why should people plant trees?
95. Where is the best place to plant a tree? Why?
96. Describe the trees where you live.
97. Why do you think this tree grew here?
98. How do you think this tree got here?
99. How did these little trees get here?

· · · · · · · · · · ·

100. Do you think trees have feelings? Why? Why not?
101. Do you think trees listen when people talk to them? Why? Why Not?
102. Do you think trees understand what people say to them? Why? Why not?

· · · · · · · · · · ·

103. What do you think "chip off the old block" means?
104. What is a forest?
105. What do you think the phrase "you can't see the forest for the trees" means?

LEAVES

1. What are leaves?
2. How do you know that's a leaf?
3. How would you describe a/the leaf?
4. How do leaves feel/smell?
5. How do leaves grow?
6. Why do you think leaves grow on trees?

....

7. Where do you usually see leaves? Why do they grow there?
8. What do you notice about leaves?
9. What do you notice about all of the leaves on this tree?
10. What do you think you would see if you looked at a leaf up close?
11. How are these leaves the same/different?
12. How does this leaf compare to that leaf?
13. What do you think you can tell about a tree by looking at its leaves?
14. Why do you think trees have different kinds of leaves?
15. Do you think a tree can grow from a leaf? Why? Why not?

....

16. How can you **sort/**match leaves by how they look?
17. Why do you think some leaves have lines/veins/bumps?

18. How do you know if one leaf is longer/wider/thinner/thicker than the other?
19. Why do you think leaves come in different shapes/sizes/colors?
20. Why do leaves change colors?
21. How do you know which part of the leaf is the top/bottom?
22. What is the difference between the top and the bottom of a leaf?
23. How do the edges of a leaf look?
24. Why are some leaf edges pointy and some curved/round/angled?

....

25. Do you think one tree can grow different kinds of leaves? Why? Why not?
26. How can you match a leaf to its tree?

....

27. How do you think leaves get food/water?
28. What happens to leaves if a plant/tree doesn't get water?
29. What would happen to a leaf if you laid it on/left it in water?
30. What happens when a leaf gets wet?
31. What do you notice about leaves after it rains/snows/a storms?

....

32. Why are these leaves on the ground?
33. Why do leaves fall from trees?
34. What happens after leaves fall from trees?
35. What do you notice about the tree/ground after the leaves fall?
36. How can you clean up the leaves that fell?

LEAVES

37. Do you think some leaves are easier to clean up than others? Why? Why not?
38. How can you find out how many leaves fell from the tree?
39. Do you think trees/leaves feel something when leaves fall? Why? Why not?
40. What can you do with the leaves you found?
41. What happens when you try to catch a leaf that is blowing/falling?
42. Can you put leaves back on a tree? Why? Why not?
43. What if you wanted to cover this with leaves? How would you do it?
44. How can you play with leaves that have fallen to the ground?

• • • • • • • • • • •

45. Why do you think the leaves are scattered?
46. What makes leaves move in the air/on the ground?
47. What happens to leaves on a windy day?
48. How can you pretend you are a falling/ floating/blowing leaf?

• • • • • • • • • • •

49. Why do some leaves break/tear when you bend them, and others don't?
50. Why do you think leaves dry out and get brittle?
51. Why do you think some leaves have tears/holes/damage?

52. What do you think would happen if trees didn't have branches/leaves?

• • • • • • • • • • •

53. Why do animals/insects eat leaves?
54. How do animals/insects use leaves to hide?
55. What would animals/insects do if there were no leaves/branches on the trees?

• • • • • • • • • • •

56. Why do you think some leaves have patterns?
57. Where else do you see patterns? How do they look?

• • • • • • • • • • •

58. Have you ever seen a leaf that looks like the one in the picture/book?
59. What can you do to remember how the leaves looked?

• • • • • • • • • • •

60. Why did you choose that leaf to add to your collection?
61. What's your favorite/least favorite leaf? Why?
62. What would happen if you rubbed over a leaf using paper and a crayon?
63. What would happen if you pressed your leaf into clay?
64. How can you make a piece of art out of the leaves you found?
65. How can you make something that looks like a leaf?

GARDENING

1. What is a garden?
2. What can you do with a garden?
3. Why do people plant gardens?
4. What is your favorite type of garden? Why?
5. How do plants grow in a garden?
6. What do you enjoy most/least about gardening?

. . . .

7. How did you learn about gardening?
8. Has you or your family ever planted a garden? Tell me about it.
9. What types of foods can grow in a garden? How do you know?

. . . .

10. How do you care for a garden?
11. Describe your garden.
12. What do you notice about the stems/leaves/vines/plants?
13. Do you have a favorite plant or vegetable in your garden? Tell me about it.
14. What are you expecting from your garden?
15. How can you make sure your garden is colorful?
16. How can you plant a garden that will attract butterflies/hummingbirds/bees?

17. Do you think plants like to hear music? Why? Why not? How can we find out?
18. What kind of songs do you think the plants would like?
19. What advice would you give to a person starting a new garden?

. . . .

20. Why do most plants need water/food/nutrients to grow?
21. What can you use to water/feed your plants? How does that work?
22. How can you get water/food to the plants?
23. What do you think happens to water when it goes into the soil and roots?
24. How do plants "drink" water?
25. How do you know when to water/feed your plants/garden?
26. What would happen if you didn't water/feed your plants?
27. What would happen if you over-watered or over-fed your plants?
28. How would your plants get water if you were going away for a while?
29. What would happen if you ignored your garden?
30. Do you need to water your plants after it rains? Why? Why not?
31. If you were a plant, how would you feel when it rained/snowed/hailed?

. . . .

GARDENING

32. What types of **plants** don't need much water/maintenance?
33. What do you know about native/cactus/succulent plants?
34. How do native/succulent plants differ from other plants?
35. Why don't native/succulent plants need as much water/care as other plants?
36. How do people benefit from planting native plants?
37. How do native plants help combat climate change?
38. How do native plants help conserve water?
39. How do native plants support local wildlife?

....

40. How do you decide what you will plant/grow?
41. What supplies do you need? How will you use them?
42. Tell me about what you want to plant in your garden.
43. How do you know when to plant?
44. What if you drew a map/plan for your garden?
45. Can you grow meat/ice cream/pasta/etc. in a garden? Why? Why not?

....

46. Tell me what you know about **dirt/soil**.
47. What can you use to keep the dirt off your hands?
48. Why do people plant gardens in dirt/soil?
49. How can you tell if the soil/dirt is dry/moist?
50. What should you do if the soil/dirt is dry?
51. How do you know if your plants need more soil/dirt?
52. What do you think happens if the plants don't have enough dirt/soil? Why?

....

53. What do you think happens if there are a lot of rocks and pebbles in the dirt/soil? Why?
54. What do you have to do to clear the dirt/soil?

....

55. What do you think happens when plants are planted too close together? Why?
56. Why do you think plants need space?
57. How can you give the plants more space to grow?
58. Why do you think people plant in rows?

....

59. What do you know about **seeds**?
60. Why do people plant seeds?
61. How can you find/buy seeds?
62. How do you know what kind of seeds you have?
63. Describe the seed you have/see.
64. How do you plant a seed?
65. How are these seeds the same/different?
66. How do you know which seeds you planted where?

GARDENING

67. How can you make a sign to tell where you planted the seeds and what you planted?
68. Why do you think seeds need time to sprout?
69. Show me how a tiny seed grows into a big, strong plant.

···········

70. What happens underground when plants are growing?
71. What do you know about **roots**?
72. What do you notice about the roots?
73. Describe how the roots look.
74. How do roots help plants?
75. How do roots collect water/nutrients for plants?
76. Why do you think roots grow in the ground?

···········

77. Why do you think plants need time to grow?
78. Why do you think some plants grow faster than others?
79. How does the sun/water help your plants?
80. Have you ever seen plants reach toward the sunlight? Why do you think they do that?
81. What if your garden didn't get sunlight or water?
82. How can you position your plant to give it more sun?

83. Why do some plants grow above the ground and others below the ground?
84. Do you think plants need to rest at night, just like we do? Why? Why not?
85. What happens if your plants get too hot/ cold?

···········

86. How has the garden changed since you first started it?
87. Describe how plants look when they sprout.
88. Why do you think some plants have really big leaves while others have small leaves?

···········

89. Describe the **tools** you use to tend your garden.
90. How do the tools help?
91. How do you use the tools?
92. Why do you have to be careful when using the tools?
93. What does the phrase "you reap what you sow" mean?

···········

94. How do you know when there are **insects/bugs**/snails in your garden?
95. How can you find out which bugs/insects are helpful/harmful/invasive to the plants?
96. What if you found **earthworms** in your garden?

GARDENING

97. How do you think earthworms get into your garden?
98. Do earthworms help or hurt your garden? How?
99. How do you keep insects/bugs/animals from eating the plants in your garden?
100. What do you know about pesticides?
101. How are pesticides harmful to insects/bugs/animals/humans?

....

102. What do you know about the **weeds** in your garden?
103. How do you know that's a weed?
104. Why don't you want weeds to grow in your garden?
105. What can you do to keep the weeds out of your garden?
106. How do you get rid of the weeds?
107. Can you eat weeds? Why? Why not?

....

108. What can you do to decorate your garden?
109. Is it a good idea to play in the garden? Why? Why not?
110. What do you think about using a lawnmower in the garden?

....

111. What do you know about fertilizer/
112. Why do people use fertilizer?
113. How does fertilizer help plants?

....

114. What do you know about **composting**?
115. How does composting help plants/the environment?

116. What does decompose mean?
117. How does composting reduce waste?
118. How can you find out how to make compost?
119. Why do you think compost is made using things we throw away?

....

120. How do plants use sunlight to make their own food?
121. What do you know about **photosynthesis**?
122. Why do you think plants need clean air to grow? (carbon dioxide)
123. How do leaves collect light and air?
124. How do you think plants make the air around us clean and fresh?

....

125. Why do living things depend on plants for food?
126. What would happen to people/animals if there were no plants? Why?
127. How do plants get destroyed/killed?
128. What can we do to protect/conserve plants?

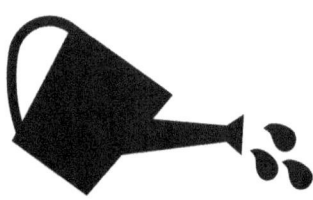

NOTES

"The important thing is not to stop questioning.
Curiosity has its own reason for existing." - Albert Einstein

NOTES

SUN · MOON

1. What do you know about the sun/moon?
2. How can you find the sun/moon?
3. How do you know where to look?
4. When is the best time to see the sun/moon? Why?
5. Describe the sun/moon.
6. Tell me about the color of the sun/moon.
7. What do you notice about the shape of the sun/moon?
8. Why do you think the sun/moon looks like that?
9. Why do you think the moon has craters?
10. Why is the sun/moon round/bright?
11. Do people need the sun to see? Why? Why not?
12. How can people make light, too?
13. Why is the sun/moon in the sky?
14. Why do you think you can't reach up and touch the sun/moon?

··········

15. What's the difference between the sun and the moon?
16. Why isn't the moon as bright as the sun?
17. Why is it hard to see the moon in the daytime?
18. What do you think makes the sun so bright?
19. Why do you think the sun shines?
20. Do you think there is a way to turn the brightness down or off like a light?
21. How do you feel when the sun shines?
22. Why do you feel the heat from the sun?

23. Do you have to be standing in the sun to feel its heat? Why? Why not?
24. What do you know about **temperature**?
25. How does the sun affect the temperature indoors/outdoors/in a car/in a bus?
26. What does it mean when the temperature is low/high?
27. Why do people want to know what the temperature is?
28. It is hot/cold today. What do you think the temperature is? Why?
29. What tools help us measure the temperature?
30. What is a **thermometer**?
31. How do people use/read a thermometer?
32. Do you think all thermometers work the same? Why? Why not?
33. Do you think everyone uses a thermometer/barometer? Why? Why not?
34. Why don't you feel any heat from the moon?

··········

35. Why can't we see the sun/moon in the sky sometimes?
36. Why do you think it is harmful to look directly at the sun?
37. How can people protect their eyes from the sun?

··········

38. How do people protect their skin/bodies from the sun?
39. Why do you think people protect their skin/bodies from the sun?
40. What happens when you are in the sun for too long?

SUN · MOON

41. What is a sunburn?
42. How can you protect your skin from getting sunburned?
43. How does a sunburn differ from other burns?
44. What do you know about using sunscreen?
45. Why do people use sunscreen?
46. How does sunscreen work?

· · · · · · · · · · ·

47. Why does the sun/moon move?
48. How does the sun/moon move?
49. What happens when the sun/moon rises and sets?
50. Why does the sun/moon rise and set?
51. Where does the sun/moon go when it rises/sets? How do you know?
52. Describe the sky when the sun sets/rises.
53. Why does the moon usually rise/move at night?
54. What if the sun/moon went away and never came back?
55. How do you know when it is daytime or nighttime?
56. When you wake up to come to school, is it daytime or nighttime? Why?
57. When you wake up from a nap, is it daytime or nighttime? Why?

· · · · · · · · · · ·

58. Why do clouds block the sun/moon?
59. How do clouds move in front of the sun/moon?

60. What do you notice when clouds block the sun/moon?

· · · · · · · · · · ·

61. How do you think animals/insects protect themselves from the sun?
62. Why do some animals/insects come out/hunt after the sun goes down/at night?
63. Do you think a cow can really jump over the moon? Why? Why not?

· · · · · · · · · · ·

64. What happens when you leave something out in the sun?
65. What happens to things that are exposed to the sun for a long time?
66. What happens to water/ice/metal/crayons/a candle/etc. when it is left in the sun?
67. Why do things get hot/melt in the sun?
68. Why don't things get hot/melt in the moonlight?

· · · · · · · · · · ·

69. Where can you go when the sun is too hot? Why would you go there?
70. How do you dress on a hot sunny day?
71. How is that different from how you dress on a cold day?

· · · · · · · · · · ·

72. What do you know about **shade**?
73. How is shade made?
74. How does the shade get here?
75. What's the difference between standing in the shade and standing in the sun?
76. How do you feel when you are in the shade?

SUN · MOON

77. Why do you think people feel cool in the shade?
78. What if you wanted to make shade? How would you do it?
79. Can you find shade anywhere? Why? Why not?

···········

80. How does the sun help people stay healthy?
81. What do you think would happen to plants/people without the sun?
82. How do you think the sun helps plants grow?

···········

83. Can people travel to the sun/moon? Why? How? Why not?
84. How would people travel to the moon?
85. What do you think would happen if you traveled to the sun/moon?
86. Do you think it would be a long trip or a short trip? Why? Why not?
87. What do you think you would see if you traveled to the sun/moon?
88. Do you think people/animals/insects live on the moon/sun now? Why? Why not?
89. Do you think people could live on the sun/moon? Why? Why not?
90. What do you think it would be like to live on the sun/moon?

···········

91. How does the moon look/change each night?
92. Why does the moon change each night?
93. What do you notice about the moon each night?
94. How do you know when a moon is full/new?
95. What does it mean to see a full/new moon?

96. Why does the moon look like a crescent?
97. What does waxing/waning mean?
98. How does the moon wax/wane?
99. What do you know about the phases of the moon? (new moon, waxing crescent, first quarter, waxing gibbous, full moon, waning gibbous, third quarter, and waning crescent)
100. Why does the moon have different phases?

···········

101. What is an **eclipse**?
102. How does an eclipse happen?
103. What do you see during an eclipse?
104. How does a shadow/blocking light make an eclipse?
105. Why does the sun/moon go dark during an eclipse?
106. What's the difference between a solar and a lunar eclipse?
107. What happens when the moon comes between the Earth and the sun? (solar eclipse)
108. What happens when the Earth comes between the sun and the moon (lunar eclipse)

···········

109. The sun is a star. Why do you think it looks different from the other stars?

···········

110. How can you find out more about the sun/moon?

RAINBOWS

1. What is a rainbow?
2. Describe a rainbow.
3. What do you notice about the rainbow's shape/colors?
4. Why do rainbows appear to bend/arc across the sky?
5. Why aren't rainbows square like a box or straight like a pencil?
6. What happened to the rest of the rainbow?

   . . . .

7. Why do you think rainbows are always the same colors?
8. Why do you think a rainbow's colors are always in the same order? (top to bottom: red, orange, yellow, green, blue, indigo, violet)
9. Why are there only seven colors in a rainbow? Why not eight or nine?
10. Why can't you find black/white/pink in a rainbow?
11. Why do you think we can see through the colors of a rainbow?

    . . . .

12. How do you feel when you see a rainbow?
13. What do you think it means when you see a rainbow?
14. Tell me about a time when you saw a rainbow.
15. Does everyone everywhere see the same rainbow in the sky? Why? Why not?

    . . . .

16. Can you touch/climb up a rainbow? Why? Why not?
17. What do you think is at the end of a rainbow? Why?
18. Do you think you can find the end of a rainbow? Why? Why not?

19. What would you have to do to find the end of a rainbow?
20. How would you get there?
21. How can you tell how far away a rainbow is?
22. Do you think there is a pot of gold at the end of a rainbow? Why? Why not?

    . . . .

23. Why do you sometimes see two rainbows?
24. Do you think a rainbow looks different from a mountain top/from a plane? Why? Why not?

    . . . .

25. How do you think rainbows are formed?
26. Why do you think you see rainbows after rain/mist/dew/fog?
27. Can rainbows appear anywhere? (room/basement/hospital/car/tunnel/cave/beach/train/etc.) What makes you think so?
28. Can you see a rainbow in the dark/at night? Why? Why not?

    . . . .

29. How can you make a rainbow of colors?
30. What if you wanted to draw/paint/mold a rainbow? How would you do it?
31. What can you use to draw/paint/mold a rainbow?

    . . . .

32. How can you find out more about rainbows?

WEATHER · CLOUDS · WIND

1. How would you describe weather/climate?
2. What do you know about weather/climate?
3. How does the weather change/stay the same?

   ············

4. Why do people look outside to check on the weather?
5. How else can people check on the weather?
6. Why should you check the weather before going outside/on a trip?
7. How can the weather change your plans for the better/worse?

   ············

8. What did you discover when you went outside?
9. What else do/did you notice?
10. How does the air feel/smell/taste/look/sound right now?
11. How does the sky look/change throughout the day?
12. What can you tell about the weather when you look at the sky?
13. Why do you think the sky changes colors?
14. What do you think the weather will be like when the sky is dark gray/bright blue?

15. What does it mean when the sky changes colors?
16. How is being outside different from being inside?
17. How does being outside make you feel?
18. What makes people warm/cold/wet when they are outside/inside?
19. How do you know what clothes to wear when you go outside?
20. What would happen if you didn't wear the right clothes?

    ············

21. How does the weather change?
22. Why isn't the weather the same every day?
23. What do you think causes the weather to change throughout the day/week/month/year?
24. Can people change the weather? Why? Why not?
25. What do you think would happen if people could change the weather every day? Why?

    ············

26. What are **clouds**?
27. How do clouds move around?
28. Why are there clouds in the sky on some days but not on others?
29. Why are clouds different colors?
30. Why are some clouds white and others gray?
31. What do you think the weather will be like when you see gray clouds/no clouds?

WEATHER · CLOUDS · WIND

32. Why are clouds in different shapes?
33. Why do clouds change shapes?
34. Sometimes clouds look like objects/ animals/insects? Why do you think that is?
35. Tell me about the different types of clouds. (cirrus, cumulus, stratus)

....

36. What do you know about **wind**?
33. What happens when the wind blows?
34. Describe the wind.
35. What do you hear/see/feel when it's windy?
36. How do you know if it's a windy day?
37. What kinds of things can you do on a windy day? Why?
38. How does the wind cool your body down?
39. How does the wind make your body cold?

....

40. How does the wind move things?
41. What's the difference between a breeze and strong wind?
42. How strong does the wind have to be for something/you to blow away?
43. How can you keep things/yourself from blowing away?
44. How can you make/build something that the wind will/won't move?

....

45. What can you do to make wind?
46. Show me how you can move things using the wind you make.

47. How can you make the wind blow harder/ softer?
48. What types of things can/can't you move with wind?
49. How can you stop the wind from moving things?

....

50. What do you think the weather might be like later/tomorrow/all week?
51. Why do people want to know what the weather will be like tomorrow/next week?
52. How can you find out what the weather will be like later/tomorrow/next week?
53. What is a weather **forecast**?
54. How do people forecast the weather?
55. What does a meteorologist do?
56. How does a meteorologist forecast the weather?
57. Is the meteorologist always right about the weather? Why? Why not?

....

58. How can you draw a picture of a windy/ cloudy/rainy/snowy/sunny/smoggy/ stormy/beautiful day?
59. What materials can you use to make your drawing/artwork?
60. What is are weather patterns?
61. Is a weather pattern something people can extend/make? Why? Why not?
62. How is a weather pattern the same/ different from the pattern on your clothes?

WEATHER · RAIN · SNOW · ICE

1. What is drizzle/rain/snow/hail?
2. How can you tell if it's drizzling/raining/snowing/hailing?
3. Describe drizzle/rain/snow/hail.
4. What is the difference between drizzle/rain/snow/hail? What are the similarities?
5. How does drizzle/rain/snow/hail sound when it falls?
6. What happens when rain/snow/hail falls?
7. Where does the water/snow/hail come from? How do you know?
8. When do you think we get the most rain/snow/hail? Why?
9. Does it matter what time/day it is? Why? Why not?
10. What do you hear/see/feel when it rains/snows/hails?
11. What do you feel/taste when you catch snowflakes/rain with your tongue?
12. How do you spend your day when it's raining/snowing/hailing/stormy outside?
13. What is your favorite thing to do when it rains/snows/hails/storms?
14. What can you do with rain water/snow?

············

15. What happens when you are "caught in the rain?"
16. What's the difference between being wet and being dry?
17. How can you stay dry when it rains?
18. What's the difference between standing in the rain and standing in a pool/the ocean?

············

19. What happens to the water that falls on the ground/in the dirt/in the sand/on your clothes?
20. Why does rain form puddles?
21. How can you capture the rain/snow/hail?
22. What can you do with the rainwater/snow/hail you collect?
23. How can you measure the rainwater you collect?
24. What happens to the rainwater when it falls in the ocean/on a lake/in the river?

············

25. What happens when there is a lot of snow/rain/ice?
26. What is a **flood**?
27. How does rain cause flooding?
28. What happens when areas flood?
29. Why are floods dangerous?
30. How can you protect yourself when it floods?
31. What if the water comes into your house/car?
32. How can you help others when there is a flood?

WEATHER · RAIN · SNOW · ICE

33. What if the hail is really big and hard?
34. What makes trees fall over when it floods?

············

35. Why do you think snow/ice is cold?
36. How can you tell how cold snow/ice is?
37. How can you tell how cold it is outside when it snows?
38. Can it snow on a hot day? Why? Why not?
39. Is it safe to stay out in the cold and snow for a long time? Why? Why not?

············

40. How do you have fun in the snow?
41. What kinds of things can/can't we do in the snow?
42. What should you wear to play in the water/rain/snow? Why?
43. How does snow feel when you touch/ step/lay/sled/ski on it?
44. Why do you think snow feels that way?
45. What happens when you squeeze/pack snow?

············

46. What can you make/build with snow?
47. How do you make a snowball/snowman?
33. Describe a snowball/snowman.
34. What happens when you throw a snowball?
35. Can you build a snowman out of water/ ice? Why? Why not?

36. What would happen if you tried to build a snowman out of water/ice?
37. What else can you use to build a snowman/a person?
38. If you wanted to make snow, how would you do it?

············

39. What happens to snow when it gets warm?
40. Where does/did the snow go? Why?
41. Why does snow melt?
42. What happens when snow melts?
43. How can you keep snow from melting?
44. What's the difference between something being hot and something being cold?

············

45. Does everyone get snow where they live? Why? Why not?
46. Why can you see snow on the mountain tops?
47. What happens when there is too much snowfall?
48. How can you find out how deep the snow is?
49. What if the snow blocks your door/buries your car?
50. What if there is too much snow on the roads?
51. How do the roads get clear after it snows?
52. What is an avalanche?
53. How do avalanches happen?
54. Why are avalanches dangerous?

············

WEATHER · RAIN · SNOW · ICE

55. What is *ice*?
56. How does water freeze/become ice?
57. What's the difference between snow and ice?
58. How does ice feel/taste/look/smell/sound?
59. What's the difference between a snowball and an ice ball?
60. Why is ice harder than water/snow?

············

61. Would you want to get hit with a ball made of ice? Why? Why not?
62. Would you rather be a person made out of snow or out of ice? Why?

············

63. What types of things can you make/build with ice?
64. Is it safe to hold/touch ice for a long time? Why? Why not?
65. How do you make an ice sculpture?
66. What do you know about igloos?
67. How do people build houses/igloos out of ice?
68. Why do people build houses/igloos out of ice?

············

69. How do people move on ice?
70. Why do they move that way?
71. What kinds of activities/sports can people do on ice? Why?
72. Describe how you walk/skate/ski on ice.
73. Why do people have to be careful when walking/skating on ice?
74. Why is ice slippery?

············

75. What happens when lakes/ponds get very cold?
76. Why does the water freeze on the surface of a lake/pond but not below?
77. What would happen if you walked on ice that was too thin to support your weight?
78. What would happen if you fell into cold icy water?
79. Why is cold icy water dangerous?
80. How cold do you think the water is under a frozen lake/pond? Why?
81. What do you think happens to the fish when the lake/pond freezes?
82. Why don't oceans freeze?

············

83. What do you know about icicles?
84. Why do you think icicles look like they do?
85. How do icicles form?
86. What happens when water drips down an icicle?
87. Why are icicles thinner at the bottom than on the top?
88. Where do you usually see icicles? Why?

WEATHER · STORMS

1. What are storms/hurricanes/tornados/blizzards?
2. What's the difference between a hurricane and a tornado/blizzard?
3. How would you describe a storm/tornado/hurricane/blizzard?
4. Why do you think there are storms/tornadoes/hurricanes/blizzards?

···········

5. What happens when there is a storm/tornado/hurricane/blizzard?
6. How do you know when a storm/tornado/hurricane/blizzard is coming/leaving?
7. How can you find out if a storm is coming?
8. What should you do before a storm/tornado/hurricane/blizzard comes?
9. How do you know what to do when there is a storm/tornado/hurricane/blizzard?

···········

10. Have you ever experienced a storm/tornado/hurricane/blizzard? What happened?
11. How does a stormy day make you feel?

···········

12. What is thunder/lightning?
13. What do you think makes thunder/lightning?
14. Describe how thunder/lightning looks in the sky.
15. Tell me about how thunder/lightning sounds.
16. Why do you hear booms and cracks when there is lightning and thunder?

17. How does thunder/lightning make you feel when you hear it?
18. What makes thunder/lightning clap/boom/rumble?
19. Why is thunder/lightning so loud?
20. How can you tell how far away thunder/lightning is?
21. Why do people hear thunder/lightning when it is so far away?
22. Can you measure a lightning strike? Why? Why not?

···········

23. Why should people stay inside when there is lightning outside?
24. What types of things attract lightning? How do you know?
25. How does thunder/lightning affect some people/animals/pets?
26. Where can people/insects/animals go when there is a storm? Why?
27. What if people/insects/animals can't find somewhere to go in a storm?
28. How do you think insects/animals feel when it storms?

···········

29. What do you know about **climate change**?
30. Why do you think the world is experiencing climate change?
31. How do people cause climate change?
32. How is climate change affecting our planet?
33. How does climate change affect people/animals/insects/the ocean?
34. Can people stop climate change? How?
35. What will happen if people do nothing about climate change?

···········

36. What do you think the phrase "the calm before the storm" means?

WEATHER · SEASONS

1. What are seasons?
2. Why do you think there are four seasons?
3. How do people know which season it is?
4. How do people know when the seasons change?
5. What do you think causes the seasons to change?
6. How can you learn more about the seasons?

· · · · · · · · · · ·

7. Which seasons are your favorite/least favorite? Why?
8. Draw a picture that shows what you do during your favorite season.
9. What do you think of when someone says winter/spring/summer/fall?
10. Describe the seasons.
11. How are the seasons similar/different from each other?
12. Which season is the coldest/warmest? How do you know?
13. Have you lived somewhere where the seasons are different? What was it like?

· · · · · · · · · · ·

14. How do you dress in the winter/spring/summer/fall?
15. What activities can/can't you do in different seasons?

· · · · · · · · · · ·

16. What does it look like where you live during the winter/spring/summer/fall?
17. What do you notice outside in the winter/spring/summer/fall?
18. What types of activities can you do in the winter/spring/summer/fall? Why?
19. How do you think the trees look/change in the fall/winter?
20. Why do you think leaves change colors in the fall/winter?
21. Why do you think leaves fall from trees in the fall/winter?
22. Why do you think the days get shorter/longer as seasons change?

· · · · · · · · · · ·

23. What does it mean to have seasonal food?
24. Does food taste better when it is in season? Why? Why not?
25. Why do farmers have to know when to plant/about seasons?
26. Why is it best to plant crops during certain seasons?
27. What would happen if people didn't plant their crops at the right time?
28. How do the seasons affect plants?

· · · · · · · · · · ·

29. Tell me about the festivals or celebrations that take place in the winter/spring/summer/fall.
30. How do you know about the festivals/celebrations?

NOTES

"*A well-educated mind will always have more questions than answers.*"
- Helen Keller

NOTES

NOTES

ANIMALS

1. What are animals?
2. What animals have you seen? Describe them.
3. How do you know what kind of animal that is?
4. Why do you think there are so many different kinds of animals?
5. What's the difference between a _____ and a _____?

    ············

6. Tell me about your favorite animal.
7. Why is it your favorite animal?
8. What do you like/dislike about this animal?

    ············

9. What makes an animal wild/tame?
10. How do you know if an animal is wild/ tame?
11. What's the difference between animals that are wild and animals that are tame?
12. How do you approach an animal that is tame/wild/growling/asleep?
13. What should you do before touching an animal?
14. What makes an animal friendly/mean/ scary/shy?
15. Why do you think animals attack?

    ············

16. How do animals find food/hunt?
17. Why do animals hunt other animals?
18. How do animals live?
19. How do animals go to the bathroom?

20. Why do you think the animal lives like that?
21. What makes their habitat a good/safe/ dangerous place for the animal to live?
22. How do animals stay warm/keep cool?

    ············

23. Why can't animals talk like people?
24. How do animals communicate with people?
25. How do animals communicate with each other?

    ············

26. Why do you think animals have stripes/ spots/fur/claws/beaks/feathers/tails/ teeth/tusks/trunks/hooves/etc.?
27. How do animals use their features?
28. How do animals hide from other animals/predators/people?
29. What do you know about camouflage?
30. Who would win in a fight between a _____ and a _____? Why do you think so?

    ············

31. How do animals move?
32. Use your body to show me how this animal moves.
33. Why do some animals run/dig/fly/climb/ jump/etc.?

    ············

34. What makes a _____ a _____?
35. How can you match/group/sort the animals by how they move/look/sound/ eat?
36. How can you group/sort the animals by their size/color/type?
37. How else can you sort the animals?

    ············

38. Describe how animals smell.
39. Why do some animals smell the way they do?

ANIMALS

40. Do you think animals care about how they smell? Why? Why not?
41. How do animals clean/bathe themselves?

· · · · · · · · · · ·

42. Do you think animals have families? Why? Why not?
43. How do animals take care of their babies/each other?
44. How can you match these animals to their babies?

· · · · · · · · · · ·

45. How can you tell if an animal is sick?
46. What can you do if you find an animal that is sick/hurt?
47. Why do you have to be careful around animals that are hurt/sick?
48. How can people keep animals safe?

· · · · · · · · · · ·

49. How do people protect animals?
50. How do people keep animals from becoming **extinct**?
51. Why do animals become extinct?
52. Why do you think we put animals in **zoos**/reserves/sanctuaries/refuges?
53. What do you think about animals being kept in a zoo/sanctuary?
54. Do you enjoy going to the zoo to look at animals? Why? Why not?
55. Do you think animals are happy living in the zoo? Why? Why not?
56. What do people do to make an animals comfortable in a zoo/on a reserve?

57. Do you think all animals live in zoos? Why? Why not?
58. Would you want to live in a zoo? Why? Why not?

· · · · · · · · · · ·

59. Which animals are the most helpful to humans? How?
60. If you could be any animal, which animal would you be?

· · · · · · · · · · ·

61. Tell me about any animals you've seen in TV shows/movies.
62. Tell me about animals you have heard about in stories.

· · · · · · · · · · ·

63. What do you notice about animals?
64. Why do cats chase mice? Dogs chase cats?
65. Why do you think a turtle goes inside/comes out of its shell?
66. Why is a giraffe's neck so long?
67. Why do elephants have tusks/long trunks?
68. Why do cats have sharp claws?
69. Why do dolphins/whales jump out of the water?
70. Why can horses run fast?
71. Why do zebras have stripes?
72. Why does an octopus have eight legs?
73. How do bats use sound to locate prey?
74. Why do owls hunt at night?
75. Why do some animals play dead?
76. What would a _____ and ___ say to each other if they could talk?

PETS

1. What do you know about pets?
2. Tell me about your pet/a pet you know.
3. Describe your pet/a pet you know.
4. How does your pet look/sound/act/feel?
5. How do you know that's a dog/cat/ snake/lizard/rabbit/ferret/bird/piglet/ hedgehog/etc.?

....

6. What's the best/worst thing about having a pet?
7. How does a pet make people feel?
8. What's your favorite/least favorite pet?
9. If you could have any animal/insect as a pet, what would it be?
10. What kind of animal makes/doesn't make a good pet? Why?
11. What makes an animal a good/bad pet?
12. Tell me about a pet you have/know.

....

13. What does it mean to **adopt** a pet?
14. How do people adopt/buy pets?
15. What do you know about adopting/ buying pets?
16. Do you think it's better to adopt or to buy a pet? Why?
17. Why do you think some pets cost a lot of money to buy?

....

18. How do you care for a pet?
19. How do you know what a pet needs?
20. Do pets need love and attention just like people do? Why? Why not?
21. How do you show your pet you care about/love him?
22. What do you think your pet is thinking of when you talk to him/hold him/pet him/ feed him/walk him/hug him/let him outside?
23. How do you clean up after a pet?
24. Why should you be kind to animals/ insects/pets?
25. Why should you be gentle with pets?
26. What do you think a pet would do if you weren't kind/gentle?
27. Which pet do you think is the easiest to care for? Why?

....

28. How do you know when your pet is hungry?
29. How do you know what to feed your pet?
30. How do you know if your pet likes its food?
31. What happens if you run out of food/ water for your pet?
32. Do pets drink water/eat the same way people do? Why? Why not?

....

33. How do pets get sick?
34. How do you know when your pet is sick?
35. What do you do if your pet is sick? Why?
36. What does a veterinarian do?

....

PETS

37. How do you hold your pet?
38. Can you pick up every kind of pet? Why? Why not?
39. Is it better to have a small pet or a big pet? Why?

··········

40. What does your pet like/dislike doing? Why?
41. What makes your pet happy/sad/angry/scared/shy/anxious/etc.?
42. How does your pet act when it is happy/sad/angry/scared/shy/lonely/hungry/anxious/etc.?
43. Why does a pet lick your face/wag its tail/jump around/growl/bark/whine/squeak/roll over/shiver/etc.?

··········

44. How do you play with your pet?
45. What kinds of toys does your pet have? How does your pet play with them?
46. How do you entertain your pet?
47. What can/can't you do with your pet? Why?

··········

48. What does your pet do while you sleep?
49. Do you think your pet dreams when sleeping? Why? Why not?
50. What types of dreams do you think your pet has? Why?

51. What does your pet do when you are away? Why?
52. Do you think your pet misses you when you are gone? Why? Why not?
53. Why do people call dogs a man's best friend?
54. Do you think dogs make better friends than people? Why? Why not?

··········

55. Cats and dogs are very common pets. Why do you think that is?
56. *Have you ever been scratched or bitten by a pet/animal? What happened?*
57. How do you stay safe around pets?
58. What should you do before approaching a pet you don't know?

··········

59. Tell me about your pet's features.
60. Why does your pet have stripes/spots/fur/claws/a beak/feathers/a tail/teeth/hooves/etc.?
61. Why do you think your pet has a wet nose/whiskers/fur/paws/claws/a shell/fins/a tail/scales/fangs/feathers/wings/a beak/etc.?
62. Show me how your pet moves.
63. How does your pet stretch/sit/roll over/walk/run/climb/swim/sleep/etc.?
64. Tell me about the strangest pet you've ever seen.

··········

65. Why do you think people put human clothes/costumes on their pets?
66. Would you allow your pet to sleep on your bed/pillow? Why? Why not?

··········

PETS

67. *Can you talk to pets? Why? Why not?*
68. *How do pets communicate with people?*
69. *How do you communicate with your pet?*
70. *How do pets communicate with each other?*
71. *If your pet could talk, what would it say?*

············

72. *Why do you think pets make noises?*
73. *What kinds of noises does your pet make?*
74. *What is growling/barking/whining/squeal?*
75. *Why do you think pets growl/bark/whine/squeal?*
76. *How do you think your pet feels when it whines/growls/barks/squeals?*
77. *How do you feel when a pet whines/growls/barks/squeals?*
78. *How do you think your pet feels when he is outside/inside/alone/with you?*

············

79. *What is the difference between a real animal and a pretend animal? Insect? Fish?*
80. *How do you know whether an animal is real or pretend?*
81. *What is the difference between a tame animal and a wild animal?*

82. *How do you know whether an animal is wild or tame?*
83. *Which animal makes a better pet, a tame one or a wild one? Why?*

············

84. *What is a **cage/enclosure/pen**?*
85. *Why do people put animals in cages/enclosures/pens?*
86. *Do you think all animals live in cages/enclosures/pens? Why? Why not?*
87. *Do you think animals like living in cages/enclosures/pens? Why? Why not?*
88. *Would you want to live in a cage/enclosure/pen? Why? Why not?*
89. *If you could design the perfect cage/enclosure/pen for our pet, what would it look like?*

············

90. *What does it mean to be allergic to animals?*
91. *Why do you think some people are allergic to animals?*
92. *Do you think you should have a pet that you are allergic to? Why? Why not?*

············

93. *Why do people train pets?*
94. *How do you train a pet?*
95. *What kinds of things can you train a pet to do?*
96. *How do people put animals to work?*
97. *What is a **service animal**?*
98. *How do service animals help people?*
99. *How do you think a service animals gets trained?*

PETS

100. Tell me about a service animal you know.

············

101. What do you think about pets pooping/peeing inside of a home?
102. Why do you think pets poop/pee inside of a home?
103. How does a pet know where it is supposed to poop/pee?
104. Why don't pets go to the bathroom in the toilet as humans do?
105. What do you think about pets chewing up things? (furniture, bed, shoes, books, belongings)
106. Why do you think pets chew/scratch on things?
107. How do you keep pets from chewing/scratching things they aren't supposed to?

············

108. What do you know about collars/chips/tags/harness/leashes?
109. Why do people put a collar/chip/tag/harness/leash on pets?

110. Can you put a collar/chip/tag/harness/leash on every kind of pet? Why? Why not?

············

111. What happens when you lose a pet?
112. What can you do to find a lost pet?
113. Why can/can't some pets find their way home when they get lost?
114. Why can't a pet call its owner when it gets lost?
115. Do you know anyone who has lost a pet? What happened?
116. What does it mean to abandon/mistreat/rescue a pet?
117. Why do you think people abandon/mistreat/rescue pets?
118. How do you feel about people who abandon/mistreat/rescue pets?
119. What happens to pets that have been abandoned/mistreated/rescued?

············

120. What do people do with their pets when they go on long trips?
121. Have you ever had to say goodbye to a pet? Why?

············

122. What kind of pet do you think I should get? Why?

BIRDS

1. What are birds?
2. How do you know that's a bird?
3. How did the bird/birds get here?
4. Describe the birds you've seen.
5. How can people tell which bird is which?
   · · · · · · · · · · ·
6. What is a **species**?
7. Why do you think there are so many different species of birds?
8. What do you notice about the colors/ shapes/sizes of birds?
9. Why are male birds more brightly colored than females?
   · · · · · · · · · · ·
10. What do you notice/see outside?
11. Listen. Tell me what you hear.
12. What do you think that bird is thinking?
13. How can you observe birds without bothering them?
14. Why won't those birds come to us?
15. Why did those birds come to us?
16. What does birdwatching mean?
17. What tools can you use to see the birds close up?
18. How do you know what kind/species of bird you're watching?
19. How will you know how many birds you see?
20. What should people do when they watch birds? Why?
    · · · · · · · · · · ·

21. Why do you think birds have these features/characteristics? (wings, feathers, beaks, bill, tails, feet)
22. How do birds use their features?
23. How do their features help them?
24. What if birds didn't have one or more of their features?
25. Why do you think their features are shaped the way they are?
26. Why do you think their features look like they do?
27. What if you wanted to match a feather to the bird from which it came?
28. How are a bird's features the same/ different from each other/other animals?
29. Do birds use their wings like people use their arms? What's the same or different?
30. What other ways are people the same/ different from birds?
    · · · · · · · · · · ·
31. Why do you think birds sing?
32. Why do you think birds sound the same/ different when they sing?
33. Can you tell a bird by the sound it makes? How?
34. What do you think is making that sound? Why? (chirps, rattles, whistles, trills, croaks, drumming, pecking, tapping)
    · · · · · · · · · · ·
35. Why do birds like trees?
36. How do you think some birds float on/ dive underwater?

BIRDS

37. *Why do birds fly in flocks together?*
38. *Why do birds fly in the shape of a V?*
39. *Why do birds fly into windows?*
············
40. *Why do birds build **nests**?*
41. *How do birds build their nests?*
42. *How do birds find the material to build their nests?*
43. *If you wanted to build a nest, what materials would you use? Why?*
44. *What would you do first, second, third…?*
············
45. *Why do birds lay **eggs**?*
46. *What happens to the eggs after they are laid?*
47. *Where do birds keep their eggs? Why?*
48. *How do birds come out of the eggs?*
49. *What happens when the baby birds come out of the egg/shell?*
50. *How do birds protect their babies?*
51. *Why do birds build nests in trees/up high?*
52. *Tell me about other animals that lay eggs.*
············
53. *How do birds take care of their babies?*
54. *What would you do if you found a baby/ fledgling bird?*

55. *Why do you think baby birds don't look like baby people?*
56. *What do you think would happen to birds if people shook trees/took their eggs/cut down trees/damaged nests?*
············
57. *What kinds of things do you think birds eat? Why?*
58. *How do birds find food?*
59. *How do birds find food for their babies?*
60. *How do birds feed their babies?*
61. *What kinds of birds/bird's eggs do people eat? How do you know?*
············
62. *How do you think birds play/ communicate/sleep?*
63. *Do you think all of the birds get along with each other? Why? Why not?*
64. *How do some species of birds learn to talk like people?*
65. *Do you think birds know what they are saying when they talk? Why? Why not?*
············
66. *What happens to birds at night?*
67. *Why are birds quiet at night?*
68. *How do some birds see at night?*
69. *How do birds stay warm in the winter or cool when it's hot?*
············
70. *Why do people put birds in cages?*
71. *What do you think about putting birds in cages?*

BIRDS

72. How do you think birds feel when they are kept in cages?
73. Why do you think people trim a bird's primary feathers?
74. How do birds get their feathers back so they can fly again?
75. Would you want your feathers trimmed if you were a bird? Why? Why not?

· · · · · · · · · · ·

76. Why do woodpeckers peck on trees?
77. Why do roosters cock-a-doodle-doo in the morning?
78. Why do flamingos stand on one leg?
79. Why do vultures eat dead animals?
80. How do you think pigeons find their way home?
81. How do pigeons help people deliver messages?
82. Why are there species of birds that can't fly?

83. Why do birds poop on cars/people?
84. Why do cats and dogs like to chase birds?
85. How do birds help us control pesky insects?
86. How do birds spread seeds?
87. What happens when birds spread seeds?
88. How do birds help people hunt?

· · · · · · · · · · ·

89. Do you think it's faster to swim/walk or to fly somewhere? Why?
90. Where would you go if you could fly? Why?

· · · · · · · · · · ·

91. What does it mean for a bird to migrate?
92. Why do birds fly south for the winter?
93. What does migrate mean?
94. Why do some species of birds migrate each year?

INSECTS • BUGS

1. What are insects/bugs?
2. How do you know so much about insects/bugs?
3. What is the difference between an insect and a bug?
4. Describe this insect/bug.
5. Why do you think this insect/bug looks the way it does?
6. Have you ever seen an insect/bug? Tell me about it.
7. How do some insects/bugs help people?
8. How can you tell if an insect/bug is real or pretend?

·············

9. What do you think about insects/bugs?
10. How do you feel about insects/bugs?
11. How do you know that's an ant/caterpillar/spider/grasshopper/beetle/moth/butterfly/bumble bee/etc.?
12. What do you think makes insects/bugs different from other animals?
13. Why do you think there are so many species of insects/bugs?
14. How did you learn about this insect/bug?

·············

15. How does this insect/bug behave?
16. What does this insect/bug do that others don't? Why?
17. What are the similarities/differences between these insects/bugs?

·············

18. What are the similar/different ways insects and bugs move around?
19. What helps insects/bugs move that way?
20. Use your body to show me how this insect moves.
21. Why do some insects/bugs have eyes/antennae/wings/stingers/thoraxes/abdomens/etc.?
22. How do insects/bugs use their eyes/antennae/wings/stingers/thoraxes/abdomens/etc.?
23. Why do you think insects/bugs have more than two legs?
24. What do you notice about this insect's/bug's body parts?

·············

25. Why do you think this insect/bug has markings/spots/these colors/a pattern/symmetry?
26. Tell me about the kinds of markings/colors/spots do people have?
27. How are people/animals different from insects/bugs?
28. Tell me what insects/bugs do that people can't, and vice versa.

·············

29. How do you know where to look for insects/bugs?
30. How do insects/bugs build their homes?
31. Why do some insects/bugs live underground/in trees/in hives/in water?
32. If you were an insect/bug, where would you want to live? Why?

·············

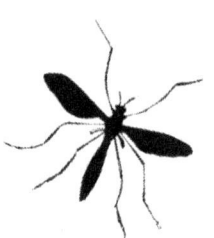

INSECTS · BUGS

33. *How do insects/bugs find food?*
34. *How do insects/bugs feed themselves?*
35. *What do insects/bugs do when they can't find food?*
36. *Why do some insects/bugs hunt for food during the day/night?*
37. *Describe something that might eat this insect/bug.*
38. *Can people eat insects/bugs? Why? Why not?*
39. *Would you ever eat a bug? Why? Why not?*
40. *What if there was nothing else to eat?*
....

41. *Tell me what you know about predators.*
42. *How do insects/bugs hide from predators?*
43. *What does* **camouflage** *mean?*
44. *How do insects/bugs hide or camouflage themselves/blend into their environment?*
45. *What happens when insects/bugs use camouflage?*
46. *Why do insects/bugs use camouflage?*
47. *Can people camouflage themselves like insects and bugs? Why? Why not?*
48. *What colors help insects/bugs blend into the environment? Why?*
49. *What do insects/bugs do when their camouflage doesn't work?*
....

50. *How do insects/bugs get inside our classrooms/homes/cars/gardens?*
51. *Why do insects/bugs enter our classrooms/homes/cars/gardens?*

52. *What do you think about insects coming inside your car/home/class?*
53. *Do you think insects/bugs are good or bad to have inside/outdoors? Why?*
....

54. *What do you think insects/bugs do all day/night?*
55. *Do insects/bugs make good pets? Why? Why not?*
56. *What do you think it might be like to be an insect/bug?*
....

57. *Why do you think insects/bugs are so much smaller than people?*
58. *How would you feel if you were as small as an insect/bug?*
59. *How can you measure how big/small an insect/bug is?*
60. *What would happen if insects/bugs were the same size as/bigger than people?*
....

61. *How do insects/bugs change in their lifetimes?*
62. *What do you know about the different stages insects/bugs go through in their lifecycle?*
63. *Why do you think some insects/bugs change their form/go through stages?*
64. *What is* **metamorphosis***?*
65. *What is the difference between a life cycle and metamorphosis?*
....

INSECTS · BUGS

66. What questions do you have about insects/bugs?

· · · · · · · · · · ·

67. Would you like to touch or hold an insect/bug? Why? Why not?
68. How does touching or holding an insect or bug feel?
69. How does an insect/bug feel when you hold it? Why? Why not?
70. Are there any insects/bugs you would want/not want to pick up/hold? Why?

· · · · · · · · · · ·

71. How do you know if it is safe to eat an insect/bug? (roasted, fried, boiled, or dried)
72. How do you cook an insect/bug?
73. How can you make a cooked insect/bug taste better?
74. More than 2 billion people around the world already eat insects. Would you ever eat an insect/bug? Why? Why not?
75. Why do you think some insects/bugs are a sustainable food source? (beetles, caterpillars, crickets, grasshoppers, locusts, and mealworms)
76. Why do you think insects are more environmentally friendly to produce than beef and pork?

· · · · · · · · · · ·

77. Why do insects bite/sting/pinch?
78. How do you treat an insect/bug bite or sting?

79. How do some insects/bugs hurt people?
80. What could happen if a person is allergic to an insect or bug?
81. Why do you think some people are afraid of insects/bugs?
82. How do you feel about insects/bugs? Why?
83. Do you think insects/bugs can be dangerous? Why? Why not?
84. Do you think it's wrong to kill an insect? Why? Why not?
85. What would happen if there were no insects/bugs anywhere in the world?

· · · · · · · · · · ·

86. How do insects/bugs communicate with each other?
87. Do insects/bugs have feelings? How do you know?
88. Do insects/bugs have friends/families? How do you know?
89. How do insects/bugs have babies?
90. How do insects/bugs take care of their babies?
91. Why do some insects lay eggs and then leave them unprotected?
92. How are insect/bug eggs similar or different from other eggs? (chicken, ostrich, fish, etc.)
93. Do you think the babies of this insect/bug look like their parents when they are born? Why do you think that?
94. What can you do to return this insect/bug to its family?

· · · · · · · · · · ·

INSECTS · BUGS

95. Do insects/bugs get up and go to work every day? Why? Why not?
96. What kinds of jobs do insects/bugs have?

············

97. What does **pollinate** mean?
98. Why do plants need to pollinate?
99. How does pollination help people?
100. How do insects/bugs pollinate? (bees, butterflies, wasps, beetles, flies, and moths)
101. How do animals pollinate?
102. Do you think insects/bugs/animals know what they're doing when they pollinate? Why? Why not?
103. How does pollinating help people?

············

104. How would people get honey if there were no bees?
105. How do ants work as a team?
106. How do ants carry things that are more than 20 times their weight?
107. How do ticks grow?
108. How do fireflies make light?
109. Why does a butterfly live for only a few weeks?
110. Why do pillbugs (rollie pollies) ball up when you touch them?
111. How do caterpillars develop into butterflies?
112. How does a caterpillar form a chrysalis?

113. What's the difference between a moth and a butterfly?
114. Why do you think this insect is called a dragonfly/rhinoceros beetle?
115. Why does a caterpillar have so many legs?
116. Where do insects/bugs go in the winter? How do you know?
117. What do insects/bugs do when there's a forest fire/snow/rain/flood/hurricane/tornado?

············

118. Why do you think some insects/bugs are attracted to light/smells/flowers/plants/fruit/leaves?
119. Why do you think certain smells repel insects/bugs? (Lavender, peppermint, and citronella)
120. What colors/foods/smells attract insects/bugs? Why?

············

121. If you could become an insect or bug, which one would you be, and what would it do?
122. If you could create a new species of insect/bug, how would it look?
123. Draw your new insect/bug.
124. If you could design a new insect/bug, what would it look like?
125. What would you name your new insect/bug? Why?
126. Do you think there are insects/bugs out there that no one has ever seen before? Why?

SPIDERS - ARACHNIDS

1. What are spiders/arachnids?
2. Describe a spider/arachnid.
3. Why is a spider called an arachnid?
4. Why aren't spiders considered insects or bugs?
5. How do spiders help us/our world?

·············

6. How do spiders catch other insects?
7. Tell me what you know about spider webs.
8. Describe a spider web.
9. Why do spiders spin webs?
10. How do spiders spin their webs?
11. How do spider webs help spiders?
12. Why are spider webs sticky?
13. How long do you think it takes a spider to spin a web? How can you find out?
14. What do you know/notice about spider webs?
15. What patterns/shapes do you see in a spider web?
16. Why do you think spider webs are very strong?
17. How does a sticky web help the spider?
18. How do spiders know the best places to build their webs?
19. Why do some spiders build their webs in trees/in front of lights/in hidden places/ up high/low to the ground?
20. Why do you think spiders design webs the way they do?
21. How could you find out how strong your web is?
22. Do spiders build webs together or by themselves? Why?

23. What do you think would happen if two spiders wanted to spin webs in the same place?
24. How do spiders that don't build webs catch their prey?
25. What happened to the spider web that was here last night/yesterday?

·············

26. How do insects/bugs get stuck in a spider web?
27. What kinds of insects get stuck in spider webs? How do you know?
28. How does a spider know when an insect gets caught in its web?
29. What happens when insects/bugs get stuck in webs?
30. Can spiders get caught/stuck in their own webs? Why? Why not?
31. What would happen if a person/animal walked into a spider web?
32. How do you think the insect/bug feels that gets caught in a spider's web?
33. Do you think there are spiders big enough to trap/eat birds and lizards? How can you find out?

·············

34. What happens when you touch a real spider web?
35. How does a spider web feel when you touch it?
36. What does the spider do when someone/ something destroys its web?

·············

37. What if you wanted to design a web? How would you do it?
38. How can you use these materials to make a web?
39. Where would you build a web to catch the most insects/bugs? Why there?

NOTES

> *"Let the questions be the curriculum."*
> **- Socrates**

NOTES

DRAMATIC PLAY ▪ PRETEND PLAY

1. Tell me about this world you created.
2. Describe the job you have.
3. Tell me about the role you are playing.
4. Why is roleplaying so fun?
5. How did you assign/select the roles?
6. What can you do to make sure everyone has a role/something to do?
7. Who is playing what role? Why?
8. How do your friends know what to do?
9. Tell me about who is supposed to do what.
10. How do you know which task is your responsibility?
11. How can you make sure everyone remembers their tasks/the rules?
   ▪▪▪▪▪▪▪▪▪▪▪
12. How can you take turns in a fair way?
13. How can you work as a team?
14. What will you do if one of you wants to switch roles?
   ▪▪▪▪▪▪▪▪▪▪▪
15. What happens here?
16. Describe what you know about being a florist/doctor/parent/postal worker/pilot/cook/etc.
17. Why do you think it's important for people to have different jobs?
18. How do you know how to do this job?

19. How does a person learn how to work/do their job?
20. Tell me about what the other workers do here.
   ▪▪▪▪▪▪▪▪▪▪▪
21. Tell me about being a _____ (occupation).
22. How do you think a _____ prepares for work/school/the day?
23. What does a _____ usually make/do/sell/build? Why?
24. What are the responsibilities of a _____ ?
25. How do you know what a _____ does/thinks/says/sees/feels/hears at work?
26. What do you think a _____ thinks about all day?
27. How do you think a _____ does their job?
28. Would a _____ ever come to your home/school? Why? Why not?
29. What would happen if a _____ came to your home/school?
30. How does a _____ help animals/insects/people/the planet?
   ▪▪▪▪▪▪▪▪▪▪▪
31. Describe the office/room/hospital/building/center where your relatives/people you know work.
32. Why can't people do that job somewhere else?
33. Can a doctor do his job in a post office? Why? Why not?

DRAMATIC PLAY · PRETEND PLAY

34. How do you know what a _____ does?
35. How do you think a doctor/florist/ firefighter/etc. remembers what to do?
    ············
36. What's a uniform?
37. Why do you think people wear uniforms to do their job?
38. Describe the uniform you are wearing.
39. Tell me about your office/clinic/kitchen/ restaurant/store/shop/cart/airport/ theater/post office/game/sport/etc.
    ············
40. What materials/tools do you need to do your job? How would you use them?
41. Why did you choose those materials?
42. How can you use this piece/part/tool/ material?
43. What do you have that will work instead?
44. How do you make/get those?
45. What makes those pieces/parts go together?
46. How can you organize the materials/ tools for the doctor/florist/firefighter/ archeologist/etc.?
47. How can you organize the materials/ tools so you can use them easily?
    ············
48. What paperwork/forms do you fill out? How?

49. Why do you use this form/receipt/bill?
50. How do you know what important information to write down?
51. What types of questions should you ask your customer/clients/patients/etc.? Why?
    ············
52. What kinds of tools/equipment does a _____ use? Why?
53. How does a _____ use their tools/ equipment?
54. How does a _____ find materials/ supplies/tools for what they do?
    ············
55. How do people know if your business is open/closed?
56. What kinds of signs would a _____ need to display?
57. How can you make a sign?
    ············
58. What services does your business/ company offer? Why?
59. How do customers know where to go/ what to do?
60. How do customers know what they can buy?
61. How do customers know how much they have to pay?
62. What can you do to keep customers from waiting too long for service?
63. What can you do to make this area comfortable?

DRAMATIC PLAY · PRETEND PLAY

64. What can customers/patients do while they wait?

65. What sort of paperwork do your customers/patients have to fill out?

66. How do you know what types of items/pieces/things/services your customers will need?

67. How do you know how many items/pieces/things/services your customers will need?

·············

68. Where have you seen a doctor/lawyer/chef/waiter/plumber/etc. before? What were you/they doing?

69. How does a hairdresser wash/rinse/cut/color/straighten/perm/curl hair?

70. How does a veterinarian help animals?

71. How does a postal worker know which mail is yours/deliver mail/find your home?

72. How does the librarian know where to find books?

73. How does a doctor know what's wrong with you?

74. How does a dentist know how to check/fix teeth?

75. How does a writer figure out what to write/make up a story?

76. How does a coder write programming for computers/games/applications?

77. How does an artist know how to draw/paint/sculpt?

78. How does architect design buildings?

79. How does a contractor know how to build/construct?

80. How does a plumber repair leaks?

81. How does a mechanic know how to fix things?

82. How do police officers find criminals?

83. How does a coach know how to train players?

84. How does a pilot know how to fly a plane?

85. How does a manager lead a team?

86. What makes people buy things from a salesperson?

87. How does a salesperson know what size shoes/clothes a customer wears?

88. How does a soldier know what to do?

89. How do you think a person becomes a prince/princess/king/queen?

90. What do you think a prince/princess/king/queen does all day?

·············

91. What can I do to help?

·············

92. What do you want to be when you grow up? Why?

DRAMATIC PLAY · RESTAURANT

1. What do people do in restaurants?
2. Why do people go to restaurants?
3. Why does it cost money to eat in a restaurant?
4. Do you think everyone can afford to eat in restaurants? Why? Why not?
5. What can people do if they can't afford to eat in a restaurant?

   ∙∙∙∙∙∙∙∙∙∙∙

6. What does a host/hostess/server/waiter/waitress/busboy/cook/chef do? How do you know?
7. How does a customer find a table at a restaurant?
8. How does a host/hostess know where to seat the customer?

   ∙∙∙∙∙∙∙∙∙∙∙

9. What does a server do?
10. How does a server/cook/chef dress for work?
11. How does a server know how many plates/napkins/spoons/forks/knives to put on the table?
12. Why do you think it's important to have clean hands/dishes/tables/silverware/menus?

13. How does a server take an order?
14. What if a customer wants something to drink?
15. What makes a good host/hostess/server/waitress/waiter/cook/chef?
16. How does the server remember what the customer ordered?
17. Why should customers be polite to the staff?

   ∙∙∙∙∙∙∙∙∙∙∙

18. How do customers know what food they can order?
19. What is the difference between a breakfast/lunch/brunch/dinner/dessert menu?
20. What is the difference between eating and drinking?
21. What is the difference between dining in and driving through/food to go?
22. How can you design/make a menu to show customers what food you have?
23. Does putting pictures of the food on the menu make it easier or harder for customers to order/be served? How?
24. How do customers know how much the food costs?
25. How does the server remember a customer's order?
26. How does the server get the dishes and food to the table?

   ∙∙∙∙∙∙∙∙∙∙∙

DRAMATIC PLAY · RESTAURANT

27. What do you know about being a cook/chef?
28. How does a cook or chef cut/mix/prepare/cook/season food?
29. How does a cook/chef know what to cook for the customer?
30. How does a cook/chef know how much food to put on a plate?
31. What happens if a customer doesn't like the food/drink that was served?
32. What if a customer wants to change their order?
33. What if a customer wants something that isn't on the menu?
34. What if a customer wants to share their order with a friend?
35. What if a customer wants to take food to go?

············

36. How do the customers know how much to pay when they finish eating?
37. Why do the servers give the customers a guest check at the end of their meal?
38. How do the servers write guest checks/bills for the food that was served?
39. How do customers pay for their food and drinks?
40. How do customers pay with cash/credit card/their phones?

41. What if the customer can't pay for their food?
42. What do you know about cash registers?
43. What do you have to do to calculate change?
44. How do servers print a receipt for the customer?
45. Why do servers give a customer a receipt after they pay?

············

46. How do you thank the server for their good service?
47. What do you know about leaving a tip?
48. Why do people leave tips for their servers?
49. How do tips help the servers?
50. How do you know how much to tip your server?

············

51. What equipment does a server/cook/chef use? (pots, pans, lids, knife, ladle, mixer, spatula, strainer, peeler, blender, sifter, stove, oven, etc.)
52. How does the equipment/tool make their job easier?
53. How does a server/busser/cook/chef/use the equipment/tool?
54. What if they didn't have the right equipment/tools to do their job?

············

55. What happens when customers complain about the food/service?
56. How can you solve a customer's problem?

BABY DOLLS

1. What can you tell me about your baby doll?
2. Describe your baby doll.
3. What is your baby doll's name? Why did you choose that name?
4. How does your baby see/smell/taste/hear/touch?
5. What will you do with your doll today? Why? How?

. . . .

6. How do you know how to take care of a baby?
7. Why can't your baby take care of itself?
8. How do you take care of a baby?
9. Why do you have to be gentle with a baby?
10. If your baby can't talk, how does it let you know it is happy/upset/sad/hungry/wet/scared/lonely?
11. How do you know what your baby needs?
12. If your baby doll could talk, what do you think it would say to you right now?

. . . .

13. How do you show your baby love?
14. What's the safest way to hold/carry your baby? Why?
15. Why do you think babies get sick?
16. What will you do if your baby gets sick?

17. Does your baby have any illnesses/disorders/diseases/challenges? Tell me about what your baby has.
18. How are you helping your baby get/feel better?
19. How do you know how to treat the illness/disorder/disease?
20. Does your baby need any special equipment? Tell me about it.

. . . .

21. How do you know when it's time to bathe your baby?
22. What do you have to do to bathe your baby?
23. How do you think your baby feels in warm/cold bathwater?
24. Why do you have to watch/supervise babies carefully when they are around water?
25. What do you do with the bath water when you are finished? How? Why?

. . . .

26. What will happen when your baby goes pee-pee/poops?
27. Why do you think a baby pees/poops?
28. How do you change a diaper?
29. What do you do after you change a diaper?
30. What will you do before/first/second/next/last/after...?

. . . .

31. What if there was no one to take care of a baby?
32. How will you divide your time between your babies?
33. What would you do if all of the babies were crying?
34. What would you do if you had to hold/feed/move/help two or three babies at the same time?

BABY DOLLS

35. What do you think would happen if you had to take care of a hundred babies?

....

36. How do you play with your baby?
37. What kinds of toys do you think your baby will want? Why?
38. What do you think your doll's favorite thing to do is? Why?
39. How can you fit all of your baby's things into one box/basket/bin/crib?

....

40. How are these babies the same/different?
41. Which baby do you think is younger/older? Why?

....

42. What's the difference between a baby doll and you/a real live baby?
43. How do you know if your baby doll is real or pretend?
44. Can you treat a real baby like you treat your doll? Why? Why not?
45. How is your baby's body/skin/eyes/etc. different from yours?
46. How are your baby's hands/feet/arms/legs/skin/body different from yours?
47. What if all baby dolls were real and alive?

....

48. How do you think your doll feels right now?
49. How would you feel if you were your doll?
50. How do you think your baby feels when you hug/talk/play/rock them?
51. Why do babies cry/laugh/stare/roll over/eat?
52. What would you do if your baby was tired/hungry/angry/lonely/crying/etc.?
53. How can you discover why the baby is crying/upset?

54. How does your doll make new friends?
55. How should your friends act so they don't frighten the baby?

....

56. Why do you think children need to take naps?
57. What do you think happens when a child doesn't take a nap/get enough sleep?
58. What does your doll dream about when they go to sleep?

....

59. How do you know if your baby is hungry?
60. How will you feed your baby?
61. Why do you think babies need help eating?
62. How do you know what food to feed your baby?
63. What do babies eat? Why?
64. How do babies eat?
65. How do you know if your baby likes the food?
66. What do you think your doll's favorite food is? Why?
67. How do you know how much food to feed your baby?
68. How do you know when to stop feeding your baby?
69. How do the bottles/spoons/bowls/containers help you feed your baby?
70. How do the bottles/spoons/bowls/containers work?
71. What if you didn't have any bottles/spoons/bowls?
72. What if your baby wanted to eat candy all day? What would you do?

....

73. Why are you patting the baby's back?
74. What is a **burp**?
75. How do you burp a baby?
76. Why do you think real babies/people burp?

BABY DOLLS

77. What happens when a baby burps?
78. Why do you have to burp a baby?

....

79. Why do you put clothes/shoes on your baby?
80. How do you know which clothes will fit your baby?
81. What do you think would happen if you tried to put your doll in those shoes/clothes? (too small or too big)
82. Tell me about the clothes your baby is wearing.
83. Does your baby have a favorite outfit? Tell me about it.
84. What if your baby doesn't want to wear what you pick out?
85. How do you know which clothes go together/match each other?
86. Why did you choose those clothes/shoes for your baby to wear?
87. Why isn't your baby wearing any shoes/clothes?
88. What would happen if you didn't wear any clothes/shoes when you went out?
89. How do you dress your baby when it's raining/cold/hot?
90. What will you do if your baby's clothes/shoes get dirty/wet?
91. Why do you think there are/is zippers/buttons/snaps/Velcro on the clothes?
92. How do the zippers/buttons/snaps/Velcro work?
93. Why do you think there are so many buttons?

....

94. What is the same/different about these baby dolls?
95. What if you lay the doll's bottles/clothes/shoes in order by size?

96. How can you find out how long your baby is?
97. How can you find out how much your baby has grown?
98. How can you find out how much your baby weighs?
99. Do you think your baby weighs more or less than you do? Why? How can you find out?
100. Do you think your doll is lighter/heavier/shorter/longer/thinner/wider than this _____? Why? How can you find out?
101. How do you know if your dolls are the same size/different sizes?
102. How many doll shoes/clothes would it take to fill this box? How can you check?
103. Can you find something that is the same length as your doll/doll's arm/doll's leg? How can you check?
104. How would you find a blanket that is as long as your doll's bed?

....

105. How can you move all of your baby's things outside/inside?
106. How can you make something to carry the baby?
107. How can you build a room/bed/playpen/toy box/chair for your baby?
108. How will you put your baby in a crib/stroller/car seat/high chair?
109. How can you seat your baby high enough to reach the table?
110. How will you fit all of your babies in the crib/stroller/tub?
111. What else can you do with a crib/stroller/tub?

....

BABY DOLLS

112. How does your baby travel in a stroller/car?
113. Why do real babies have to sit in a car seat/stroller?
114. What could happen if babies didn't sit in car seats?

···········

115. What story will you read to your baby? Why did you pick that story?
116. Tell me about your story.
117. Do you think your baby likes your story? Why?
118. What do you think your baby likes/dislikes about the story? Why?
119. What's your favorite story to read to your baby? Why?
120. What is your baby's favorite bedtime story? Tell me about it.

···········

121. What if you wanted to sing to your baby? How would you choose/learn a song?
122. How does your baby react when you sing?
123. Do you sing quietly or loud to your baby? Why?
124. Does your baby have a favorite song? Let me hear it.

···········

125. What if we were all babies?
126. What if there were no babies anywhere?

···········

127. What's the most exciting thing that has happened to your doll recently?
128. Tell me about your baby's family/friends.
129. What's your doll's favorite game to play/puzzle?
130. What secret talents or skills does your doll have?

131. Tell me about the places your doll has been.
132. What did you teach your baby today?
133. What's your doll's favorite thing to do/learn?

···········

134. How do parents/caregivers take care of their children/families?
135. What do you know about being a parent/mommy/daddy/guardian/caregiver/babysitter?
136. Is being a parent/mommy/daddy/guardian/caregiver/babysitter a job? Why? Why not?
137. Do you think being a parent is easy or hard? Why?
138. Do you think people should get paid to be parents? Why? Why not?

···········

139. Will you want to be a parent/caregiver one day? Why? Why not?
140. Will you put/enroll your baby in a school when they are older? Why? Why not?
141. How do you think going to school will help your baby?
142. What do you think your baby will do when they grow up?
143. What kind of job/career does your baby want to have as an adult?
144. What would you like your baby to do as an adult?
145. What if they don't want to do that?

NOTES

"*Question everything. Learn something. Answer nothing.*"
- Euripides

SUPERHEROES · SUPERHEROINES · ACTION FIGURES

1. What is a superhero/superheroine?
2. What does super/hero/heroine mean?
3. What makes a person a superhero/heroine?
4. Tell me about the special abilities superheroes/heroines have.
5. What else makes a superhero/heroine? Why?
6. What can you tell me about superheroes/heroines?

....

7. Describe your favorite superhero/heroine.
8. Why do you like what your superhero/heroine does?
9. What kind of person is your superhero/heroine? Why do you think that?
10. Tell me what your superhero/heroine can do that no one else can do.
11. How did your superhero/heroine get powers?
12. Are superhero/heroine powers/heroes real or pretend? Why? Why not?
13. How do you know if your superhero/heroine is real or pretend?
14. Do you think there are any real-life superheroes/heroines? Why? Why not?
15. What do you think people would do if they saw a real-life superhero/heroine flying around? Why?
16. What if you could talk to a real superhero/heroine? What would you say?

17. What if you could ask a superhero/heroine questions? What would you ask?
18. What would happen if your superhero/heroine didn't have a shield/cape/spider web/super suit/mask/ring/hammer/wand/etc.?
19. What would happen if your superhero/heroine lost all of his/her powers?
20. Would you rather be able to fly/shoot webs/shoot arrows/be strong/see-through things or something else? Why?

....

21. What makes a superhero/heroine stronger/weaker than other superheroes/heroines?
22. What is the hardest/easiest thing your superhero/heroine can do? How does he/she do it?
23. What types of problems does your superhero/heroine have? How do you think your superhero should solve them?
24. What's the best/worst thing about superheroes/heroines? Why?

....

25. Tell me about the clothes/outfit your superhero/heroine wears.
26. Why does your superhero/heroine dress like that?
27. How do you know what clothes to put on your superhero/heroine?
28. What if it was cold/hot/raining/snowing?

....

SUPERHEROES · SUPERHEROINES · ACTION FIGURES

29. What is your superhero's/heroine's name? How do you think he/she got his name?
30. What is a secret identity?
31. Why do you think superheroes/heroines have secret identities?
32. What does your superhero/heroine do to keep his real name/identity a secret?
33. Since your superhero/heroine has a secret identity, what would happen if people found out who he/she was?
34. What would happen if everyone knew where your superhero/heroine lived?
35. What would happen if everyone knew your superhero's/heroine's phone number?
36. Would you ever call your favorite superhero/heroine? What would you say?

....

37. What are villains/criminals/bad guys?
38. Tell me about the villains/criminals superheroes/heroines fight.
39. Who fights villains/criminals in real life? How?
40. Why do you think superheroes/heroines fight villains/bad guys?
41. Who is your superhero's/heroine's worst enemy? Why? What happened to cause that?

42. If you had superpowers, would you be a superhero/heroine or a supervillain? Why?
43. How do you think the police would feel about superheroes/heroines solving crimes/catching bad guys/fighting criminals? Why?

....

44. Have you seen your superhero/heroine in a television show/movie/story? Tell me about the story.
45. How does your superhero/heroine behave in the television show/movie/story/comic book?
46. Tell me about your favorite/least favorite superhero/heroine TV show/movie/story/comic book.
47. What can you learn from the shows/movies/books/comics you watch or read?
48. Have you seen/met a superhero/heroine in person/costume? How did they act?
49. What happened when you met the superhero/heroine?

....

50. What is an action figure?
51. How is your action figure similar to/different from the superhero/heroine.
52. How do you play with an action figure?
53. How does your action figure feel/smell/look in your hand?
54. Does your action figure have any moving parts? Tell me how they work.
55. What will you do before/first/second/next/last/after with your action figure?
56. What if you had more than one/too many to carry or move?

....

SUPERHEROES · SUPERHEROINES · ACTION FIGURES

57. Can real people like you and I be superheroes? Why? Why not?

58. Do you think a real person could do what a superhero does? Why? Why not?

59. Do you have to have superpowers to be a superhero/heroine? Why? Why not?

60. Do you think a regular person with no super powers can be a superhero/heroine?

61. Do you have to be rich to be a superhero/heroine? Why? Why not?

62. If there are real-life superheroes/heroines, how do they help people?

63. What's the difference between your favorite superhero/heroine and a real person like you and me?

64. How is/are your superhero's/heroine's eyes/arms/legs/head/body/clothes different from yours?

65. What if you could become a superhero/heroine? What would you do?

66. What superpower would you like to have? Why?

67. What would you call yourself? Why?

68. How would your clothes/costume/outfit look?

69. Would you rather be a tiny superhero/heroine or a huge one? Why?

· · · · · · · · · · ·

70. What kinds of feelings do you think your superhero/heroine has?

71. Do you think your superhero/heroine would ever cry/laugh/get sick/get scared/get tired/have an accident/fall down/make fun of someone? Why? Why not?

72. What if someone was being mean/destructive/hurtful? What do you think your superhero/heroine would do?

73. What do you think would hurt your superhero's/heroine's feelings?

74. Why do you think superheroes/heroines are supposed to be strong/powerful?

75. What makes someone strong/powerful/weak?

76. What do you think would happen if a superhero/heroine lost his/her/their powers?

77. How would you help your superhero/heroine if he/she told you they were tired/hungry/angry/lonely/sick/sad/etc.?

· · · · · · · · · · ·

78. How can you find out how tall/short/big/strong your superhero/heroine is?

79. How much do you think your superhero/heroine weighs? What would you have to do to find out?

80. Which is more important, how big your superhero/heroine is or how strong? Why?

81. How does your superhero/heroine stay fit and strong? Do you think your superhero/heroine eats healthy food or junk food? Why?

SUPERHEROES · SUPERHEROINES · ACTION FIGURES

82. What do you think your superhero/heroine eats? Why?

83. If you had to prepare a meal for your superhero/superheroine, what would you make? Why?

· · · · · · · · · · ·

84. What do you think would be hard/easy about being a superhero/heroine?

85. Do you think superheroes/heroines could have real families/children/homes/friends/cars/pets? Why? Why not?

86. Do you think your superhero/heroine ever went to school? Why? Why not?

87. How do you think superheroes/heroines get paid/make a living?

· · · · · · · · · · ·

88. If you could give your superhero/heroine more powers, what would they be? Why?

89. If you could give your superhero/heroine another name, what would it be? Why?

90. Which superhero/heroine would make the best/worst friend? Why?

91. Would you want to be friends with a superhero/heroine? Why? Why not?

92. What do you think you could learn from a superhero/heroine?

93. What do you think your favorite superhero/heroine would say about you?

· · · · · · · · · · ·

94. Which story would you read to your superhero/heroine? Why did you choose that one?

95. Why do you think your superhero/heroine would like that book/story?

96. What if you wanted to make up a story/song for or about your superhero/heroine?

97. How would the song or story begin/end?

98. Would your song or story be funny or sad? Why?

99. How would you draw a picture of/for your superhero/heroine?

100. Why don't you write a letter to your superhero/heroine?

· · · · · · · · · · ·

101. How can you make something to carry/move/transport your superhero/heroine?

102. How can you organize your superheroes/heroines?

103. How will you fit all of your superheroes/heroines into one bin/box?

· · · · · · · · · · ·

104. How do you take care of a superhero/heroine toy?

105. What would happen if you didn't take care of your superhero/heroine toy?

106. How do you keep your superhero/heroine toy clean?

107. What would happen if your superhero/heroine toy got wet/dirty/broken?

ARTS · CRAFTS

Materials: clay, paint, crayons, markers, water, food coloring, blocks, rocks, sticks, leaves, pinecones, acorns, seashells, cookie cutters, pipe cleaners, beads, buttons, shaving cream, foam, fabric, string, tongue depressors, popsicle sticks, cardboard, pom poms, plastic tubing, wire, ice, etc.

1. Tell me about your artwork/craft.
2. How would you describe what you created?
3. If you could give your art a name/title, what would you call it? Why?
4. Would you enjoy making more of these? Why? Why not?
5. Is this something real, imaginary, or a little of both? Tell me about it.
6. Tell me a story that goes along with your artwork.
7. I'd be happy to write the story behind your art/craft. What would you like me to write?

···········

8. How did you make/create your art?
9. How did you think of that design?
10. How did you get this idea?
11. How is this different from the last art/piece you made?

12. Why did you put the _____ on the top/bottom/inside/outside/surface?
13. What made you think to put this beside/around/in between/on top of/under this?

···········

14. What did you do before you started?
15. What steps did you take to make this?
16. What did you do first/second/next/last?
17. What do you have to do to finish this?
18. What will you do after you finish?

···········

19. What do you like/dislike about your artwork?
20. If you had more time, what else would you do/make?
21. What would you change/add/take away from your work?
22. If you did this again, what would you do the same/differently?
23. If you could add/take away anything from your artwork, what would it be?

···········

24. How can/did you make this shape/color/line/size/piece/thing?
25. Describe the lines/colors/shapes/material you used.
26. What comes to mind when you see this color/shape/line/image/material in your artwork?
27. How would you describe this color/shape/line/material?
28. Why did you decide to use this color, shape/line/image/material?

ARTS · CRAFTS

29. How are these colors/shapes/lines/images/materials the same/different?

30. Why do the colors/shapes/lines/images/materials look different now?

31. Why do you think some colors/shapes/lines/images/materials are harder/easier to work with?

32. Why do you think these colors are darker/lighter than those?

33. Tell me about the different lines you used in your drawing. (straight, wavy, or zigzag, curved)

34. Why are some lines straight/wavy/zigzag/curved and some not?

35. Where have you seen something like this before? Tell me about your experience.

36. What are some ways you could fill up this paper?

· · · · · · · · · · ·

37. What **materials/tools** did you use to make your art/craft/piece/design? Why?

38. How could you make these stay/adhere/stick together?

39. How do you use glue/tape?

40. What can you do with glue/tape?

41. What steps do you take when you glue/tape something?

42. What happens when you use too much or not enough glue/tape/glitter/material?

43. What happens when you don't wait for the glue to dry?

44. What happens when you get glue or tape on your hands/clothes/the table/the wrong things?

45. How does the glue/tape/tool/material feel on your hands?

46. When you touch your artwork, what do you notice about the texture?

47. Why do you think your artwork feels like that?

· · · · · · · · · · ·

48. What do you like/dislike about using the materials/tools?

49. What do you think you could do with these colors/shapes/pieces/materials/mediums/tools?

50. What if you used this instead of that?

· · · · · · · · · · ·

51. How can you sort the colors/shapes/pieces/materials/medium to make it easier to work?

52. How can you separate/connect/mix/combine/add to those?

53. What happened when you did that?

54. How did you make that color/design?

55. What do you think would happen if you used/combined/mixed/changed the colors, pieces, shapes, or materials?

56. How many ways do you think you can use the colors/shapes/pieces/materials/medium?

57. What if you didn't have this color/shape/material?

58. What else could you use? Why? How?

59. What can you do with the leftover material/pieces?

· · · · · · · · · · ·

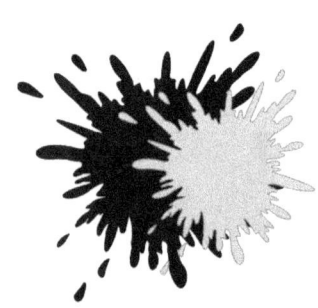

ARTS · CRAFTS

60. How would your art/craft look if you worked on the ground instead of the table? Inside instead of outside?
61. How would your art/craft look if you turned it over/upside down/sideways?
62. How would your art/craft look if you used a different tool?

············

63. Why do you think your artwork/craft/piece is or isn't flat/raised?
64. What is 2-dimensional/3-dimensional artwork?
65. What is the difference between 2-D and 3-D artwork?
66. Is your artwork 2-D or 3-D? How do you know?
67. What can you do to make your art 3-D?

············

68. How were you feeling when you were making this art/piece?
69. How do you think others will feel when they look at your art?
70. If art could talk, what do you think your art would say?

············

71. What is your favorite/least favorite part of the art/craft/piece? Why?
72. What do you plan to do with your art/craft/piece?

73. Where should we keep/store this art/craft/piece? Why?
74. What would you do if someone wanted to buy your art/craft/piece?
75. Is there anything else you would like to make/design? Tell me about it.

············

76. How do you feel when you look at this artist's work?
77. What is mysterious/strange/unusual/scary/creepy/sad/calming/realistic/boring/exciting/memorable/etc. about this art?
78. How do you think this was made?
79. What do you notice about this artist's style?
80. What do you think is missing from this art/piece?
81. What does this piece tell you about the artist?
82. What do you think this artist is trying to tell us?
83. If you could ask this artist one question, what would you ask?
84. Who do you know that would really like/dislike this art? Why?
85. If you could step into this artwork, what would you do?
86. What does this artwork say about our community/town/city/world?
87. What do you know about the culture in which this art/craft was made?

SCISSORS

1. What are scissors?
2. Why do we use scissors?
3. Describe the scissors.
4. How do you use scissors?
5. How do scissors work?
6. How do scissors help us?

....

7. Why do scissors open and close?
8. How do you open and close the scissors?
9. How do you know where to put your fingers/hands?
10. How do the scissors feel in your hands?
11. How do the scissors cut the paper?

....

12. Why do you think scissors are sharp?
13. Do all scissors look the same? Why? Why not?
14. Why do you think you should be careful with the scissors?
15. Why do you think scissors come in different sizes/styles?
16. Are scissors sharp everywhere? Why? Why not?

....

17. What types of things can you cut with scissors?
18. How does it feel when you cut this?
19. What if you wanted to cut a desk/car/chair in half? Could you do it with scissors? Why? Why not?
20. What if the scissors were bigger/longer than you?
21. How does it feel to cut the _____?

22. What's the difference between cutting paper and cutting cardboard/fabric/wire?
23. How are the materials you cut the same/different?
24. Why do you think it's harder/easier to cut this material with scissors?
25. Does it matter whether the material was thin or thick? Blue or red? Hard or soft? Smooth or rough? Light or heavy? Why?
26. How do you know how much to cut?
27. What if you cut too little/much?

....

28. Tell me about what you're working on/cutting/doing.
29. Why did you have to cut these?
30. How are you going to use the pieces you cut?

....

31. What did you notice before/during/after you cut with the scissors?
32. How does the material look after you cut it?
33. Why do you think the pieces you cut look the same/different?
34. Why do you think your material/project looks different now?

....

35. What was easy/challenging about using the scissors? Why?

....

36. How else can you cut the material?
37. Will it be this neat if you tear it instead of cutting it? Why? Why not?
38. How can you cut the pieces smaller/larger/thinner/wider/bigger/shorter/longer?

....

39. What sorts of things should not be cut with scissors? Why?
40. Who do you know that uses scissors when they work? Tell me about them.

NOTES

> *"What children can do today with assistance,*
> *they will be able to do by themselves tomorrow."* - Lev S. Vygotsky

NOTES

MUSIC · SOUND

1. What is music/sound?
2. How do people make music/sounds?
3. Why do people listen to music?
4. What do you hear when you listen carefully?
5. What do you think of when you hear this?
6. How does music remind you of things?

· · · · · · · · · · ·

7. How does this music/sound make you feel?
8. What kind of music makes you calm/crazy/happy/sad/agitated/nervous/scared/etc.?
9. Do you think music can change your mood/the way you feel? Why? Why not? How?
10. What makes a song sound happy/sad/angry/exciting/relaxing?
11. Why do you think people feel like singing and dancing when they hear music?
12. Does the music/song make you feel like jumping/swaying/sleeping/dancing/clapping/patting/stomping/etc.? Why? Why not?
13. How would you move/dance to this music/sound?
14. What if we all followed you when you moved?

15. How can you make sure everyone gets a turn to be the leader?
16. How would you move to the song if you were a soldier/kangaroo/bunny/turtle/bird/snail/tiger/elephant/etc.?

· · · · · · · · · · ·

17. What is it you like or dislike about the music/song/instrument you're hearing/feeling? Why? Why not?
18. How would you describe the music/songs/sounds you like/dislike?

· · · · · · · · · · ·

19. How can you tell when the music starts/stops?
20. What do you hear when the music starts/stops?
21. How does the music change?

· · · · · · · · · · ·

22. What do you know about singing?
23. How can you use your voice to make music?
24. How can you change your voice to match the sound you hear?
25. How can you use your voice to sing high/low/fast/slow/loud/soft?
26. How are our voices the same/different?
27. Why do you think our voices are the same/different?
28. How about if you use a silly/funny/different voice to sing?

· · · · · · · · · · ·

29. What are **lyrics**?
30. How do you learn the lyrics of a song?
31. How does knowing/memorizing the lyrics help you sing along?
32. How would you sound if you hummed the song instead?

MUSIC • SOUND

33. How can we sing your name in the lyrics/song?
34. How would it sound if we sang/clapped the syllables of your name?
35. What if we added other names?

  ············

36. What do you know about the steady **beat**? (demonstrate)
37. Is it easy to find/follow the beat? Why? Why not?
38. How can you walk/tap/pound/drum/stomp/march/clap/wiggle your fingers to the steady beat?
39. How can you clap/move in different ways?
40. How do you think the beat helps people keep time?
41. How do you think the beat helps people play/sing/move/play together?
42. How can we all play music/move to the steady beat?
43. How can we all start clapping/singing at the same time/simultaneously?
44. What happens when we all play an instrument/sing together?
45. What does it sound when we all clap/sing together?
46. What's the difference between playing/singing together and playing/singing alone?

47. What if we all took turns making different sounds?
48. What do you think we would sound like if we all played to a different beat?
49. What would we sound like if we didn't play/sing the song together?

  ············

50. What is the slowest/fastest/highest/lowest/loudest/quietest part of the song/music? How can you tell?
51. Tell me where the music gets faster/slower/louder/softer/higher/lower.
52. Does the music or song speed up/slow down/stay the same? How can you tell?

  ············

53. What do you know about **instruments**?
54. Tell me about the instruments with which you are familiar.
55. Describe this instrument.
56. Which instruments do you recognize? Why? How?
57. Why are there so many different instruments?
58. Do you think your voice is an instrument? Why? Why not?
59. How can you use your voice as an instrument?

  ············

60. Which instrument would you like to play? Why?
61. What do you have to do to play an instrument properly?
62. How can you learn to play an instrument?
63. What happens when you beat a drum/blow a horn/shake a shaker/tap the sticks/etc.?
64. What do you think is making the sound in/on/from this instrument? Why?

MUSIC ▪ SOUND

65. *How do you know when to hit the drum/play the instrument/shake the shaker?*

66. *How do you know when to start/stop?*

67. *What is your favorite/least favorite instrument? Why?*

....

68. *Why do you think instruments are played together/separately?*

69. *What is a band/orchestra?*

70. *How many instruments are playing? How do you know?*

71. *How can you tell which instruments are playing?*

72. *How do you think the instrument is being played? (struck, blown, strummed, bowed, plucked, drummed, etc.)*

73. *Show me what sounds the instrument makes.*

74. *How can you imitate the sound this instrument makes?*

75. *How do you change the sounds the instrument makes?*

76. *What's happening with your mouth/ fingers/hand/arm/feet when you play?*

77. *How is this instrument different from that one?*

78. *What do you have to do to take care of this/an instrument?*

....

79. *What is a **melody**?*

80. *How do you know that's the melody?*

81. *What if you wanted to hum/sing the melody? How would you do it?*

82. *Would the melody be easy or hard to hum/sing? Why? Why not?*

83. *Is the melody easy to remember? Why? Why not?*

84. *What makes you like/dislike a song? Is it the melody, lyrics, style, singer, or something else? Why?*

....

85. *What is the **pitch** of the song/music? (high vs. low tone)*

86. *What's the difference between the pitch of a big dog's bark vs. a small dog's bark? A cow vs. a bird? A big bell vs. a small bell?*

87. *Does it matter how small or big an animal/instrument is when it comes to the sound that it makes? Why? Why not?*

88. *Why do you think a little bell makes such a high-pitched sound?*

....

89. *What do you know about the tempo or speed of the music/song?*

90. *Does the music/song speed up, slow down, or stay the same? How can you tell?*

91. *How can we sing or clap to the song?*

92. *What if we sang/clapped faster/slower?*

93. *How does it sound when we sing/clap faster or slower than the song is playing?*

94. *How do you feel when the song speeds up/slows down?*

95. *What if we counted while we sang/ clapped?*

MUSIC · SOUND

96. *Do you think this music would make the wind blow hard like a storm or soft like a gentle breeze? How can you show me with your body?*

97. *If this music was a car, would it move at a slow pace or zoom down the road?*

· · · · · · · · · · ·

98. *How can you find the rhythmic pattern that repeats in the music/song?*

99. *What if you wanted to drum/tap/clap out the rhythm? How would you do it?*

100. *Where do you hear breaks/changes in the music/song? Describe them to me.*

101. *Can you identify when one section ends and the next begins? How?*

· · · · · · · · · · ·

102. *How can/did you make an instrument?*

103. *How can you make an instrument out of these boxes/tubes/bells/sticks/lids/pans/etc.?*

104. *What did you use to make your instrument?*

105. *How do you think the instrument makes that sound?*

106. *How can you change the sound this instrument makes?*

107. *How did you make those sounds?*

108. *Why is the sound quiet/loud/high/low?*

109. *What would happen if you changed the objects inside of the shaker?*

110. *What can you do to play/sing the music softer/quieter/louder/faster/slower?*

· · · · · · · · · · ·

111. *What kind of music do you listen to at home/in the car/at school?*

112. *How often do you listen to music? Why?*

113. *Do you think music helps you pay attention or distracts you? Why?*

114. *What is your favorite/least favorite song/style of music? Why?*

· · · · · · · · · · ·

115. *What do you know about musicians?*

116. *Describe the musicians you know.*

117. *How do you think musicians compose/write/sing/play?*

118. *How do you think musicians/artists/bands prepare to play music/perform?*

119. *How long/often do you think musicians practice? Why?*

120. *Do you think musicians practice together or apart? Why?*

121. *Who is your favorite musician/artist/band?*

122. *Why do you think musicians/artists/bands have albums/CDs/concerts?*

123. *What do you have to do to see your favorite musician/artist/band?*

· · · · · · · · · · ·

124. *What kinds of music does your family like to listen to?*

125. *What do you think about the music your family listens to?*

126. *How does your family listen to music?*

COMPUTERS

1. What are computers?
2. How does a computer work?
3. What can you do on a computer?
4. How do you know so much about computers?
5. Why should you wash and dry your hands before using the computer?
6. What's the difference between a tablet/iPad/laptop/desktop?

....

7. What do you like/dislike about using the computer?
8. What is your favorite/least favorite thing about using a computer? Why?

....

9. Do you have a computer at home? How does it look?
10. What types of things can you do on your computer?
11. Do you have to own a computer to use one?
12. What if you don't have a computer? Where can you go to use one? How do you know?
13. Do you think a cell phone is a computer? Why? Why not?
14. How is the computer you've seen/used the same/different from this one/others?
15. How do you know if a computer is on/off?
16. Why do we turn computers on and off?
17. How do you turn a computer on and off?

....

18. What is a computer **mouse**?
19. Why do you think this is called a mouse?
20. Is this a real mouse? How do you know?
21. How does the mouse work?
22. What happens on the screen/monitor when you move/click the mouse?
23. What would you do if you didn't have the mouse?
24. Do you need a mouse to use this computer, or can you use your finger? How does that work?

....

25. What is a **cursor**?
26. How do you make the cursor move?
27. Why does the cursor move when you move the mouse/your finger?
28. How does a cursor/mouse/screen/monitor help you?
29. How did you turn on the monitor/screen/printer?
30. Why is this blinking/swirling/spinning?
31. How did you get the cursor/objects/numbers/letters/shapes to move on the screen/monitor?
32. How can I help you?

....

33. Where do you type when you use a computer? Why?
34. How do you type letters/words/symbols on the screen?
35. What does **typing** mean?
36. What is a keyboard?
37. What do you notice about the keyboard?
38. What happens when you type/press buttons on the keyboard?

COMPUTERS

39. Why are all of those letters and numbers on the keyboard?
40. What do those other buttons on the keyboard do?
41. What do you think will happen if you start typing on the keyboard?
42. How do you know where to click to make letters and numbers appear on the screen?
43. How do you think the keyboard works?
44. How can you use the computer to write your name?
45. How did you get that to appear on the screen?

....

46. What would happen if you weren't gentle with the computer/mouse/keyboard?
47. Should you eat or drink around the computer? Why? Why not?
48. What would happen if the computer/keyboard/mouse got wet?

....

49. Tell me about your work.
50. What was the first/second/third thing you did on the computer?
51. How do you find what you're looking for on the computer?
52. How do you save your work on a computer?
53. What are **files/folders**?
54. How do you name a file/folder?
55. How do you find a file/folder?
56. How do you open a file/folder?
57. What's the difference between a paper folder and a folder on a computer?

....

58. What is making the sound coming out of the computer?
59. How can you turn up/down the speaker?
60. What can you do if you don't want to disturb/distract others with the sound?

61. How can you listen to music/watch a video on a computer?
62. What are headphones?
63. How do headphones keep you from disturbing/distracting others?
64. What will happen if your headphones are too loud?

....

65. How do you think computers help people in school/at home/at work?
66. Do computers make life easier or harder? How?
67. What can you learn when you use a computer?
68. How do you learn things on your computer?
69. What new thing did you learn on the computer today?
70. What did you have to do to get the answer?
71. How do you know where to put the answer?

....

72. What types of games can you play on a computer?
73. Describe how you play the game.
74. Tell me about the game you're playing.
75. What if friends wanted to learn how to play? How would you teach them?
76. What types of things are you learning from this game?

....

77. What type of computer would you like to have in the future?

LETTERS · ALPHABET · PHONEMES

1. What do you know about shapes/lines/letters?
2. How do shapes and lines make letters?
3. How do you know this symbol is a letter?
4. How do you know which letter this is?
5. Describe the letter/letters.
6. What do you notice about these letters?
7. Tell me about the letters you see/wrote/used.
8. What is the difference between this letter and that letter?
9. How can you copy/write this letter?
10. What else can you use to make this letter?
11. Show me where you see this letter.
12. What is your favorite/least favorite letter in the alphabet?
13. Tell me about the first letter of your name.
14. Can you think of a word that starts with the same sound as your name?
15. How do you know this name tag is yours?

· · · · · · · · · · ·

16. What if you made up a chant/song about the letter ___?
17. What can we do to help you remember your chant/song?

· · · · · · · · · · ·

18. What is the **alphabet**?
19. What do you know about the alphabet?
20. How can you remember the order of the letters in the alphabet?
21. What happens when you sing the alphabet?
22. How does singing the alphabet help you remember the order of the letters?
23. What if we sang the alphabet song together?
24. What if you made up a dance to go with the alphabet song? (Like the Macarena)

· · · · · · · · · · ·

25. How do these letters/words sound?
26. What if you repeat the sounds you hear?

27. How do you think these letters/words look/sound the same/different?
28. How can you rearrange/sort/make a word out of these letters?
29. What happens when you say these letters separately/together?
30. Why do you think these words have the same beginning/middle/ending sounds?
31. What if you looked for names/objects with the same beginning/middle/ending sounds?
32. Which word is shorter/longer/has the most/least letters? How can you tell?
33. How would this word sound if you added/took away the letter ___?
34. How would these words sound if you changed the first/middle/last letter to ___?

· · · · · · · · · · ·

35. How can you tell the difference between upper and lower case letters?
36. How do you match an uppercase letter with its lowercase partner?
37. How are upper and lower case letters similar/different from each other?
38. Why do these uppercase and lowercase letters sound the same?

· · · · · · · · · · ·

39. What do you know about **syllables**?
40. How can we separate this word into parts/beats?
41. How can you count the syllables of your name/this word?
42. What if you clapped/stomped/moved when you counted?

· · · · · · · · · · ·

43. What do you know about long/short **vowels**? (a, e, i, o, u)
44. How does a vowel say its short/long sound?
45. Describe the difference between the sounds long and short vowels make.

WRITING

1. What does it mean to write something?
2. Why do you think people write things down?
3. What do you have to do to write?
4. How does writing help us?
5. What do you need to know if you want to write something?
6. What can you do if you don't know how/ are unable to write?
7. Have you ever seen anyone writing? Tell me about what they were doing.
8. What do you like most/least about writing? Why?
9. What do you notice when you write?
10. Where do you start/stop writing? Why?

....

11. What are words/sentences?
12. How do you put letters together to make words?
13. How do you put words together to make sentences?
14. How do you know that is a sentence?
15. How do words help tell a story?
16. What if there were no letters/words in the story/book?
17. How does labeling things/objects help you learn words?
18. What else helps you learn words?

....

19. What do you know about writing implements/tools?
20. Which writing tools have you used? How did they work?
21. How do you hold a writing tool? (crayon, marker, pencil, pen, paintbrush, stick, etc.)

22. How does the writing tool feel in your hands?
23. What else can you use to write besides this tool?
24. What's the difference between writing with this tool and writing that one?
25. Which tool do you like to write with the most/least? Why?

....

26. Do you have to write on paper? Why? Why not?
27. What materials do you need in order to write?
28. How can you write on other surfaces/ with other materials? (paper, sand, shaving cream, dirt, wood, tablet, etc.)
29. What if you wanted to scratch or scrape the letters/numbers/shapes/lines/etc. onto a surface? How would you do it?
30. Where is a good/bad place to write? Why?
31. When is the best/worst time to write? Why?
32. Where are you most comfortable writing? Why?
33. How can you use a machine/computer to write?

....

34. What do you know about shapes/lines/ dots/the alphabet/letters/numbers/ words/sentences/punctuation?
35. How do lines form letters/numbers/ shapes?
36. How do you draw shapes/lines/dots?

WRITING

37. How does tracing letters/numbers/shapes/lines help you write?
38. How would you describe this line/letter/number/shape?
39. What if you made up a chant/song to remember how to write this letter/number/shape?

....

40. How do you write the first letter of your name/letters/numbers/words?
41. Show me the letters in your name.

....

42. What would you like to write about today? Why?
43. What made you think of writing about that?
44. Tell me about what you wrote.
45. Is what you wrote real-life or make-believe?

....

46. How did you write this?
47. What made you think of doing this?
48. What does this mean?
49. What if you drew a picture to go with what you wrote?
50. How can you turn your writing into a story/book?
51. If you wanted to take a picture with a camera to go with what you wrote, what kind of picture would you take?
52. I used to be able to read this sort of writing (scribbles), but I've forgotten how. What does it say?

53. Tell me about your drawing so I can write down/dictate what you say.

....

54. What kinds of characters/events/things will you write about this/next time?
55. Describe these characters/events/things.
56. Tell me about the words/pictures you used.
57. How do words/pictures help people understand what you write?

....

58. What would you want to say if you wrote a greeting card/note/letter?
59. To whom would you send the card/note/letter? Why?
60. How would you decorate your card/note/letter/envelope?
61. What materials would you need to decorate your card/note/letter/envelope?
62. Why do people send cards/notes/letters?
63. If you wanted to send a card/note/letter to someone, how would you do it?

....

64. How will people know who wrote this?
65. How can you sign your work?
66. How will you remember when you wrote this?

....

67. What do you like the most/least about what you've written?
68. If you could change anything you wrote, what would you change?

RHYMES

1. What does rhyming mean?
2. Tell me about what you hear.
3. How do you know when words rhyme/ sound the same?
4. Why do you think rhyming words sound like they go together?
5. Do rhyming words sound the same at the beginning or the end of the word? Why?

. . . .

6. What do you notice about the words you are saying/hearing?
7. How do the rhyming words sound to you?
8. How do these words sound the same/ different?
9. Where have you heard words that rhyme? Tell me about them.
10. Why do you think many songs and books have words that rhyme?

. . . .

11. What if the words didn't rhyme at all? (provide example)
12. How would you feel if I changed the words so that they did/didn't rhyme? (provide an example)?
13. How can you change a word that doesn't rhyme to a word that does rhyme with this word?
14. How do rhyming words help you guess/ remember which word will come next?

15. What do you think of when you hear the word/s ____ and ____? Why?
16. Which word rhymes with _____? How do you know?
17. What made you think of that word?

. . . .

18. What is the easiest/hardest thing about creating a rhyme? Why?
19. What do you think is the most important thing to remember when writing a rhyme? Why?
20. Do you think there are any special rules for writing a rhyme? What would they be?
21. What's the difference between saying a rhyme and singing a rhyme?
22. How can you make up a word that rhymes with your name?
23. What if you wanted to make up a silly rhyme? How would you do it?
24. How can you make your silly rhymes into a song/chant/story?
25. How can we each add a rhyming word?
26. How can you act out/move to these rhyming words?

. . . .

27. Share a nursery rhyme that you know.
28. Share a nursery rhyme in your home language.
29. What is your favorite/least favorite nursery rhyme? Why?
30. What do you think makes a rhyme fun to listen to?

BOOKS · READING

1. What do you know about books/ reading?
2. Why do people read books?
3. Why do you think people like to read books?
4. What do you like most/least about reading?
5. What can people learn from reading books?
6. Do people have to learn something when they read a book? Why? Why not?
7. How do you think books are made?
8. Why do you think books are made differently? (board book, paperback, hardback, spiral bound, lift-a-flap, etc.)

....

9. How do you hold a book properly to read it?
10. Why can't you read it this way? (flipped upside down or backward)

....

11. What do you notice about the **cover**?
12. What do you think about the illustration/ image/characters on the cover?
13. How does the cover illustration make you feel?
14. What is the picture trying to tell you?
15. What do you notice about what's on the top/bottom/in the corner of the cover?
16. What do you think this story will be about by looking at the cover/hearing the title? Why?

17. Why do you think there is a description written on the back of the book?

....

18. Why do you think books have **titles**?
19. Why do you think the title is printed on the cover?
20. What do you think the title means?
21. Why do you think the author gave this book that title?
22. Why do you think the title is printed on the book's spine?

....

23. How do you know who wrote the book/ illustrated the book?
24. What do you know about authors/ illustrators?
25. What does an author/illustrator do?

....

26. Why do you have to turn the pages to read the story?
27. Which direction should you turn the pages? Why?
28. What would happen if you turned the pages the opposite way/from back to front?

....

29. What do you see happening in this picture?
30. Why are or aren't there letters/words on the pages?
31. Do people need words or pictures on a page/in a book to tell a story? Why? Why not?

BOOKS · READING

32. How can people tell stories without words/pictures/books?
33. Do people have to know how to read to enjoy books? Why? Why not?
34. Do people have to read books, or can they read something else? Why? Why not?
35. How else can people read if they don't have a book?
36. What if we didn't have books? How would we learn about things?
37. What if a book was written in a different language than yours?

··········

38. What do you think this word/sentence/phrase/statement means?
39. Why do you think that?

··········

40. What do you know about **genres**? (fantasy, fairy tale, humor, drama, fiction, nonfiction, science fiction, horror, mystery, mythology, poetry, etc.)
41. What are the differences between these genres?
42. Why do you think there are so many genres of books?
43. What genre do you like most/least? Why?

··········

44. How do people find books?
45. What do you know about **ISBNs,** International Standard Book Numbers?
46. How do ISBN numbers help people find/buy books?
47. What do you think would happen if every book had the same ISBN number?
48. Why do you think books are assigned ISBN numbers?

··········

49. What can you do to keep from losing your place when you read? (tracking)
50. What is a bookmark?
51. What else can you use to hold your place? How will it work?
52. What if you wanted to design a bookmark? How would you do it?
53. Where is the best/worst place to read a book? Why?
54. What is the best/worst time to read a book? Why?
55. What can you do to make it easier to focus on reading your book?
56. What happens if you get distracted when you are reading?
57. How do you feel when you get distracted?

··········

58. What's the difference between reading words on paper pages versus on a tablet?
59. Which kinds of stories do you prefer to read? Why?

NOTES

> *"It's better to know some of the questions than all of the answers."*
> **- James Thurber**

NOTES

STORIES

1. What are stories?
2. How do people tell stories?
3. What happens in your mind when you hear/read a story?
4. What do you know about this story?
5. Why did you choose this story?
6. What do you remember about this story?
7. How can we sit so everyone can see the pictures/hear the story?

....

8. Tell me about when the story takes place. (past, present, future)
9. How do you know when this story takes place?
10. What if the story happened in the present/past/future? How would it be different?

....

11. Tell me about the **characters**.
12. Describe the characters. (personality, clothing, appearance, etc.)
13. Why do you think the author made the characters/people/animals/insects/robots/objects so unique/etc.?
14. What do you think of the characters in the story? Why?
15. Who do you think the main character is in the story? Why?

16. How much younger/older do you think this character is than you? Why?
17. How is the character similar/different from you?
18. Which character do you like the most/least? Why?
19. What do you like/dislike about this character/story? Why?

....

20. How do you think the characters met?
21. Why do you think these characters are/aren't friends?
22. How do the characters feel about each other?
23. Which character in the book would you most like to meet/avoid? Why?
24. Who is the leader/follower in the story? How can you tell?

....

25. Do you think the character/story is real or pretend/make-believe? Why? Why not?
26. Do you think this story could happen in real life? Why? Why not?
27. If this story was real, what would this situation be like for us?

....

28. What do you think about how the character acted/spoke/did things?
29. Do you think this character is good/bad/honest/scared/happy/sad/mean/etc.? Why?
30. What do you think the character is or was feeling/thinking/seeing/touching/tasting/smelling/hearing? Why?

STORIES

31. *Tell me about a time when you might have felt like the character is feeling.*
32. *Why do you think the character said/did/ thought that?*
33. *Why do you think the character made that choice?*
34. *What would happen if someone really said/did/thought that?*
35. *What could happen to make this character feel better?*
36. *How would you react/feel if this happened to you? Why?*
37. *What would you do in a situation like that?*
38. *What's another way the character could have...?*
39. *When have you or a friend felt the same way as this character? Tell me about it.*
40. *Would you want to be friends with this character? Why? Why not?*
41. *If you were a character in the story, what would you do the same/differently?*
- - - - - - - - - - -
42. *What is happening/did happen to the character? Why?*
43. *Then what happened in the story?*
44. *What is the character's situation at the beginning/middle/end of the story?*
45. *What is the major problem/conflict/ incident in the story?*

46. *What/Who caused the problem/trouble? How?*
47. *Why do you think there was a problem/ trouble/conflict?*
48. *What happened to make the situation better/worse?*
49. *What do you think the character would have preferred to have happened?*
50. *What is the character trying to do? Why?*
51. *What did the character/s do to solve the problem?*
52. *What would you have done to solve the problem/fix things?*
- - - - - - - - - - -
53. *Tell me about the **plot**/sequence of events.*
54. *What happened in the beginning/middle/ end of the story?*
55. *What happened first/second/next/ before/after/last/etc.?*
56. *How did one event cause/affect another?*
- - - - - - - - - - -
57. *What do you know about the **setting** of the story... where the story takes place?*
58. *Describe the setting.*
59. *Is this a setting/place you would find in real life? Why? Why not?*
60. *How does the setting make you feel?*
61. *What would you do if you went to a place like this?*
62. *What do you think you would see/hear/ smell/do in such a place? Why?*
63. *Would you enjoy being in this setting? Why? Why not?*
64. *Would you want to visit a place like this? Why? Why not?*

STORIES

65. Have you ever been to/seen a place like this? Tell me about it.
66. How is this place the same/different from where you live?
67. What would be appropriate to wear in this setting? Why?
68. What would make the setting more comfortable/enjoyable/fun/interesting/believable? Why?
69. How does/did the setting change throughout the story?
70. What would you change about where the story takes place if you could? Why?

....

71. Do you feel like this story is believable? Why? Why not?
72. How would you change the beginning/ending of the story if you wrote it?
73. What else would you change about the story?

....

74. How do you think this story will end?
75. What have you learned so far?
76. What has happened so far?
77. What do you think will happen next/last?
78. What message do you think the author was trying to share with us?

79. What questions do you have about this story?
80. What part of the story will you remember the most?
81. What part of the story would you like to forget?

....

82. What would you tell a friend about this book?
83. How would you describe this story to a friend?

....

84. What do you think about the beginning/ending of the story?
85. Did you like the beginning/ending of the story? Why? Why not?
86. Why do you think the story started/ended this way?
87. What did you think of the story?
88. How do you feel about the story?
89. What about the story did you like the best/least? Why?
90. Do you think this story is sad/funny/tragic/mysterious/scary/romantic/etc.? Why? Why not?
91. Would you want to be a part of this story? Why/Why not?
92. Now that you've heard the story, would you give the book another title? What? Why?
93. What stories have you heard that are similar to/different from this one? How are they similar/different?

....

94. What can you do to remember this story?
95. What if you drew a picture/acted in a play/made a puppet about this story?

SUPPORTING CHANTS & LULLABIES

Song: *Pat-a-Cake*

Pat-a-cake, pat-a-cake baker's man.
Bake me a cake as fast as you can.
Roll it and pat it and mark it with a "B."
And put it in the oven for baby and me.

Suggested open-ended questions:
- *Why is the baker being asked to bake the cake fast?*
- *How do you make a cake?*
- *Why do you think the cake will be marked with a "B?"*
- *What letter would you put on the cake? Why?*
- *How would you decorate the cake?*
- *How do you think the cake will taste?*

Song: *Where Has My Little Dog Gone*

Where? Oh, where
has my little dog gone?
Where? Oh, where can it be?
With its ears cut short
and its tail cut long.
Where? Oh, where can he be?

Suggested open-ended questions:
- *Why do you think the dog ran away?*
- *Describe the dog that ran away.*
- *Where do you think the dog went? Why?*
- *How does the owner feel about their dog?*
- *What can the owner do to find their dog?*
- *Do you think the dog will come back on its own? Why? Why not?*
- *How can the owner keep the dog from leaving again?*

Chant: *Humpty Dumpty*

Humpty Dumpty sat on a wall,
Humpty Dumpty had a great fall.
All the king's horses
and all the king's men
couldn't put Humpty together again.

Suggested open-ended questions:
- *Why was Humpty sitting on a wall?*
- *What happened to Humpty?*
- *Why do you think Humpty fell?*
- *Why couldn't the horses or men put Humpty back together?*
- *What would you do to fix Humpty?*
- *How can you keep Humpty from falling next time?*

Song: *My Birdie Flies Over the Ocean*
Adaptation of *My Bonnie Lies Over the Ocean*

My birdie flies over the ocean
My birdie flies over the sea
My birdie flies over the ocean
Oh, bring back my birdie to me.

Suggested open-ended questions:
- *Tell me about the birdie.*
- *What did the birdie do?*
- *How does the birdie fly?*
- *Why can't anyone find the birdie?*
- *Why doesn't the birdie fly over land?*
- *Who can bring the birdie back home? How?*
- *How would you feel if you lost your birdie?*

SUPPORTING PICTURE BOOKS

Book: Pete the Cat and His Four Groovy Buttons
      by Eric Litwin

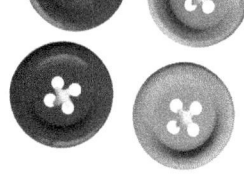

1. How do you know Pete is a cat?
2. Have you ever seen a cat? How did it look/smell/sound/feel?
3. Describe how Pete looks.
4. How are the cats you've seen the same/ different from Pete?
5. Describe what Pete is wearing.
6. Tell me about what Pete is doing in this picture.
7. Where do you think this story takes place? How do you know?
8. Why do you think Pete is singing?
9. Do you think this story is real or pretend? What makes you think that?

· · · · · · · · · · ·

10. What are buttons?
11. How do buttons work?
12. What do you notice about Pete's buttons?
13. Why are Pete's buttons different colors?
14. What do you think about Pete's colorful buttons?
15. Why do you think Pete's buttons are round?
16. How can we tell how many buttons are on Pete's shirt?
17. Why do you think Pete's buttons are popping off?
18. What would you do if you found Pete's buttons? Why?
19. How do you make buttons stay on clothes?
20. What happened to the buttons after they popped off Pete's shirt?

· · · · · · · · · · ·

21. Did Pete cry when he lost his buttons? Why? Why not?

22. Why wasn't Pete worried about losing his buttons?
23. What can Pete do to find his buttons?
24. What if Pete never finds his buttons?
25. How can we replace Pete's buttons?

· · · · · · · · · · ·

26. Are you wearing more buttons than Pete? How do you know?
27. What would happen if all of the buttons popped off your clothes?
28. How would you feel if your buttons popped off?
29. How could you close your clothing with no buttons?
30. What else could you use to close your clothes?

· · · · · · · · · · ·

31. What's a belly button?
32. Why do you think people have belly buttons?
33. What can Pete do with his belly button?
34. Can you button your clothes with a belly button? Why? Why not?
35. How is Pete's belly button the same/ different from the buttons on his shirt?
36. How is Pete's belly button the same/ different from your belly button?

· · · · · · · · · · ·

37. What does "groovy" mean?
38. If you could design groovy buttons, how would they look?
39. How would you use this material to make a button?
40. How would you use these buttons to make a picture/art/something?

NOTES

NOTES

NOTES

NOTES

NOTES

NOTES

INDEX

INDEX

INDEX

INDEX

INDEX

INDEX

RESOURCES

- Brendtro, L. & Longhurst, J.E. (2005). *The resilient brain. Reclaiming Children & Youth*, 14 (1), Pgs. 52-60.
- De Rivera, C., Girolametto, L., Greenberg, J., and Weitzman, E. (2005). *Children's responses to educators' questions in day care play groups.* American Journal of Speech-Language Pathology,14, Pgs. 14–26. doi: 10.1044/1058-0360(2005/004).
- Dewey, J. [1910] 2008. *How we think.* New York: Book Jungle. Duster, S. (1997). *Classroom questioning: How teachers use it to promote creativity and higher level thinking.* (Unpublished master's thesis). The Faculty of Pacific Lutheran University, America.
- Gall, M. (1984). *Synthesis of research on teachers questio*ning. Education Leadership, November, Pgs. 40-47.
- Gestwicki, C. (2016). *Developmentally Appropriate Practice: Curriculum and Development in Early Education*, Ch. 7, Pg. 169.
- Gullo, D. F., and Hughes, K. (2011). *Reclaiming kindergarten: Part I. Questions about theory and practice.* Early Childhood Education Journal, Pgs. 38, Pgs. 323-328.
- Jones, E., & G. Reynolds. (2011). *The Play's the Thing: Teachers' Roles in Children's Play.* 2nd Edition. New York: Teachers College Press, Pg. 35.
- Kohn, A. (2001). NAEYC—Young Children. *Five Reasons to Stop Saying "Good Job!"* September 2001.
- Lee, Y. (2010). *Blended Teacher Supports for Promoting Open-ended Questioning in Pre-K Science Activities.* (Unpublished doctoral dissertation). University of Virginia, USA.
- MacNaughton, G., and Williams, G. (2004). *Teaching young children choices in theory and practice.* Australia: Ligare Pty. Ltd.
- Massey, S.L., Pence, K.L., Justice, L.M., and Bowles, R.P. (2008). *Educators' use of cognitively challenging questions in economically disadvantaged preschool classroom contexts.* Early Education And Development, 19(2), Pgs. 340–360. doi:10.1080/10409280801964119.
- McNeil, N. M., & Jarvin, L. (2007). *When Theories Don't Add Up: Disentangling the Manipulatives Debate.* Theory Into Practice, 46(4), Pgs. 309-316.
- NAEYC. *Principles of Child Development and Learning and Implications That Inform Practice.* https://www.naeyc.org/resources/position-statements/dap/principles
- Nilsen, B. A. (2017). *Week by Week: Plans for Documenting Children's Development.* 7th Edition. Cengage Learning, Pg. 155.
- NAEYC, Sept. 2011. *A Conversation with Vivian Gussin Paley*, Young Children, Pg. 92.
- Thompson, R.A. (2002). *The Roots of School Readiness in Social Emotional Development.* The Kauffman Early Education Exchange 1, 8-29.
- Walsh, B., and Blewitt, P. (2006).*The effect of questioning style during storybook reading on novel vocabulary acquisition of preschoolers.* Early Childhood Education Journal, February, 33, 4. doi:10.1007/s10643-005-0052-0.